Troubled Paradise

Troubled Paradise

Limited Salvation and the
Problem of Heavenly Grief

ERIC REITAN

CASCADE Books • Eugene, Oregon

TROUBLED PARADISE

Limited Salvation and the Problem of Heavenly Grief

Copyright © 2024 Eric Reitan. All rights reserved. Except for brief quotations in critical publications or reviews, no part of this book may be reproduced in any manner without prior written permission from the publisher. Write: Permissions, Wipf and Stock Publishers, 199 W. 8th Ave., Suite 3, Eugene, OR 97401.

Cascade Books
An Imprint of Wipf and Stock Publishers
199 W. 8th Ave., Suite 3
Eugene, OR 97401

www.wipfandstock.com

PAPERBACK ISBN: 978-1-6667-6533-5
HARDCOVER ISBN: 978-1-6667-6534-2
EBOOK ISBN: 978-1-6667-6535-9

Cataloguing-in-Publication data:

Names: Reitan, Eric [Author].

Title: Troubled paradise : limited salvation and the problem of heavenly grief / Eric Reitan.

Description: Eugene, OR: Cascade Books, 2024 | Includes bibliographical references and index.

Identifiers: ISBN 978-1-6667-6533-5 (paperback) | ISBN 978-1-6667-6534-2 (hardcover) | ISBN 978-1-6667-6535-9 (ebook)

Subjects: LCSH: Universalism. | Salvation—Christianity. | Hell—Christianity. | Heaven. | Grief. | Future punishment. | Philosophical theology.

Classification: BX9946 R45 2024 (print) | BX9946 (ebook)

Scripture quotations are from New Revised Standard Version Updated Edition. Copyright © 2021 National Council of Churches of Christ in the United States of America. Used by permission. All rights reserved worldwide.

In memory of M. Reidun Reitan, whose steadfast love, formidable spirit, and passion for ideas and music have helped to shape every contour of my life.

Table of Contents

Preface ix

Acknowledgments xiii

Chapter 1. Introduction to the Problem 1

Chapter 2. Portraits of Grief 25

Chapter 3. Sympathy for the Damned 51

Chapter 4. The Love of the Blessed 70

Chapter 5. Moral Sanctification, Emotions, and Grief 94

Chapter 6. Purported Solutions: Limited Love 119

Chapter 7. Purported Solutions: Unfitting Grief 149

Chapter 8. Escaping the Problem 184

Bibliography 211

Index 217

Preface

I WAS POLISHING THE final draft of this book when my mother passed away. Because this is a book about grief, and because I believe we cannot think well about grief without taking seriously the *experience* of grief, I have made an effort in these pages to be more personal than is typical for academic books in philosophy of religion and theology. That is, I have not shied away from sharing, as appropriate, my own experience with grief.

I thought about revising the book to reflect this most recent, and hence my rawest, loss. But I decided against it for both personal and practical reasons. Hence, the main body of this book says nothing about the death of my mother, even in those places where that might be especially fitting or appropriate.

That said, my family has been losing my mother piecemeal to dementia over the course of the last dozen years, and I do make mention of this where the subject matter made it impossible for me *not* to think about and reflect on this tragic vitiation of a beloved parent. That has been my rule while writing this book: where I cannot help but think about how the arguments and ideas in the book connect with my own experiences of loss, I have allowed these experiences to influence what I say and how I say it. I have done so because I am convinced that, although doing so may not add to the academic *rigor* of these pages, it will make my reflections *wiser*.

This point connects with another important aim I had while writing this book: accessibility. I want this work to make an original scholarly contribution to the problem of heavenly grief and the challenge it poses for the doctrine of limited salvation. But I want to do so in a way that is accessible to educated readers, not merely to academics specializing in philosophical theology and its neighboring disciplines. When I gave a public talk at my university on this topic, a student in attendance told me afterwards that she was "very excited" when she saw the announcement for the talk, because she'd been chewing for years over the question of how the blessed in heaven could be perfectly happy if their loved ones were eternally damned. Wouldn't they grieve for them? Wouldn't that tarnish their joy?

She isn't alone. This is not some abstract scholarly puzzle. It is something lay Christians find themselves asking about, and something clergy need to confront both in their own lives and in their ministries. While my own view is that universalism offers the best way out of the problem, I mean for this book to be of value to those who reach a different conclusion. That is, my aim is to be clear enough in formulating the problem of heavenly grief, and clear enough in explaining why I find non-universalist solutions unsatisfying, that critics can identify where their presuppositions differ from those that point me towards universalism as the least costly way out.

To be clear enough for this purpose requires rigor—but it doesn't call for the kind of rigor at every level that sometimes leads philosophers to add so many qualifiers and clarifications that readers not trained to parse this kind of writing can no longer identify the main point. In the editing stages, I have found myself occasionally pausing before a sentence and thinking, "That's not exactly right. What's exactly right is expressed by this much more complicated sentence." And then I kept the original, less exact phrasing, because analytic philosophers and theologians would know what I meant to say and everyone else would have an easier time following my thinking in the simpler guise.

I have also avoided the philosopher's habit of introducing acronyms to conveniently refer to principles or doctrines, and I have largely avoided formalized arguments laid out with numbered premises in favor of a more narrative approach.

But the most significant deviation from the norms of academic writing (at least in my discipline) has been the inclusion of personal stories of grief, both from my own life and from some of the most honest, wise, and eloquent memoirs about loss and grief that I know. I have allowed my thinking in these pages to be shaped by immersion in these human experiences of loss. And because of that, the absence of any mention of my mother's recent death feels, at least to me, like a glaring omission.

For a few weeks now I have been sitting with a mostly finished manuscript and the reality of my mother's death, and I have been wondering what I might say about her loss, in this preface, that contributes in some small way to the arguments that follow.

There *is* something distinctive about the way we lost my mother: bit by bit to dementia over the course of a dozen years. And there is something distinctive about the grief associated with that kind of loss. In chapter 2, I talk about Mark Doty's insight that grief is a bit like new love: in both cases, *novelty* calls the loved one to our attention. Human beings have this propensity to notice shiny new things, to pay more attention to the new than to the familiar. And this propensity keeps us from taking a new love for granted. Because their presence in our lives is novel, we notice them and their role in our lives.

In the case of grief, what is novel is their absence. But it is in precisely this respect that my mother's death differs from other deaths I have grieved. For a dozen years I have been incrementally acclimating myself to my mother's loss, by confronting it piecemeal. For example, while my habit of calling my mother to share good news did not stop with the withering of her capacity to grasp and retain the news, those calls became steadily less meaningful to me: they became mere habits. And with time, the urge to let her know about my kids' achievements—children whose existence she could not remember—faded away.

By the time she died, so many of the ways I had, through my life, connected with my mother were no longer ways I *could* connect with her. It would be wrong to say I had already come to terms with these losses before she died. In fact, because my mother was still alive, it didn't feel as if I could fully grieve. The truth, rather, is that I got used to these losses. They became familiar.

More than that: *one more thing being gone* became familiar. Since I live far from her, I saw my mother once or twice year. Each visit featured a striking change: some new diminishment. I came to expect it. I can almost recall how shocking those early losses were, the way I was shaken by them. But by the end I was no longer shocked or shaken. I'd gotten used to one more thing gone.

In chapter 7, I discuss Dan Moller's idea that we have an "emotional immune system" that attenuates our grief, but that the cost of this emotional immune system's work is the severing of a fitting connection to loss. We become disconnected from reality, from the real value of what has been lost. In other words, our propensity to "get over" loss is tied to something we would not want to attribute to the blessed in heaven, who according to Christian teachings are morally perfected. If the attenuation of grief depends upon losing touch with the value of what we've lost, because familiarity breeds indifference if not contempt, then we should not expect the grief of the blessed to attenuate.

If there is a single way in which the experience of my mother's loss fits into the arguments of this book, it is here: the emotional immune system that kicked in long before my mother died, that made *loss itself* so familiar that new losses hit with less and less force, was no gift. While it was, perhaps, necessary in order to live my life, there is a sense in which it deprived me of my grief. The level and degree of grief I ought to feel, that I have a *right* to feel, that I *need* to feel in order to be in tune with the truth—that grief is elusive. I am fighting to claim it even as I write these words.

Grief is about proper emotional attunement to lost value. In that sense, it is a relative good: when tragic things happen, it is better to feel the tragedy with fitting emotions than to be out of touch with it. To lose a loved one and *not* grieve is thus to lose this relative good on top of the loss of the loved one: a magnification of loss.

My mother is dead. But because I've been losing her piecemeal for a dozen years, I've gotten used to it. I feel wrong inside because my emotions are out of touch with reality, shut down by my emotional immune system. I grieve for what the slow grind of my mother's dementia has taken from me in terms of my ability to fully experience her loss. And through *that* grief, I struggle to reclaim the grief I should feel for the loss of my mother, the grief that is a fitting response to everything she meant to me.

That struggle is a struggle towards moral improvement. Because, in order to be good, we must weep for goods that are gone. And we can't let familiarity with loss steal that from us.

The blessed in heaven, being morally perfected, would not have their grief stolen from them by the familiarity of loss. And this means that, were anyone they love lost forever, I can only believe that *they would never get used it*.

Acknowledgments

SOME PARTS OF THIS book were adapted, generally with quite extensive revision, from earlier works of mine previously published elsewhere. Portions of chapter 4 were adapted from material originally published in *The Triumph of Love* (Cascade, 2017). Portions of chapter 6 were adapted from material originally published in "Eternal Damnation and Blessed Ignorance: Is the Damnation of Some Incompatible with the Salvation of Any?" *Religious Studies* 38 (2002) 429–50. And portions of chapters 7 and 8 were adapted from material originally published in Al Kimel's blog, *Eclectic Orthodoxy*. The revisions to this material were partly shaped by feedback on the earlier works, for which I am grateful.

I am also grateful for the helpful comments, feedback, and suggestions provided at two public lectures where drafts of the main ideas in this book were presented. The first was at the St. Louis University Graduate Student Philosophy Conference in October 2022, where I delivered a keynote address on this topic. The second was at an Oklahoma State University "Friends of the Forms" lecture in October 2023.

As always, I am deeply grateful to John Kronen for talking through philosophical ideas with me, reading my work when asked, and pressing me to deepen my thinking. And I am grateful for the support of my philosophy colleagues at Oklahoma State University and my editor at Cascade Books, Robin Parry.

1

Introduction to the Problem

AN INITIAL STATEMENT OF THE PROBLEM

HISTORICALLY, MOST CHRISTIANS HAVE thought that some of us are *saved* while others are not. The saved experience eternal life in heaven while the unsaved experience eternal damnation in hell or, according to some, annihilation: a final death for which there will be no resurrection.

This book addresses a problem faced by this view. Briefly stated, the problem is this: if any are lost forever, whether through damnation or annihilation, it seems the joy of the saved would be marred by grief. Being perfected in love, they would love and so grieve for the unsaved—especially those among the unsaved who were beloved friends and family in this life. And this grief would be unmoored from the consolation of Easter's promise. Without hope of heavenly reunion with the unsaved, the saved would face a *permanent* loss. The tragedies of this earthly life, rather than being left behind, would follow them into heaven. But isn't salvation supposed to fulfill the promise, found in Revelation 21:4, that God "will wipe every tear from their eyes," and that death "will be no more; mourning and crying and pain will be no more, for the first things have passed away"?

This, then, is the *problem of heavenly grief*. Like the more well-known problem of evil, it is the problem of responding adequately to an argument. The problem of evil arises from the argument that the evils of our earthly lives count decisively against the existence of a good and almighty God. The argument poses a *problem* because of its plausibility:

it isn't easy to explain why such a God would permit the Black Death, the Holocaust, and all the routine tragedies and cruelties that litter our lives.

Obviously, the problem of evil is not a *problem* for atheists. Similarly, the problem of heavenly grief is not a problem for universalists who think all are saved. Instead, it is a problem for those who think some are forever unsaved. The argument that generates the problem—the *argument* from heavenly grief—targets this traditional *doctrine of limited salvation*.

DEFINING TERMS

Let me define some key terms more fully. By "the doctrine of limited salvation," I mean the traditional Christian teaching that only some created persons are saved. By the "saved," I mean those freed from sin and death who enjoy eternal life, perfect happiness or joy, and moral sanctification in community with God and one another, a community called "heaven." I will call those who enjoy this state "the blessed" and the state itself "perfect blessedness."[1]

Significantly, this state includes more than just eternal life and perfect happiness. It also includes moral sanctification.[2] To be saved is to be liberated not just from death and suffering but from sin. Within the Christian tradition, sin is a corruption, a vitiation of our humanity caused by alienation from our creator and our own nature. As such, it is *bad for us*. Virtue is good for us—*intrinsically* good, not just good as a means to pleasant experiences. So, salvation removes everything that limits our good—especially suffering, death, and sin.

It also involves relationships: the blessed have mutually loving relationships with God and one another. Not only, then, are they freed from death, suffering, and sin, but from isolation and loneliness. And the heavenly relationships are perfected ones, undiminished by moral failings like pettiness or envy. Nor are they unrequited. In heaven, we love and are loved. This community of mutual love is made possible by moral sanctification and is a main source of heavenly joy. First and foremost, the saved take joy in loving union with God. But they also take joy in loving relationships with one another.

In sum, "perfect blessedness" consists in the possession of at least these goods: eternal life, moral sanctification, perfect happiness or joy,

---

1. For a more detailed explication of the elements traditionally thought to constitute perfect blessedness, see Kronen and Reitan, *God's Final Victory*, 28–29.

2. For a classic articulation of this view, see Augustine, *City of God* 22.30.1–3.

and perfected loving relationships with God and the blessed. By "the doctrine of perfect blessedness," I mean the view that all the saved come to enjoy perfect blessedness in this sense.

The unsaved are those deprived of such blessedness. On traditional Christian teachings, this dispossession is total or nearly so. They lack not only perfect happiness but happiness of any kind. Not only are they not morally sanctified; sinfulness is the final note of their existence. Not only do they fall short of perfect relationships with God and the blessed; they are cut off. Beyond this, Christians vary in their views about what the unsaved endure, resulting in different versions of the doctrine of limited salvation. On the most traditional view, the doctrine of hell, the unsaved exist eternally in a state deprived of the goods that make existence worth having. This is "hell," and those who endure it are "the damned." The doctrine of hell thus denies the unsaved all heavenly goods *except* eternal existence—but an existence so miserable we might not want to call it *life*.

Those who embrace this doctrine are often called traditionalists. But traditionalism has different versions, some more traditional than others. The most traditional, sometimes called infernalism, holds that God *casts* the damned into hell as a punishment for sin and that, beyond the suffering that naturally accompanies being cut off from heaven's goods, they endure further torments inflicted by God, especially the agony of unquenchable burning.[3]

But there are more moderated versions of the doctrine. Typically, those who back off from the image of hell as a place of infernal torment also back away from the idea that God *inflicts* it as a punishment. Instead, the damned impose it on themselves by rejecting God's grace and love. As C. S. Lewis puts it, "the doors of hell are locked on the *inside*."[4] The damned cut themselves off, too proud or hateful or spiteful to welcome God's offer of loving communion. By their choices they alienate themselves from everything that makes existence worth having. Their suffering, while extreme, consists in the natural outcomes of this self-inflicted separation.[5]

Although traditionalism is the most common form of the doctrine, there is another form, namely annihilationism (or conditionalism). Again

---

3. See, for example, Augustine, *City of God* 21.9.1–2; Aquinas, *Summa Theologica*, Suppl., Q. 97, Art. 1–5; Baier, *Compendium Theologiae Positivae*, 209–11.

4. Lewis, *Problem of Pain*, 115.

5. For a clear statement of this view, see Davis, "Universalism, Hell, and the Fate of the Ignorant," 178–79.

there are different versions, but the dominant one holds that eternal life is a supernatural blessing bestowed by God only on those who have repented of their sins and embraced Christ as savior. Those who have not done so by the time of their earthly deaths cease to exist (perhaps after enduring a finite hell as punishment for sin, and perhaps not until after the day of judgment).[6] Other versions hold that those who reject divine grace orient themselves towards non-being in such a way that, eventually, they cease to exist: their own rejection of God, the source of being, leads to a steady vitiation of their being until they wither into nothingness.[7]

These doctrinal perspectives share the conviction that some are eternally excluded from heaven: there are extraordinary goods that *would* have been part of their lives (and part of God's creation) *had* they been saved, but which are not. It will be useful to have a general term for these eternally unsaved persons, whether damned or annihilated. I will call them "the lost."

In contrast, the doctrine of universal salvation, or universalism, holds that all are saved. Universalism is compatible with some being lost *for a time*—for example, by enduring a finite hell. What universalism excludes is the view that separation from God and the blessed, through banishment or self-chosen exile or annihilation, is anyone's *final* state. Hence, universalism rejects all versions of the doctrine of limited salvation. Since it will be useful to talk generically about adherents to the doctrine of limited salvation in any form, the simplest thing is to refer to them collectively as "non-universalists" and their shared view as "non-universalism."

THE ARGUMENT FROM HEAVENLY GRIEF

The argument from heavenly grief holds that the perfect blessedness of anyone is incompatible with limited salvation and that the doctrine of limited salvation should therefore be rejected. While I develop my preferred version of this argument in chapters 3–5, it will be helpful to offer an initial overview. The argument concludes that, were any eternally lost,

---

6. For a seminal defense and explication of this view, see Fudge, *Fire That Consumes*. Fudge's view is that there is a general resurrection of all for the final judgment, after which the unsaved perish eternally (p. 378).

7. For a development and defense of this view, see Griffiths, "Self-Annihilation or Damnation?" Kvanvig favors a similar view but is open to the idea that "some never get to the end of the road toward annihilation," suggesting that some may be ultimately annihilated while others suffer eternally. See Kvanvig, *Problem of Hell*, 152.

their loss would cause persistent grief in the saved, thus precluding their perfect blessedness. The case for this conclusion relies on a few key premises. First, there is the *love premise*, which holds that by virtue of their moral sanctification, the blessed will love all the lost in a general sense and some in a more personal way. Second, there is the *awareness premise*, holding that if any are lost, the blessed will be aware of this. Third, the *fitting grief premise* holds that some degree of enduring grief is a morally fitting response to the eternal loss of those one loves (meaning the blessed would feel grief were they aware of the loss). Finally, the *incompatibility premise* holds that enduring grief is incompatible with perfect happiness.

Given these premises, which enjoy an initial plausibility for most Christians, the doctrines of limited salvation and perfect blessedness are incompatible. The argument thus pushes non-universalists to wrestle with how they can coherently affirm both doctrines. The *problem* of heavenly grief, then, is the problem faced by non-universalists of providing a satisfactory response to the *argument* from heavenly grief.

While universalism might be construed as one solution to the problem, I think it better to distinguish between *solutions* and *escapes*. For non-universalists, the challenge is to provide a *solution* that permits continued endorsement of limited salvation without giving up the doctrine of perfect blessedness. Such a solution would offer reasons to think Christians can reject one or more of the premises of the argument from heavenly grief without paying too high a cost.

For universalists, however, the problem of heavenly grief does not arise: universalists *escape* the problem. Of course, there is another escape: rejecting the doctrine of perfect blessedness. Can Christians live with the idea that, while the saved escape annihilation or damnation, they do *not* escape the pain of grief and so fall short of perfect happiness?

In chapters 6–7, I will look systematically at proposed solutions to the problem in order to assess their costs and limitations. I will conclude that all of these solutions are costly. In chapter 8, I will argue that while escaping the problem by rejecting the doctrine of perfect blessedness is clearly costly, the universalist escape is less costly than it has typically been taken to be—and so should be taken more seriously than it has been historically.

That said, this book is not a systematic defense of universalism. I have co-authored such a defense,[8] but the main aim here is to wrestle seriously with the issues that arise from the problem of heavenly grief. Serious

---

8. Kronen and Reitan, *God's Final Victory*.

engagement with this problem will, I hope, help all Christians—universalists and non-universalists—to think more deeply about the nature of heaven, the scope of the call to love our neighbors as ourselves, and the place of emotions like grief in the kind of fully actualized life that Christianity takes the blessed to enjoy.

THE PROBLEM OF HEAVENLY GRIEF, THE PROBLEM OF EVIL, AND THE PROBLEM OF HELL

Since the problem of heavenly grief is less familiar than the problem of evil and the associated problem of hell, situating it in relation to these other problems—showing how the current discussion bears on them—may be helpful. As already noted, the problem of evil is the problem theists face of formulating an adequate response to the argument from evil—really a cluster of arguments that purport to show an incompatibility between the existence of a perfectly good and almighty God and the world's evils. Marilyn McCord Adams famously argued that Christians who embrace the doctrine of hell face a unique version of this problem, namely the problem of hell, that arises because damnation constitutes an evil God would presumably want and be able to prevent.[9]

Just as there are proposed responses to the problem of evil, there are proposed responses to the problem of hell. But one of Adams's aims is to show that the magnitude of the evil posited by the doctrine of hell makes that problem harder to solve than the more terrestrial problem of evil. This aim coheres with Adams's broader work on the problem of evil. Adams thinks an adequate Christian response to the problem of evil must do more than just explain why God permits evil. Some evils are what she calls horrendous evils or *horrors*—evils "the participation in ... which constitutes *prima facie* reason to doubt whether the participant's life could (given their inclusion in it) have positive meaning for him/her on the whole."[10] An adequate Christian response to the problem of evil must explain how a loving God could be good to those caught up in horror despite its apparent meaning-obliterating significance.

Her answer is that God can both *engulf* and *defeat* horror. To "engulf" it is to fill the horror victim's life with so much good it becomes worth living despite horror's presence—something God could do by

---

9. Adams, "Problem of Hell," 301–2.
10. Adams, *Christ and Horrors*, 32.

bestowing the good of loving union with God, a good so great (in fact, the *only* good so great) it swamps all finite evils, even horrors. To "defeat" horror is to build up around it something of great value, a good of which the horror is an organic and inextricable part, thereby rendering the horror a meaningful part of a whole so good even the victims would rather have it than forego the horror.[11]

Her most developed example of the latter comes in her book, *Christ and Horrors*, in which she conceives Christ's atonement as a means of defeating horror. While I cannot do justice to her account here, a brief sketch will be helpful. As Adams conceives it, Christ's crucifixion is a horror. By becoming incarnate and enduring such evil, God comes to suffer horror in solidarity with horror's human victims. By so doing, God transforms participation in horror into a unique pathway to solidarity and community with God in God's most accessibly human form.[12]

Adams thinks that for any terrestrial horror, God both can and will engulf and defeat it, thereby redeeming the lives of those caught up in it. None of this explains why God would permit horror in the first place. But God's ability and willingness to redeem the lives of horror's victims through engulfing and defeating horror shows that God can be good to them despite permitting horror. And this is *necessary* for a satisfactory solution to the problem of evil even if not sufficient.

But when it comes to the evils of hell, this necessary feature of a satisfactory solution is elusive. As traditionally conceived, damnation is the ultimate horror, beside which terrestrial horrors pale—a horror that, according to the doctrine of hell, God either cannot or will not marshal divine resources to engulf and defeat. Horrendous evil that is engulfed and defeated by God does not threaten our image of a God who loves us and desires our good, because God works to render such evil compatible with our good. But the doctrine of hell posits the existence of horror that dwarfs the worst terrestrial horrors and that God never redeems. If this is right, then the problem of hell appears to be vastly more serious than the terrestrial problem of evil.[13]

---

11. See Adams, "Horrendous Evil," 306–9, for a concise development of these ideas. For a fuller development, see Adams, *Horrendous Evil*, ch. 8.

12. See especially Adams, *Christ and Horrors*, ch. 3.

13. Annihilationism, too, magnifies the difficulty of solving the problem of evil. If someone caught up in horror in this life is then annihilated, that person's existence ends absent the good of union with God, the only good that can outweigh horror. And, presumably, the annihilated include only those who have not come to believe in Christ in the deep way that leads them to experience solidarity with Christ in the midst of horror.

A second difference between the problem of terrestrial evil and the problem of hell is this: hell is a theological doctrine rather than a tragic fact of our lived experience. So, unlike the problem of evil, the problem of hell does not challenge God's existence based on a fact of our lives, but posits an incompatibility between doctrines. And if Christians must choose between belief in God and belief in hell, it's the latter that has to go.

So how does the problem of heavenly grief relate to these more widely discussed problems? First, like the problem of hell, the problem of heavenly grief does not challenge God's existence. These problems, unlike the problem of evil, challenge Christians to wrestle with *how to formulate* their theology, not with whether they should have any theology at all.

Another similarity is this. The problem of hell presents us with a magnified version of something—evil—that troubles us in this life. Absent the doctrine of hell, all evil is limited and potentially subject to divine redemption. But the doctrine of hell posits horror that is unlimited and will never be redeemed. Similarly, the problem of heavenly grief presents us with a magnified version of something we confront in this life: the anguish of losing those we love. Absent the doctrine of limited salvation, terrestrial grief admits of consolation in the form of a divine promise that death's separation is not final. The doctrine of limited salvation *eliminates* this consolation with respect to the lost: for them, separation *is* the final word. Christianity's Easter promise laces hope into the pain of grief. But the doctrine of limited salvation just *is* the doctrine that for some, *this hope and this promise will never be fulfilled*.

Despite these parallels, the problem of heavenly grief is not a variant of the problem of hell. First, even though neither problem challenges God's existence, the problem of hell follows the *structure* of the problem of evil by pitting God's existence against the existence of hell. The problem of heavenly grief, instead, pits the doctrine of limited salvation against the doctrine of perfect blessedness. And the doctrine of perfect blessedness is clearly *less* central to Christian faith than God's existence. In the case of the problem of hell, while there are technically two *escapes* from the problem—universalism and atheism—no Christian would opt for the latter. But when it comes to the problem of heavenly grief, the two escapes are universalism and a modified understanding of the heavenly state which includes enduring grief as a component. When those are the options, it is less obvious that, absent a solution to the problem, Christians should choose universalism. Despite the challenges to doing so, perhaps a non-universalist could build a case for a non-traditional view of heaven in which grief is an enduring feature.

Another important difference between the problem of hell and the problem of heavenly grief emerges when we consider the terrestrial problems to which they are related. The problem of hell parallels the terrestrial problem of evil: the two arguments have the same form, but focus on different evils. But when it comes to the problem of heavenly grief, there is no terrestrial problem of grief that it parallels. Instead, we find a tension between what traditional teachings say about the heavenly state and two *facts* about the human condition in this life: we lose people we love, and in the wake of such loss we suffer. The doctrine of limited salvation *affirms* a heavenly correlate for the first fact, while the doctrine of perfect blessedness *denies* any such correlate for the second fact. The problem of heavenly grief arises precisely because of this disconnect between the terrestrial and the heavenly and because the two facts we encounter in this life are intimately connected: we grieve *because* we lose loved ones.

To imagine someone who *doesn't* grieve the loss of a loved one is to imagine an emotionless android or shallow cad, not a morally perfected person. This is why Eleonore Stump rejects the "stern-minded" attitude endorsed by Teresa of Avila when she treats her propensity to grieve for lost loved ones as a defect in her relationship with God. Stump disagrees, noting that "there is something bad and lamentable, something worth tears, something whose loss brings affliction with it, about the death of any person whom one loves—one's father, or even one's neighbour, whom one is bound to love too, as Teresa thinks." As such, "Unmoved tranquillity at the death of another person is thus incompatible with love of that person."[14]

The problem of heavenly grief arises precisely because loss and grief are facts of our terrestrial life that seem to fittingly go together—but traditional theologies *pry them apart* in the heavenly realm. This view of heaven invites comparison to those dystopian tales of an idealized future in which everyone is happy all the time, not because bad things have stopped happening but because people take happy pills to keep their spirits up while tragedy continues unabated. The intuition that leads us to view such tales as *dystopian* is this: negative emotions like grief *properly accompany* evils like death. To eliminate the negative emotions without eliminating the evils is actually to *put more evil into the world*—namely

---

14. Stump, "Problem of Evil and the Desires of the Heart," 204.

the evil character trait of being emotionally insensitive to the reality of evil.

In short, there is no problem of terrestrial grief in the sense of there being a distinct evil—grief—whose existence we need to reconcile with God's existence. Instead, we have the problem of terrestrial *loss*—the problem of explaining why God permits death and other forms of wrenching separation on this mortal coil. And we have the parallel problem of eternal loss, a version of the problem of evil that arises for Christians who believe in limited salvation.

Of these two version of the problem of evil, the latter is more serious because the loss is everlasting. The blessed will never be reunited with damned or destroyed loved ones, and since they will never die themselves they will experience their loved ones' absence forever. The problem of heavenly grief *arises out of* this problem of eternal loss. Hence, even though the problem of heavenly grief is not a version of the problem of evil, it is closely wedded to one. A problem of eternal loss generates the problem of heavenly grief because traditional Christianity affirms that the blessed in heaven will be perfectly happy *despite this eternal loss*. My contention is that we should *not* affirm this. If the blessed are morally perfected, they will fittingly grieve the eternal loss of inherently valuable persons.

One way to construe my argument in these pages, then, is as follows: The consolation offered in Revelation 21:4 is best construed as the promise that all proper *occasion* for grief will be wiped from God's creation. But the doctrine of limited salvation rejects this promise.

BROADLY ARMINIAN PRESUPPOSITIONS

Before moving on to some points about methodology, I want to make a point about my default assumptions in this book. As already mentioned, one premise of the argument from heavenly grief is what I am labeling the love premise: the moral sanctification of the blessed entails that their love extends to the lost.

But that means I am presuming—and hence, directing my argument primarily towards—versions of non-universalism that hold that *God* loves the lost. After all, we cannot construe the moral sanctification of the blessed in a way that puts their wills and desires at odds with God's. They will love the damned only if God does. And given the understanding of love I will be defending—a love that values the being and welfare of the loved one and union with them—a God who loves all will *desire* the salvation of all, just as 1 Timothy 2:4 proclaims.

For this reason, and for further reasons enumerated below, my argument will focus primarily on versions of non-universalism that adopt what I will call a broadly Arminian theology. By this, I mean a species of non-universalism characterized by the following features. First, God loves all persons and desires their salvation and so extends grace to all persons with the aim of achieving their salvation. Second, if all are not saved, this is because there is something at work *other than God's sovereign will* that determines final outcomes (presumably because God judges the existence of this *something-else-at-work* to be good and designs the world accordingly). Third, this "something else" is *human freedom*. If some are saved and others lost, it is not because of a difference in what God has offered them but because the lost made free choices different from those made by the saved, and this difference is what accounts for the fact that they are lost. Fourth, the fact that the lost made salvation-precluding free choices is not the case because God *determined* them to make these choices but, rather, on account of an exercise of human freedom permitted but *undetermined* by God, a "libertarian" freedom that allows us to act contrary to God's will.[15] Finally, God imbuing us with such freedom, and respecting the choices we make through its exercise, is an expression of divine love. More: it is such an important expression of God's loving nature that God permits the natural outcomes of our free choices even when those outcomes clash with God's desires, even the desire that each of his beloved human children be saved.

None of this means we can be saved apart from divine grace. Instead, it means that God has so ordered things that in addition to a grace that extends to all and makes salvation possible for all, there has to be the right sort of undetermined free response. For the purposes of this book, I will not specify the character of that response. My own Lutheran conviction is that the only free response required for salvation is *non-resistance* to divine grace: so long as we do not actively rebuff God's saving grace, it will operate to secure our salvation. But others may view the undetermined free response in more active terms, locating it in, say, the decision to accept Christ as Lord and Savior, or in the decision to repent of our sins, or in the choice to *accept* God's saving grace. So long as a theology holds there is some undetermined free choice that, if made, would

---

15. I will offer a fuller discussion of different philosophical accounts of freedom—especially "libertarian" and "compatibilist" freedom—in chapter 6.

preclude our salvation—and so long as we would be saved but for how we have deployed our freedom in relation to this choice—I will categorize the theology as *broadly* Arminian.[16]

This theological perspective can be usefully clarified using the distinction between God's antecedent and consequent wills. Eleonore Stump concisely explains the distinction as follows:

> Many of the things which happen in the world are not in accordance with God's *antecedent* will. Roughly put, God's *antecedent* will is what God would have willed if things in the world had been up to God alone. God's *consequent* will is what God in fact wills, given what he knows that his creatures will. God's consequent will is his will for the greatest good available in the circumstances which are generated through creaturely free will.[17]

God's will reflects God's desires, which are always for *the good*. God's *antecedent will* reflects God's *all-else-being-equal* desires—for the individual goods God would realize if circumstances permitted. God's *consequent* will reflects God's *all-things-considered* desires—for the highest good realizable given circumstances that are, in part, what they are because of human free choices. For simplicity, we can use the antecedent/consequent nomenclature for both God's will and God's desires.

There are at least two reasons why circumstances might not permit the realization of God's antecedent desire for the salvation of all. First, it might not be *possible* for God to realize this desire apart from an undetermined free choice. One might think the essence of salvation is loving union with God and that loving union by its nature requires the undetermined free participation of each party. God desires that they choose to love God but cannot *make* them, because anything God makes happen would undermine one of the conditions for loving union.[18]

The second reason why circumstances might not permit the realization of God's antecedent desire for the salvation of all is that those circumstances put some of God's antecedent desires into conflict, such

---

16. It is worth noting, however, that the Lutheran view is a middle ground between the view that we must make an active choice to be saved and the view that we are saved by God apart from our choices. For Lutherans, if we are saved it is entirely on account of God: we have done nothing, and so God's grace operates unimpeded to secure our salvation. If we are unsaved, it is entirely our doing: we have rebuffed the grace that would have saved us had we simply been quiescent.

17. Stump, "Problem of Evil and Desires of the Heart," 209.

18. This appears to be Eleonore Stump's view. See Stump, *Wandering in Darkness*, ch. 6.

that they cannot all be realized at once. Even if we suppose God *could* cause us to love God, God might antecedently desire that such love be a matter of undetermined free choice. But if God also antecedently desires loving union, then a creature failing to freely do their part in creating such union produces circumstances in which God cannot realize *both* antecedent desires.

Or suppose God desires the salvation of everyone on account of love for them but also desires that justice be done—and Betty, by freely sinning but freely failing to repent, comes to deserve a fate incompatible with her salvation. Or perhaps God has made it possible for justice's demands to be met vicariously on the cross, but only if persons freely put their faith in Christ—and Betty has failed to do so. In such cases, God might not be able to satisfy both the desire to save Betty and the desire that justice be done in relation to her.

We thus have a cluster of non-universalist views I am labeling "broadly Arminian" because they share Jacobus Arminius's conviction—contra the Calvinists—that God so loves humanity that God would save all *but for free choices undetermined by God*. But in presupposing this broadly Arminian theology, I am presupposing something *opposed* to Calvinist versions of non-universalism—versions that hold that what ultimately distinguishes the saved from the lost is not some difference in their undetermined free choices but in a sovereign decision of God.

Someone who rejects what I am here calling a broad Arminian theology has at least three alternative theological perspectives they might adopt instead. First, they could hold that human free choices play *no* role in determining who is saved and who isn't. That is determined entirely by God, who saves some and damns others apart from any choices they make (presumably for the sake of achieving some other divine goal, such as creating a world containing vessels of both divine mercy and divine wrath, as traditional Calvinism holds).

Second, they could hold that, while there is a difference between the free choices of the saved and the unsaved, who exhibits the "saving" choices" and who doesn't is determined by God. In other words, although the damned and the saved make different choices, the reason they make different choices is because God causes the difference—by, say, bestowing on some but not others the grace needed to repent (again, presumably, for the sake of achieving some goal such as creating vessels of mercy and wrath). This latter view supposes a "compatibilist" view of freedom distinct from the "libertarian" freedom presumed in broadly Arminian theologies.[19]

Third, they could hold that all of those who make the right undetermined free choices are saved, and some (but not all) of those who fail to do so are then determined by God to make the right choices and so are saved. The idea is this: God imbues humans with the capacity for undetermined or libertarian free choices and saves all those who exercise that freedom appropriately (by, say, not resisting God's resistible grace). Of those who misuse this freedom, God deploys an irresistible grace in relation to some, saving them despite their undetermined free choice to rebuff. But God withholds such grace from others, allowing them thereby to damn themselves (again, for some purpose such as ensuring there are vessels of both mercy and wrath).

Traditional Calvinism, as I understand it, endorses the second of these options, but all three share the view that what distinguishes the damned from at least *some* of the saved has nothing to do with the undetermined free choices they made and everything to do with a divine sovereign decision made for reasons apart from respect for creaturely freedom. And that means, on this view, that God's moral character does not *require* respect for the undetermined free choices of human beings. Such respect for freedom is thus not what ultimately accounts for why some are unsaved. While calling views that fall into any of these three categories "broadly Calvinist" may cause some to balk (especially those who lean towards the third option), for the sake of parity and simplicity I will use that terminology here.

My formulation of the argument from heavenly grief relies on the love premise—a premise that broadly Arminian non-universalists will accept but broadly Calvinist non-universalists should reject. I say *should* reject, not that they always do, for a pair of reasons. First, because their theological commitments *appear* to be at odds with the premise. Second, because if they accept it despite these appearances, they *magnify* the problem of heavenly grief.

With respect to the first point, if at least some of the unsaved are no different from at least some of the damned in terms of their undetermined choices—if what distinguishes them is a matter of sovereign divine will—then *God* elected some for salvation but not others. Thus, God has brought it about, through an exercise of sovereign will, that some are eternally lost, suffering at best a brief and incomplete existence in which

---

19. Again, this is a distinction I will explore more deeply in chapter 6.

they never actualize their potential (on annihilationism), and at worst a fate of eternal suffering (on traditionalism).

But this certainly does not sound like something a loving parent would decide with respect to their beloved child. And the description of God as a heavenly Father immediately suggests that God's love is like a parent's. Loving parents want their children to flourish, to actualize their potential, to be happy and virtuous. And they want to cultivate loving relationships with their children. To will that some be eternally lost is to will that, for some, all or most of these goods that loving parents desire for their children will never be theirs. We can certainly imagine loving parents who watch their children make terrible choices that deprive them of these goods and who don't act to stop it, out of respect for those choices or simply because they don't have the power to fix things. But it is harder to picture loving parents who decide, apart from any choices made by their children, to act in ways that guarantee that some are eternally deprived of happiness, virtue, or existence, while acting decisively to bring these blessings to others. Such parents appear to be playing favorites: loving some of their children with this parental love but not others. Likewise, on a broadly Calvinist non-universalism, it seems God loves some in this way but not others.[20]

If God does not love the lost, there is little reason to think the blessed would. Hence, if broadly Calvinist theologies do imply that God is selective in whom God loves, it follows that these theologies reject the love premise of the argument from heavenly grief. That is, they reject the moral framework on which the argument from heavenly grief depends and from which the eternal loss of the unsaved is most obviously tragic. If this appearance is right, the argument from heavenly grief developed here primarily targets a broadly Arminian non-universalism.

But in saying this, I am *not* saying I won't consider the broadly Calvinist view. I will consider it *as a potential solution* to the problem of heavenly grief. So, I will develop and frame the problem from within a broadly Arminian perspective that affirms the love premise—and I will offer reasons *for* affirming the love premise. I will then consider the broadly Calvinist view as a possible basis for solving the problem. In considering this broadly Calvinist solution, I will offer my reasons for being skeptical of any theology that denies the love premise.

Let me stress, furthermore, that I do not think the broadly Calvinist affirmation of divine sovereignty *by itself* clashes with the love premise. It

---

20. For a rigorous development of this view, see Walls, *Does God Love Everyone?*

only clashes with it when paired with non-universalism. My view is that without something undetermined by God (such as free choices) shaping the circumstances in which God exercises the divine will, *there is nothing to pry apart God's antecedent and consequent wills*. God's antecedent and consequent wills would align—and so, if God does not save all, it is because God's *antecedent will* is not to save all. That is, God wills antecedently that some persons be eternally deprived of goods loving parents antecedently desire their children to have.

But at least some Calvinist thinkers disagree with this apparent implication of their theology, arguing that God can and does love and desire the salvation of all—while deciding not to save all as an act of sovereign divine will. John Piper, for example, holds that God sincerely desires the salvation of all but *also* desires "the manifestation of the full range of God's glory in wrath and mercy (Romans 9:22–23)."[21] Fully manifesting God's glory is more important to God than fully expressing divine love and so prevails over God's love in relation to those God has chosen as vessels of wrath (persons predestined by God for eternal torment).

Still, Piper insists the desire for the salvation of all is real, manifesting as "a real and deep compassion for perishing sinners" and "a genuine inclination" to spare them. These "longings and desires" are real in the sense that "they tell us something true about [God's] character," even if they don't govern God's actions.[22]

On Piper's theology, there is reason to embrace the love premise: if God loves even those God predestines to damnation, then presumably so would the blessed. But unlike the interpretation of Calvinism that denies the love premise, Piper's interpretation offers no solution to the problem of heavenly grief. Arguably, it makes the problem worse. Piper builds into God's very nature an inescapable conflict among divine desires. *No matter what*, God will preside over a world where one or another of God's real desires cannot be fulfilled; one or another of the genuine goods God wants to obtain in the world must be excluded from it. For Piper, the tragic ending in which some goods are eternally unrealized, and God never gets every good thing God wants, has the character of *a foregone conclusion*. What for broadly Arminian theologies is a contingent tragedy, avoidable if only creatures made better choices, is for Piper an *essential* tragedy written into God's immutable character. If it is fitting for the blessed to grieve circumstances in which goods God sincerely desires

---

21. Piper, *Does God Desire All to Be Saved?*, 39.
22. Piper, *Does God Desire All to Be Saved?*, 48–49.

are eternally excluded from creation, then Piper's theology implies it is fitting for the blessed to grieve under *all* circumstances.

Let me unpack this reasoning just a bit. On Piper's view, the salvation of all is something God genuinely desires out of love for creatures. Since God only desires what is good, the salvation of all must be good. What keeps God from acting on this desire and realizing this good is that God has a second desire for an incommensurable good: to fully manifest God's glory through a display of divine justice achieved through inflicting eternal torment on some of those God loves. This second desire is essentially at odds with the first: they clash *under all circumstances*.[23] It isn't the case that if only people would make better choices, God could save all without incurring a conflict with other divine desires. It isn't true that if only everyone would repent and turn to Christ, God could then achieve every good God desires to achieve. Instead, God *needs* for there to be some who don't make the right choices in order for God to realize God's second desire. To achieve the second desire, God must design the world such that the first desire is eternally unfulfilled—and vice versa. Even if we concede Piper's point that there is a hierarchy among God's desires that decides *which* will be fulfilled, it remains true that something God desires—the realization of a genuine good—simply *cannot* be realized. Instead of escaping the problem of heavenly grief, this perspective appears to simply relocate its source, writing the tragedy into the very nature of God (and of reality).

Think of it this way. J. I. Packer describes God's love as follows: "This is what God does for those he loves—*the best He can*; and the measure of the best that God can do is omnipotence!"[24] Thomas Talbott works with this initial definition, noting that doing the best God can for Jacob means God will act in Jacob's best interest to the extent God can.[25] But even if *power* puts no limits on the extent to which God can do this, power may

23. One might question the coherence of Piper positing such an inescapable clash given his penal substitutionary theology. This theology affirms not only that God desires to fully manifest both divine justice and divine love, but also that God has overcome the conflict between these desires on the cross. Christ, in an act of divine love, has met justice's demands in our stead. If this is correct, why would God's desire to manifest justice conflict with God's desire to save all, especially if creaturely freedom imposes no impediment? Given the cross, God has found a way to fully manifest justice *while saving all*. Of course, this solution would require Piper to embrace universalism. For a full development of an argument along these lines (albeit in terms of a Lutheran vicarious atonement theology), see Kronen and Reitan, *God's Final Victory*, 116–23.

24. Packer, *Knowing God*, 115. Cited in Talbott, *Inescapable Love of God*, 124.

25. Talbott, *Inescapable Love of God*, 124.

not be the only potential source of limits. What if God loves both Jacob and Isaac, and what if their best interests are opposed? Then, while God could do what is best for one of them, God could not do what is best for both.[26] This represents a kind of conflict among God's desires—specifically, a conflict between God's desire to maximize Jacob's best interest, and God's desire to maximize Isaac's. What Piper posits is *this* kind of limit on the best God can do for those God loves. God's desire to manifest the divine glory precludes God from maximizing the best interests of all those God loves. Given God's desire to manifest divine glory, the *best* God can do for the non-elect is *eternal conscious torment*.

Suppose God really loves Janet. If the best God can do for her is to predestine her to hell, isn't *that* a tragedy? Isn't it deeply tragic that God, who sincerely loves Janet and so aims to do the best God can for her, *can't* do better for Janet than damnation? If the best I could do for my daughter was arrange for her a fate in which a car accident leaves her blind, paralyzed, and covered head to toe in agonizing burns for the rest of her life, I would fittingly weep, as any loving parent would if this was the best they could do for their child. I would also weep were her death the best I could do for her. If God sincerely loves the unsaved and damnation (or annihilation) is the best God can do for them given God's other priorities, wouldn't God fittingly weep—and the blessed, who love God, fittingly weep along?

In short, Piper's version of Calvinist non-universalism—which affirms a divine love for all but puts it in inescapable conflict with other divine motives—appears to magnify the problem of heavenly grief *through its inescapability* rather than offer the promise of a solution. Hence, I will hereafter assume that those non-universalists who embrace the love premise adopt a broadly Arminian theology. I will thus be primarily positing this broadly Arminian perspective as the target of the argument from heavenly grief, and I will be taking up a broadly Calvinist theology only insofar as it offers a potential solution to the problem of heavenly grief in the form of denying the love premise.

SOLUTIONS, THEODICIES, AND DEFENSES

One final issue I want to explore in this introductory chapter has to do with my methodology. Once I have constructed what I think is the

---

26. Talbott, *Inescapable Love of God*, 125–26.

strongest version of the argument from heavenly grief, I will look at various attempted solutions. But what do I mean by a *solution*? One way to construe a *solution* to the *problem* of heavenly grief is to identify it with a convincing *objection* to the *argument* from heavenly grief. But I think more needs to be said, given some of the ways in which solutions to the problem of evil have been construed.

In contemporary philosophy of religion, it has become common to talk about two ways of responding to the problem of evil: by providing a *theodicy* or a *defense*. This distinction was first articulated by Alvin Plantinga in response to J. L. Mackie's attempt to argue that the existence of a perfectly good and almighty God is logically incompatible with the existence of the world's evils.[27] Plantinga notes there are two ways to address such a claim. First, you can offer a *theodicy*: an attempt to explain why God, despite being almighty and perfectly good, permits the world's evils. If your explanation makes sense of why God would permit the world's evils without giving up on God's goodness or power—and without requiring you to endorse claims that seem to you clearly false, so that you can in good conscience stand behind the explanation and endorse it—then it would obviously count as a *solution* to the problem of evil.

But you might instead offer something more modest: a *defense*. By a defense, Plantinga means an attempt, not to actually explain why God permits the world's evils, but to show that their existence is logically compatible with God's existence. A defense does this by putting forward something that's *possibly* true—a proposition or set of propositions—that *resembles* the explanation offered in a theodicy: it provides the basis for a picture of how things are, one that includes God's existence and the existence of evil without entailing any contradictions. But the explanation you offer in a defense—which I'll call a "reconciling story"—needn't be something you think is actually true. You're not giving an account of why God permits evils. Instead, you're saying something like this: "Suppose things were *this way*. Things being this way is coherent—it *might* be true that things are this way, even though I'm not claiming they are. And if things *were* this way *and* God existed (a conjunction that is itself logically coherent), it follows that God would permit the world's evils."

If you can come up with such a reconciling story, you have shown that there is no strict logical incompatibility between God and evil. But have you offered a *solution* to the problem of evil, given that you've done nothing to support the *truth* of the reconciling story?

27. See Mackie, "Evil and Omnipotence"; Plantinga, *God, Freedom, and Evil*.

Philosophers generally agree there is something you *have* done: you have refuted what has come to be called "the logical argument from evil," an argument that purports to demonstrate a logical or quasi-logical incompatibility between evil's existence and God's. But the problem of evil might persist even if, taken in isolation, evil's existence is logically compatible with God's existence. This fact manifests in the history of philosophical discussion of the problem of evil through the emergence of so-called "evidential" arguments from evil in the wake of Plantinga's "free will defense" against the logical argument.[28] It became clear that even though Plantinga had done something important, the problem of evil persisted: it had not been *solved*.

Although I could explain why by digging more deeply into the problem of evil, it may be more helpful to shift to a simpler example to show why a defense is rarely enough to "solve" a problem like the problem of evil . . . or the problem of heavenly grief.

Suppose I confront two claims: (a) "Andre is a surgeon's son"; (b) "Andre's father is not a surgeon." Suppose I don't see how both can be true. But you happen to know that Andre's mother is a surgeon. You tell me so and thus show me he *is* the son of a surgeon, even though his father is no surgeon. You have offered the equivalent of a theodicy: an account of the way you actually believe things to be that reconciles the two claims.

But suppose you know absolutely nothing about Andre or his family. You might still say, "Those two things are perfectly compatible! Maybe Andre's mother is a surgeon." You have no clue whether this is true. But it is possible, it's compatible with Andre's dad not being a surgeon, and the whole picture implies Andre is a surgeon's son. Have you *solved* the problem?

That depends. Rarely, if ever, do we care only about the strict logical compatibility of two propositions in isolation. We also care about the coherence of affirming both within the context of background conditions we take to be true. Sometimes, a reconciling story as simple as "Maybe Andre's mother is a surgeon" will solve the problem because it calls attention to the fact that I've been operating unconsciously with false background assumptions. Maybe I am sexist and out of touch with recent history, and so I have been blithely assuming that women aren't surgeons—and this is why I've been having trouble reconciling the claims. In challenging my assumptions by asserting that a counterexample could be true,

---

28. See especially Rowe, "Problem of Evil"; Russell, "Persistent Problem of Evil."

INTRODUCTION TO THE PROBLEM   21

you've forced me to acknowledge something I was implicitly denying: some women are surgeons. The problem has been solved.

But suppose that, unlike you, I actually know a few things about Andre, and this background information is contributing to my problem. Specifically, I know that he lived in early nineteenth-century France, and his mother was a famous opera singer. In addition to these facts about Andre, I also have some historical knowledge, including that the first woman admitted into medical school in France was Madeleine Brés in the 1870s, years after Andre's death. I also have general knowledge about human capacities that tells me it would be hard to pursue a career both as a surgeon and as a successful opera singer, given the demands of both jobs.

With this background information, the fact that Andre's mother *could* have been a surgeon is not enough to solve my problem. Even if I acknowledge that this is a picture of things that *might* be true, and even if I concede that on this picture Andre would be a surgeon's son even were Andre's father not a surgeon, I'll still have trouble reconciling the claims that Andre is a surgeon's son but his father is no surgeon—because I have reason to think the reconciling story, while *possibly* true, is *actually* false. Given the background information, it seems *unreasonable* to believe the reconciling story.

Still, you might modify your reconciling story to account for these background facts: Andre's mother disguised herself as a man by day to study medicine, while continuing her opera career at night. You have no evidence that she did these things, but they are possibly true and accommodate the background information. While not the most likely scenario, I've heard stories of women masquerading as men in more sexist times to pursue vocations from which women were excluded. So I take your suggestion seriously, digging into archival documents to see if I can learn more about Andre's mother.

Suppose I learn she was a busy socialite, routinely seen in cafes and salons by day and at post-opera parties late at night. How, then, could she be disguising herself as a man by day to attend medical school? Once again, further background information derails the reconciling story. But suppose you modify your story even further to accommodate these additional facts: maybe she had a secret lover who was a surgeon and taught her in private late at night.

I might respond, "I suppose that is theoretically possible, but it seems highly unlikely. When did she sleep?" I return to the archives and find no record of the ill health that chronic sleep deprivation would produce. In fact, she lived to a ripe old age and was still performing in her sixties, reportedly looking as young and beautiful as women half her age. Armed with this further information, I dismiss the late-night private surgery lessons theory.

Now suppose you answer with, "Maybe she was genetically modified by space aliens so that she didn't need sleep."

At this point I'm not going to head back to the archives. Instead, I'll roll my eyes. Even though you've constructed a reconciling story consistent with all background information, one that isn't *impossible* (intelligent aliens meddling in human affairs is surely *possible*), I'm likely to conclude that if Andre's *father* wasn't a surgeon, Andre wasn't a surgeon's son. And I would be justified in doing so, even though you have presented me with a defense that "works" in the technical sense of showing that there is no strict inconsistency between the original propositions.

Your defense fails as a *solution*, even though it achieves what a *defense* is intended to achieve, because the reconciling story has become increasingly *implausible*. As we gathered more background information, we discovered that the path to our two propositions both being true became increasingly narrow: the world had to be arranged *just so* in order for Andre to remain a surgeon's son despite his father being no surgeon. And this just-so arrangement isn't a commonplace just-so arrangement but a conjunction of highly rare occurrences. We don't typically find early nineteenth-century French women pursuing successful opera careers and full social calendars while studying surgery under a lover's tutelage in the dead of night, fighting off sleep deprivation with the help of space aliens (or some implausibly robust constitution, etc.). In fact, this reconciling story is so deeply at odds with the way we think the world ordinarily operates that, absent paradigm-shattering evidence that would force us to revise our basic belief system, *we shouldn't believe it*. And since we shouldn't believe it, it doesn't solve the problem of reconciling the original propositions.

The defense we arrived at was the outcome of a series of modifications introduced to address additional background information, with each subsequent iteration of the defense becoming less plausible than the one before. Had there been no relevant conflicting background information to drive a further modification, we could have stopped with the more plausible defense.

What this shows is that defenses admit of varying degrees of plausibility. In light of this, I am inclined to think the distinction between a theodicy and a defense is not the most important or useful one. Instead of a binary distinction, it may be better to envision a continuum. When confronted with the challenge of reconciling two propositions that appear incompatible given relevant background conditions we take to be true, there will be reconciling stories of greater or lesser plausibility, with a "theodicy" falling on the most plausible end of the continuum. Whether a reconciling story counts as a solution will depend on where it lies on this continuum and thus may itself be a matter of degrees.

We might say that some solutions come with minor costs, while others come with more significant costs—where a "cost" is a modification to our broader network of reasonable beliefs that the solution forces us to make, which involves either accepting as true something we have reason to think false or rejecting as false something we have reason to think true. In other words, we can ask *how costly* a solution is, in terms of how much it challenges our network of reasonable beliefs. We can then compare the costs of any given solution with the costs of escaping the problem by rejecting one of the apparently conflicting propositions. If the costs of a solution are greater than the costs of escape, the solution doesn't work.

There is a clear relationship between investigating proposed solutions to a problem of this kind and evaluating an argument: the problem of reconciling two propositions arises because we can formulate an argument that has one proposition as a premise, has the negation of the other as a conclusion and has as its additional premises things drawn from our network of reasonable beliefs. Reconciling stories are pictures of the way things might be arranged that call into question one or more of these additional premises. In the initial sexist version of the above narrative, I am deducing that Andre is not a surgeon's son from the premise that Andre's father is not a surgeon and the hidden premise that women are not surgeons. The very simple reconciling story raised in that case—maybe his mother is a surgeon—exposes the hidden premise. Once it is exposed, it is quickly seen to be false. The argument is refuted and the problem solved.

But when arguments involve more defensible background assumptions, reconciling stories may be less successful. If Andre lived in nineteenth-century France, the simply story, "Andre's mother was a surgeon," won't derail a formulation of the argument featuring, first, the premise that a woman living at that time and place could not become a surgeon unless she pursued extraordinary means, and, second, that Andre's mother did not pursue such extraordinary means. Assuming we have good reasons to suppose the second is true absent the intervention of gene-altering aliens or a similarly implausible hypothesis, the argument remains compelling even in the face of a reconciling story that posits just such an implausible hypothesis. Put simply, the costs of accepting the reconciling story are higher than the costs of sticking to the premises of the argument the story aims to challenge.

Based on all of this, we might define a "clear solution" to the problem of heavenly grief as *an uncostly picture of the way things are* that exposes an error in the premises of the argument from heavenly grief, an error that cannot be readily fixed by introducing further background information (that is, by making uncostly modifications to existing premises and/or introducing uncostly additional premises). But even absent a *clear* solution in this sense, one might have a compelling solution if *all* the options—including the *escapes* from the problem—are costly, and the reconciling story is the least costly. Hence, a fully satisfactory assessment of a purported solution can't take place absent an evaluation of the costs of other solutions and escapes.

In this book, I will pursue this kind of dialectical approach to the problem: developing what I take to be the strongest version of the argument from heavenly grief, considering the costs of purported solutions, and exploring the costs of escape. I say I will *pursue* this task. I cannot pretend my examination is the final word in the discussion. But I hope readers will gain three things from this work: first, a deeper understanding of the relevant issues and arguments; second, a framework for thinking about the problem of heavenly grief that can facilitate future discussion; and, finally, a better sense of why a Christian (like me) might reasonably think the universalist escape is the least costly path to follow.

2

Portraits of Grief

SLUMBER PARTIES IN THE SHADOW OF DEATH

IN THE SPRING AFTER my father's death, on the night before Easter, my kids announced they wanted to have a slumber party. It would involve bringing my younger child's stuffed "lion-bear" across the hall. And maybe her pillow.

The two were anxiously awaiting my blessing. My youngest clung to my leg saying, "Can we, Daddy? Can we?" while the older one shouted, "It's Easter Eve! It's a special occasion!"

As I looked down at my joyful children, it was hard not to see in this eager spring moment the shadow of October—hard not to hear that same request, born then from the need for comfort in the dark.

It came, that previous time, while I was packing for an unexpected flight. I'd originally been scheduled to travel later in the week: a visit to my ailing father. But my sister's urgent phone call inspired a change of plans. "I told him you were coming on Thursday," she said. "I asked if he could hold out that long. He said yes, but his eyes . . . I don't think he'll make it."

As I was packing, my children handed me a Perry the Platypus baseball cap. They knew my father had a thing for interesting hats. "Take this. Fafa will like it." As I threw it in my bag, I imagined sitting by my father's sick bed with that absurd hat perched on my head.

"Can Sissy stay with me tonight? Like when we're on vacation?"

"Sure," I said, blinking against a surge of feeling.

As I put them to bed I reminded them I'd be gone before they woke. I could see in their faces the weight of it, the awareness of this enormous and inevitable thing.

The call came half an hour later. I thought of waking the kids, giving them the news before I left. Instead, I went to their door just to look at them. I held close the image of those two faces, so alike in the darkness, so at peace in the restless night.

The next morning I was on a plane. The trip had changed from a last chance to say goodbye into something full of anguish. I reached into my bag for a book, something to distract me from the waves of pain, but my hand closed instead on the Perry the Platypus hat. I rocked in my seat, hugging myself and sobbing and imagining my childhood home without my father in it.

It proved hard to do because so much of him still littered the house. I'd round a corner and I'd see something of his, set aside as if at any moment he'd return to reclaim it: his reading glasses on an end-table, his well-worn slippers set neatly side-by-side near the recliner. I fled the house to escape the triggers for my grief, but as I walked the neighborhood, I confronted the old corner building that used to house the first barber I visited. I pictured my father leading me inside, helping me into one of the green polyester chairs. I turned onto Main Street and saw the pub where I'd taken him for Father's Day the year after I became a father.

Escape only came when I flew home to a world he'd never inhabited, a home he'd never visited because we moved into it months before he died. There, it was almost possible to forget. I could pretend he was still around, still a plane ride or phone call away.

And here I stood, six months later, and my kids were asking for a slumber party. I stumbled with the weight of unexpected grief. My children jumped and pleaded and spun, their spirits full of the promise of tomorrow: stories of an empty tomb, the unfurled "Alleluia!" banner, the pastel Easter outfits, and spring grass littered with brightly colored eggs. Yesterday we sat in silence as the bell tolled three times, as the altar went dark, as the Good Friday service reminded us of crucifixion. But tomorrow there'd be trumpets.

In the light of Easter's promise, my grief changed. Two slumber parties in the shadow of death, one born from its anticipation, the other from anticipation of its transcendence. I saw my children's smiles and recalled their sleeping faces in the dark. I was trembling at the edge of the numinous.

"Can we, Daddy? Can we? Can we? It's Easter Eve!"

I blinked against the pain and comfort that were here at once: the vivid reminder of my father's absence paired with this joy, this unspeakable joy.

TAKING EMOTIONAL EXPERIENCE INTO ACCOUNT

I begin with these trembling feelings on the eve of an Easter celebration because this is a book about grief and the scope of Easter's promise. But it is also an academic book written by an analytically trained philosopher. And it is easy in such a book to get caught up in the gristle of arguments, logic-chopping one's way to a place so far removed from our human experience of love and loss and consolation that the point of the exercise is lost.

I begin here because I take seriously Marilyn McCord Adams's words at the close of her essay, "The Problem of Hell: A Problem of Evil for Christians"—specifically her claim that "feelings are highly relevant to the problem of evil and the problem of hell, because they are one source of information about how bad something is for a person."[1] She concedes that feelings are not an infallible source. But, she goes on,

> Where questions of value are concerned, reason is not an infallible source either. That is why so-called value calculations in abstraction from feelings can strike us as "cold" or "callous." I do not believe we have any infallible faculties at all. But our best shot at valuations will come from the collaboration of feelings and reason, the latter articulating the former, the former giving data to the latter.[2]

In this spirit, she invites all who think "the saved can in good conscience let their happiness be unaffected by the plight of the damned because the destruction of the latter is self-willed" to spend time "visiting patients who are dying of emphysema or of the advanced effects of alcoholism, to listen with sympathetic presence, to enter into their point of view on their lives, to face their pain and despair."[3]

From this emotional space, Adams thinks we cannot "in good conscience dismiss their suffering with 'Oh, well, they brought it on

---

1. Adams, "Problem of Hell," 326.
2. Adams, "Problem of Hell," 326.
3. Adams, "Problem of Hell," 326.

themselves!'"[4] From a place of love, we attend empathetically to their suffering and thus grasp it more truly. She sees this point as "an extension of the old Augustinian-Platonist point, that where values are concerned, what and how well you see depends not simply on how well you think, but on what and how well you love."[5]

Or consider these words from C. S. Lewis in *A Grief Observed*, in which he records his grief journey in the wake of his wife's death:

> From the rational point of view, what new factor had H's death introduced into the problem of the universe? I knew already that these things, and worse, happened daily. I would have said that I had taken them into account. . . . The faith which "took these things into account" was not faith but imagination. The taking them into account was not real sympathy. If I had really cared, as I thought I did, about the sorrows of the world, I should not have been so overwhelmed when my own sorrow came.[6]

Nicholas Wolterstorff expresses something similar in his *Lament for a Son*, as he grapples with the loss of his twenty-five-year-old son to a climbing accident. Like Lewis, he articulates the irreplaceability of direct emotional experience when it comes to understanding the significance of loss and suffering:

> The suffering of the world has worked its way deeper inside me. I never knew that sorrow could be like this. Six months before, I had gone to the funeral of the twenty-three-year-old son of friends. I tried to imagine the quality of their grief. I know now that I failed miserably.
>
> Each person's suffering has its own quality. No outsider can fully enter it. Yet more of suffering is now accessible to me.[7]

Adams is right to warn us against a purely intellectual engagement with matters of Christian soteriology. Human feelings—the data they provide, however flawed and fallible—are essential for reflecting wisely on these matters. In the case of the present study, they are also a starting point for extrapolation. To assess whether grief for the lost would diminish the joy of the blessed, we need to extrapolate from the human experience of grief. But here, we must take seriously another warning.

---

4. Adams, "Problem of Hell," 326.
5. Adams, "Problem of Hell," 327.
6. Lewis, *Grief Observed*, 31.
7. Wolterstorff, *Lament for a Son*, 72.

Unlike the blessed, we are not morally sanctified. Hence, our extrapolations from our own experience must be guided by the effort to bracket all those dimensions of this experience that spring from moral imperfection.

When Lewis considers the twin Christian promises of heaven—the "mystical union" with God and "re-union with the dead"—he warns that the ideas we have of them are extrapolations. "The reality of either," he says, "would probably blow all one's ideas about both (how much more one's ideas about their relations to each other) into smithereens."[8] The same can surely be said about the emotional lives of the blessed. We must be careful, then, about extrapolating too confidently from this-worldly emotions in our efforts to understand what those in heaven would feel. But to treat this as a reason to ignore our experience with grief is folly. It would mean untethering our reflections from reality. Love and grief are not abstract intellectual curiosities but realities deeply woven into the human condition. Better to extrapolate from imperfect data than from none at all. As Wolterstorff puts it, "I shall look at the world through tears. Perhaps I shall see things that dry-eyed I could not see."[9]

A GRIEF OBSERVED

One of the most powerful literary portraits of grief we have is C. S. Lewis's *A Grief Observed*, in which Lewis journals his way through shattering loss. The result is a series of raw reflections on grief by one of our most gifted writers and thinkers.

As powerful as it is, there is an important limit on its value for the present study. The problem is this: Lewis's grief journey is one in which the Easter promise, initially obscured by the magnitude of his loss, steadily creeps back in. As he struggles out of the self-focused pit of his initial torment, it is towards a vision in which "She is in God's hand."[10] Lewis does not imagine his wife damned or annihilated, and so does not grieve for her as he would had he believed her to be *eternally* lost.

The closest he comes to doing so is at the very beginning of his grief journey, where he is in the grip of "maudlin tears" and feels disgusted by his own "bath of self-pity, the wallow, the loathsome sticky-sweet pleasure

---

8. Lewis, *Grief Observed*, 55–56.
9. Wolterstorff, *Lament for a Son*, 26.
10. Lewis, *Grief Observed*, 50.

of indulging it."[11] In this state, both God and his wife seem wholly absent. With an earlier friend's death, one that hit less close to home, Lewis had "a most vivid feeling of certainty about his continued life." But now, his wife gone, there is no such assurance: "I have begged to be given even one hundredth part of the same assurance about H. There is no answer. Only the locked door, the iron curtain, the vacuum, absolute zero."[12]

The very question of whether she is "with God" strikes him as "not after all very important in relation to grief." In response to those who tell him her life goes on beyond this world, he declares, "But my heart and body are crying out, come back, come back. . . . [T]he thing I want is exactly the thing I can never get. The old life, the jokes, the drinks, the arguments, the lovemaking, the tiny, heartbreaking commonplace."[13]

In short, Lewis finds himself focused inward. This stage of his grief journey, where he cannot see his wife's death through the lens of the Easter promise, is also the stage at which he is wallowing in anguish over the loss of the joys of his life with her. In other words, his disconnect from Easter's promise is wedded to a fixation on what *Lewis* has been deprived of.

Such a fixation is natural and human, and since these are real losses, there is nothing unfitting or improper about grieving them. In this, Lewis is surely too hard on himself. Still, we wouldn't expect the morally sanctified to be narrowly fixated on the personal goods *they* have lost on account of someone else being lost. Wouldn't they also—and perhaps primarily—grieve the fact that the loved one is *gone*, that the good of their very being has been vitiated or destroyed, apart from how that affects *them*?

Lewis's grief, at its early stages, betrays the limitations of our imperfect state. Lewis knows as much. In response to a friend who quotes to him, "Do not mourn like those that have no hope," he responds, "It astonishes me, the way we are invited to apply to ourselves words so obviously addressed to our betters." He sees how far he is from the moral condition of the saints: "What St. Paul says can comfort only those who love God better than the dead, and the dead better than themselves. If a mother is mourning not for what she has lost but for what her dead child

---

11. Lewis, *Grief Observed*, 8.
12. Lewis, *Grief Observed*, 11.
13. Lewis, *Grief Observed*, 22.

has lost, it is a comfort to believe that the child has not lost the end for which it was created."[14]

Lewis's immunity to comfort comes from the self-focused character of his grief—paired with his intellectual honesty. He can find no comfort in "all that stuff about family reunions 'on the further shore,' pictured in entirely earthly terms," because the truth couldn't be like that. "Reality never repeats. The exact same thing is never taken away and given back."[15] His fixation is on the exact life he had before—not just on a relationship with his wife, but one with all the familiar contours. Whatever the Easter promise means, it isn't the restoration of *that*. His grief is thus not just egoistic but tied to a kind of *toxic nostalgia*.

This is why he finds his faith irrelevant to his grief: "Talk to me about the truth of religion and I'll listen gladly. Talk to me about the duty of religion and I'll listen submissively. But don't come talking to me about the consolations of religion or I shall suspect that you don't understand."[16]

In the course of journaling about his loss, he transitions out of this self-focused, toxically nostalgic state into one more like that of the imagined mother, consoled by the promise that her child hasn't lost the end for which they were made. But this transition is almost perfectly aligned with a restored sense of his wife's persistence beyond death.

A pivotal moment in his grief journey happens when a good night's sleep and pleasant weather lift him from his wallowing. He suddenly has something "better than memory" of his wife: "an instantaneous, unanswerable impression. To say it was like a meeting would be going too far. Yet there was that in it which tempts one to use those words. It was as if the lifting of the sorrow removed a barrier."[17]

This experience becomes a recurring theme. He describes "a sort of unobtrusive but massive sense that she is, just as much as ever, a fact to be taken into account."[18] His earlier, self-focused grief was an impediment to this contact: "Passionate grief does not link us with the dead but cuts us off from them."[19] And so he decides to "turn to her as often as possible

---

14. Lewis, *Grief Observed*, 24.
15. Lewis, *Grief Observed*, 23.
16. Lewis, *Grief Observed*, 23.
17. Lewis, *Grief Observed*, 37.
18. Lewis, *Grief Observed*, 42.
19. Lewis, *Grief Observed*, 44.

in gladness. I will even salute her with a laugh. The less I mourn her the nearer I seem to her."[20]

Lewis releases his longing for the way things were, for the specific joys of their prior relationship. His love becomes more about the reality of *her*: "The earthly beloved... incessantly triumphs over your mere idea of her. And you want her to; you want her with all her resistances, all her faults, all her unexpectedness. That is, in her foursquare and independent reality. And this, not any image or memory, is what we are to love still, after she is dead."[21]

In this space of other-directed love, Lewis's grief abates. But the object of that love, for Lewis, is the woman he imagines a sword in God's hand: "Now perhaps He grasps the hilt; weighs the new weapon; makes lightnings with it in the air. 'A right Jerusalem blade.'"[22] But what if this "foursquare and independent reality" that "we are to love still" were defined instead by eternal conscious torment, or eternal entrenchment in stultifying vice, or annihilation? What if the reality we are to love is precisely the opposite of what Lewis concedes might comfort the mother who loves her dead child well? What if that mother, who selflessly loves her child, learns that this child has eternally *lost* "the end for which it was created"?

This is the possibility the problem of heavenly grief asks us to confront, and it is precisely this possibility about which Lewis's powerful memoir has essentially nothing directly to say. There is only one moment in his memoir when, from a standpoint of selfless love for his wife's being, he imagines eternal separation from her: "If I knew that to be eternally divided from H. and eternally forgotten by her would add a greater joy and splendor to her being, of course I'd say 'Fire ahead.'"[23] But eternal separation as a way to *magnify* someone's joy and *add splendor* to their being is hardly what we confront with respect to the lost. Far from adding splendor to their being, the separation of the lost diminishes or destroys it.

What if, with the perfected love the blessed possess, we love someone who is not just cut off from us but cut off in a way that permanently diminishes or harms them? What if they have, in the end, become a locus

---

20. Lewis, *Grief Observed*, 45–46.
21. Lewis, *Grief Observed*, 52.
22. Lewis, *Grief Observed*, 50.
23. Lewis, *Grief Observed*, 54.

of *eternally* unrealized potential, a focal point not merely of actual goods forever lost but of potential goods that will never be realized?

JOURNEYS OF GRIEF

Even if Lewis's reflections on grief provide no direct answers to these questions, they provide important lessons valuable for the sake of extrapolation. First, and most obviously, grief is intimately tied to love. We may regret the loss of those we don't love and perhaps feel a momentary sadness. But absent love, we do not grieve.

Second, even if Lewis disgusts himself with the "sticky-sweet pleasure" of wallowing in his loss, the truth is that what has been taken from him is a rich set of authentic goods: laughter and intimacy, honest connection, a person who challenged him with her otherness. These are goods Lewis *should* value. And to value them and *not* grieve their loss would be a mark of callousness. If there is *progress* in Lewis's grief journey, it lies not in losing touch with these losses but situating them within the context of more profound objective values (his wife's *being* and her self-actualization) and the Easter promise that what he's lost will be restored in a new, more perfect form. In the immediate aftermath of loss, especially given the ambiguity of our terrestrial lives, the raw fact of death can shatter our capacity to appreciate that context.

This points to another feature of grief that Lewis's account illuminates: its progressive nature. As Lewis puts it,

> I thought I could describe a *state*; make a map of sorrow. Sorrow, however, turns out to be not a state but a process. It needs not a map but a history, and if I don't stop writing that history at some quite arbitrary point, there's no reason why I should ever stop. There is something new to be chronicled every day. Grief is like a long valley, a winding valley where any bend may reveal a totally new landscape.... Sometimes the surprise is the opposite one; you are presented with exactly the same sort of country you thought you had left behind miles ago. That is when you wonder whether the valley isn't a circular trench. But it isn't. There are partial recurrences, but the sequence doesn't repeat.[24]

Although the journey of grief is not one that ends, there is a forward movement that can even look like "getting over it," a kind of healing. But

---

24. Lewis, *Grief Observed*, 47.

even with the healing, Lewis notes that grief's pain and impact persist in new forms. He likens it to a man who loses a leg. Even after it heals, "he will probably have recurrent pains in the stump all his life, and perhaps pretty bad ones; and he will always be a one-legged man. There will be hardly any moment when he forgets it."[25] If we lose a loved one, grief will endure—including pain and awareness of what their absence means—even if it ceases to be all-consuming.

But for the blessed in heaven, it seems the journey of grief *can* reach an end through heavenly re-union—even if, as Lewis warns, relationships in heaven will be unlike relationships in this life. Given their sanctified state, the blessed would be free of toxic nostalgia. Hence, restoration of relationships in a new and perfected form would end grief's journey and its pains.

In other words, we can imagine grief itself as but a stage in a larger journey of human relationship transformed in the light of sanctifying grace. But that would apply only to the blessed in relation to one another. If non-universalism is true, there would be no next stage in the journey of human relationship with *the lost*. There would be no transition out of the grief-stage and into the stage of heavenly reunion. And if grief is not superseded (and so ended) by the next stage in human relationship, why suppose it would end at all for the blessed who love the lost?

It is worth noting here that, for Lewis, the connection between grief and love cannot be limited to those on this side of death's divide: "If, as I can't help suspecting, the dead also feel the pains of separation (and this may be one of the purgatorial sufferings), then for both lovers, and for all pairs of lovers without exception, bereavement is a universal and integral part of our experience of love."[26]

Lewis's parenthetical remark that the pains of separation might be purgatorial suggests that grief can be part of God's means of sanctifying the saved. His own experience with grief supports this view: his grief makes him confront his imperfections and pushes him towards a love less self-focused and toxically nostalgic. While each stage of his grief features vivid emotional awareness of loss, the earliest stage is bound up with *how her participation in his life impacted him*. His love for her was surely not limited to these things. Surely he valued her existence and happiness in themselves. But such non-instrumental love is hard for flawed people in

---

25. Lewis, *Grief Observed*, 43.
26. Lewis, *Grief Observed*, 41.

this life to disentangle from a more instrumental love in which one values how the lost loved one contributed to one's own quality of life. So many of the joys of Lewis's life, once his wife became a part of it, were joys she played a role in producing. In the first stages of grief, Lewis fixates on these losses. He defines his life so much in relation to her that, with her gone, his life unravels and he finds he can't do anything—what he calls "the laziness of grief."[27]

Because such misery cannot be endured, the suffering *forces* a change. The bereaved must choose between self-destruction and transformation. Lewis's grief journey teaches him to love in a way that acknowledges the reality of the other *as other* and values the other *as other*. This is grief's purgatorial nature: like a refiner's fire, grief perfects his love. Towards the end of his reflections, Lewis articulates "one of the miracles of love," namely its "power of seeing through its own enchantments and yet not being disenchanted."[28] He likens it to seeing as God does: "His love and His knowledge are not distinct from one another, nor from Him. We could almost say He sees because He loves, and therefore loves although He sees."[29] If there is a mature grief at which Lewis arrives despite the grief journey continuing on, it is one informed by this kind of love.

Wolterstorff's grief journey, described in *Lament for a Son*, looks different. In fact, Wolterstorff warns that "each grief over death has its own character—its own inscape."[30] At one point, Wolterstorff explicitly contrasts his grief journey with Lewis's:

> C. S. Lewis, writing about the death of his wife, was plainly angry with God. He, Lewis, deserved something better than to be treated so shabbily. I am not angry but baffled and hurt. My wound is an unanswered question. The wounds of all humanity are unanswered questions.[31]

But in addition to this stated difference, another difference emerges when we read the works side-by-side: Wolterstorff's grief, from the start, combines an awareness of what *he* has lost in losing his son Eric with a deep sense of what *Eric* has lost, and the way the world itself is diminished by Eric no longer being in it.

27. Lewis, *Grief Observed*, 8.
28. Lewis, *Grief Observed*, 56.
29. Lewis, *Grief Observed*, 57.
30. Wolterstorff, *Lament for a Son*, 56.
31. Wolterstorff, *Lament for a Son*, 68.

It is the being and well-being of his son that he grieves. For Wolterstorff, this less self-focused grief—grief for what is gone, what will never be, for potential unrealized—does not emerge alongside assurances of the loved one's persistence in God's hand. Rather, it is born in the earliest stages of loss, amidst the inescapable awareness of his son's absence: "In all the crowds and streets and rooms and churches and schools and libraries and gatherings of friends in our world, on all the mountains, I will not find him. Only his absence."[32] And yet, in that vivid consciousness of absence, there is more than sticky-sweet self-pity. Wolterstorff's grief is tied to "the hole in the world" created by his son's absence:

> There's nobody now who saw just what he saw, knows what he knew, remembers what he remembered, loves what he loved. A person, an irreplaceable person, is gone. Never again will anyone apprehend the world quite the way he did. Never again will anyone inhabit the world the way he did. Questions I have can never now get answers. The world is emptier.[33]

And his grief is not confined to the lost *being* of his son, but also extends to what Eric has lost through death:

> Loss is his as well. How very strange! Yet I feel it acutely. His sudden early death is not just our loss but his: the loss of seeing trees, of hearing music, of reading books, of writing books, of walking through cathedrals, of visiting friends, of being with family, of marrying, of going to church, and—dare I say it—of climbing mountains.[34]

Wolterstorff grieves what has been taken from the world and from Eric: "All the rich future that he held—gone in those tumbling seconds. His death is things to do not done—never to be done."[35] Wolterstorff's grief encompasses the *opportunities* lost with the death of his child.

If the blessed in heaven are human, then surely they will love in this beautiful human way—a love that values the *being* of the loved-one, that cares about their welfare not just in terms of the goods those loved ones in fact enjoy but in terms of their potential and its realization. The grief associated with such love would not be limited to the self-focused grief that cries out, "Something I've wedded my welfare to has been taken

---

32. Wolterstorff, *Lament for a Son*, 14.
33. Wolterstorff, *Lament for a Son*, 33.
34. Wolterstorff, *Lament for a Son*, 49.
35. Wolterstorff, *Lament for a Son*, 30.

away!" Instead, it will be a grief that cries out for the good that is gone and the potential snuffed out—a grief that cries out with Wolterstorff, "I lament all that might have been, and now will never be."[36]

Such a love will not just care about the loved one's *being* and *well-being* but also the good of mutual love—the *intimate relationship* that unites loved ones. While blessed love won't be nostalgically tethered to a particular form such relationship took in the past, it will grieve the loss of such relationship. At least as significantly, it will grieve the ways such relationship failed to be fully realized. This, too, finds expression in Wolterstorff's grief:

> What do I do now with my regrets—over the time I neglected to take him along hiking, over the times I placed work ahead of being with him, over the times I postponed writing letters, over the times I unreasonably got angry with him—over all the times I hurt him, times I noticed the hurt and times I didn't but should have. . . . When the person is living we can make amends. . . . But when the person is dead, what do we do with our regrets?[37]

Although Wolterstorff only mentions his own shortcomings here, relational failures are always mutual in this life (even if, in abusive relationships, violation and exploitation are usually one-sided). And no matter who fell short and how, the unrealized potential is something to grieve. For Wolterstorff, the awareness of that unrealized potential—of all the what-might-have-beens in his relationship with Eric—is brought into focus by regret. He commits to allowing his regrets "to sharpen the vision and intensify the hope for that Great Day coming when we can all throw ourselves into each other's arms and say, 'I'm sorry.'"[38] Wolterstorff's faith hopes for such a day: "The God of love will surely grant such a day. Love needs that."[39]

The love that cries out for such a day is the mature love that yearns for the continued existence, welfare, and full actualization of the beloved, and for the flowering of perfected human relationship. For Wolterstorff, this "Great Day" is the only true consolation for grief, the only thing that can bring it to an end:

---

36. Wolterstorff, *Lament for a Son*, 22.
37. Wolterstorff, *Lament for a Son*, 64.
38. Wolterstorff, *Lament for a Son*, 65.
39. Wolterstorff, *Lament for a Son*, 65.

> I did not grieve as one who has no hope. Yet Eric is gone, *here* and *now* he is gone; *now* I cannot talk with him, *now* I cannot see him, *now* I cannot hug him, *now* I cannot hear of his plans for the future. *That* is my sorrow. A friend said, "Remember, he's in good hands." I was deeply moved. But that reality does not put Eric back in my hands now. That's my grief. For that grief, what consolation can there be other than having him back?[40]

Lewis's reflection on his grief journey takes us through a dark place woven through with human finitude and failings. Even so, his grief evolves into one we might fittingly attribute to the blessed. We find that same virtuous grief in Wolterstorff: a grief born out of a love that values the being and well-being of the beloved, as well as a relationship free from sin and its regrets. When death tears the beloved away, all these goods are lost. But where the Easter promise holds sway, grief has a final destination and so an end: sanctified restoration and reunion.

If universalism is true, the Easter promise holds sway for every loss. But what if the more traditional doctrine is correct? What if, for some, the great day of reunion that love needs will never be granted? In that case, will not the blessed, who love perfectly, forever feel that unmet need?

NOVELTY, PRETENSE, AND GRIEF

There are further features of the human experience of grief that warrant attention, features highlighted by another masterful memoir: *Heaven's Coast*, in which poet Mark Doty tells the story of the loss of his life partner, Wally, to AIDS.

Wally's death was something they saw coming from a distance. In the late 1980s, a positive HIV test meant death. Perhaps sooner, perhaps later, but inevitably. As Doty puts it, "the virus was a kind of chill, violent current, one which was eroding, at who knew what speed, the ground upon which we stood. If you watched, you could see the edges crumbling."[41]

And so they saw death coming years before Wally's sickness and the demands of his care came to dominate their lives. One lesson of Doty's story is that such advance warning has little bearing on the depth of the grief that follows loss. If any suppose the eternal loss of unsaved loved

---

40. Wolterstorff, *Lament for a Son*, 31.
41. Doty, *Heaven's Coast*, 2.

ones can be seen coming, and that this somehow inoculates the blessed against grief (as if grief depended on surprise), I think we can confidently set that notion aside.

A less obvious lesson of Doty's narrative has to do with how loss can refocus our love. "Being in grief," Doty says, "is not unlike being in love." He goes on:

> In both states, the imagination's entirely occupied with one person. The beloved dwells at the heart of the world, and becomes a Rome: the roads of feeling all lead to him, all proceed from him. Everything that touches us seems to relate back to that center; there is no emotional life, no place outside the universe of feeling centered on its pivotal figure. . . .
>
> In grief and in love—so allied, perhaps, as to be severe gradations of *one* state?—the places and things associated with the beloved take on a shine, a numinosity which radiates out all the energy, the depth of emotion and meaning with which they have been invested.[42]

Lewis experiences this same reality, of course: his total absorption with his lost love, his inability to think of anything else. But where Lewis is struck by how her loss strips him of the assurances of his faith, Doty—an agnostic—faces Wally's death without any such assurances. What strikes him instead is how similar grief is to the first wild rush of new love.

This similarity is tied to something Lewis realizes later in his grief journey: "I think I am beginning to understand why grief feels like suspense. It comes from the frustration of so many impulses that had become habitual. Thought after thought, feeling after feeling, action after action, had H. for their object. Now their target is gone."[43]

Doty's analogy to new love is striking because both states feature an element of *novelty*. The reality of loss can transform our love by reminding us of our loved one's importance, driving home the significance of what their presence in our lives means by replacing it with something novel: their absence. We can no longer take them for granted amidst the routines of daily life—or, in the case of Mark Doty's relationship with Wally, the rhythms of terminal illness and caretaking:

> In the years before Wally's death, our life together came to center around his illness, and whatever questions or issues might have

---

42. Doty, *Heaven's Coast*, 38.
43. Lewis, *Grief Observed*, 39.

> arisen between us, whatever evolutions might have occurred in the normal course of a relationship, were simply covered over or set aside, obscured by the reality of a more pressing condition. That, I think, is one of the real tragedies of illness; you cannot know the life you might have had....
>
> After Wally died I realized there was a new quality in my feeling for him, something that didn't have anything to do with taking care of him. It was, in fact, not something new, but the reemergence of an original feeling, from years before: I was falling in love with him again.[44]

For Doty, Wally's death had the surprising effect of making him love Wally as he had at the beginning, when nothing was routine or assumed, when this person was a fresh wonder. As Simone Weil has powerfully observed, a crucial element of love is *attention*.[45] But human beings are finite and imperfect creatures: out attention drifts. We get caught up in other things. Paying attention to our intimate partner is easy at first, because what is new in our environment draws our gaze in ways familiar things do not. But as the novelty fades, so does our attention.

But when a loved one dies, a familiar feature of our landscape is ripped away. There is an empty space once filled by a person. As Wolterstorff puts it,

> We took him too much for granted. Perhaps we all take each other too much for granted. The routines of life distract us; our own pursuits make us oblivious; our anxieties and sorrows, unmindful. The beauties of the familiar go unremarked. We do not treasure each other enough.
>
> He was a gift to us for twenty-five years. When the gift was finally snatched away, I realized how great it was.[46]

But if familiarity breeds contempt—or at least a distracted loss of attention—then it does so in a way that erodes not only the wonder of new love but also our grief over loss. In the midst of grief, we pay attention. Our love is enlivened, activated in a way analogous to what we experience with new love. But then the novelty of their absence fades. If our grief fades with it, how much of that is rooted, not in "resilience," but in the same moral weaknesses that lead us to take our loved ones

---

44. Doty, *Heaven's Coast*, 42.
45. Weil, *Gravity and Grace*, 173.
46. Wolterstorff, *Lament for a Son*, 13.

for granted—that same propensity to pay attention mostly to shiny new things and hence forget what a miracle our loved ones and loving relationships are?

If blessedness means being morally sanctified, the grief of the blessed will not be diminished by such weaknesses. If an inherently valuable loved one is lost eternally, the familiarity of loss and the lure of new things won't distract the blessed from the loss.

So, what does that say about heavenly grief? Whatever it says will be shaped by the context of heaven itself: union with God and the rest of the blessed. These are extraordinary goods. But on the doctrine of limited salvation, even this blessed community will be shaped by absence. Not a finite absence culminating in heavenly reunion, as Christians are inclined to imagine when they consider the deaths of loved ones. And not a finite experience of absence that comes to an end when our terrestrial lives end, as atheists are inclined to imagine things. What would such eternal absence, eternally experienced, mean for the blessed if they aren't sinfully distracted from fully appreciating the inherent worth of their missing loved ones?

In addressing this question, it may help to reflect on the following fact: my grief over my father's passing was far less all-consuming, far less disruptive to my life, than what we find in the accounts of Lewis, Doty, and Wolterstorff. Why?

Lewis and Doty both confront the loss of a life partner, someone with whom they built a shared life. Their daily routines featured the loved one's presence. When my father died, that loss had little impact on the life I'd created with my wife and children, the home we'd built a thousand miles away. None of *that* life unraveled. But in the days and weeks after the death of their partners, Doty and Lewis describe the struggle of coming to grips with just such an unraveling.

Like all who grieve, Doty finds himself inhabiting a new world, one without Wally in it. But unlike me at my father's death, the reality of that absence isn't muted by the distance that had already, painlessly, become a routine feature of the relationship. If anything, Wally's illness erased more ordinary kinds of distance. The relational characteristic of lovers became overlaid with those of the caretaker. Doty devotes much of *Heaven's Coast* to recounting the evolution of his relationship with Wally, from lovers enjoying new love to lovers facing the erosion of their future, to lovers looking for distraction and intimacy under the shadow of looming death, to a relationship increasingly characterized by the demands of caring for Wally:

> More and more, Wally doesn't want anyone else around, just Darren or me. Where I used to need to get away, and so take advantage of the time the home health aides would come to do errands, to swim or ride my bike or walk, I don't seem to need that now; Wally and I are drawing together into something enormous and quiet, spacious but almost unexplainably intimate.[47]

Perhaps something similar characterized the final stage of Lewis's relationship with his wife, who died of cancer. Care for a dying loved one often entails intense attention and a range of caretaking routines that are severed all at once by death.

But when my father died I'd already forged a life apart from my parents, one I could and did return to in the wake of my father's passing. And when I returned to "my life," it seemed as if I'd returned to a world where my father remained alive, still there in New York state, just a call away if I could be bothered to pick up the phone.

The death of my father was a death that allowed for easy *denial*.

That denial was even easier with my grandparents. Because they were in Norway in the years preceding their deaths, it was a simple matter, even long after their passing, to pretend they still lived their lives in that distant place. Even now I can picture them in their bi-level Oslo condominium. I can imagine my grandfather cranking the handle that unfurls the balcony's cloth canopy, or resetting the cuckoo clock before bed by yanking down the pinecone-shaped counterweight. I can see them setting out on an afternoon walk in the Østmark woods, that sprawling forest that comes to the edge of their neighborhood.

I do not grieve for them, because they're still there, still alive, still doing all the mundane, lovely things they used to do. Grief overcome, or set aside, by pretense.

Physical distance and distance from the routines of daily life can mute grief. So can distance in time, especially as new routines are forged and old ones forgotten. Even so, there are moments when the reality of absence hits—like that moment, several years after his death, when I learned that the last of my father's siblings had passed away. I found myself looking at a picture of all of them together: these humans who'd grown up together, who'd known each other longer than anyone and

---

47. Doty, *Heaven's Coast*, 253.

surely had countless untold stories no one now would ever hear. That photograph stripped me of my pretenses. I wept as if I'd just heard the news of my father's passing.

In the stories Doty and Lewis tell, pretense is impossible. They cannot go back to their daily lives and pretend their loved one is still there, because the features of their lives have been utterly transformed by loss. For Wolterstorff, the story is different. The routines of daily life do not preclude pretense, since his son was grown and living on his own when he died. Instead, habits of imagination—picturing what his son is doing now—collide with the reality of absence:

> Imagination and thought are out of phase. Sometimes it's as if he's not dead, just away. I see him. Then thought intervenes and says, "Remember, he's dead now." For twenty-five years I have been imagining what he's doing. That keeps on going. In me now there is this strange flux of spontaneously picturing him and then painfully reminding myself.[48]

What is the difference here? Why is it so much easier, in the case of deceases parents and grandparents, to allow routine and pretense to put their *gone-ness* out of mind? Wolterstorff asks this question, noting that burying his father was nothing at all like burying his son. Part of the difference he attributes to expectations: we expect to bury our parents but not our children.

But that is only part of the story. Another part is that, with our children, more of who they might have been goes unrealized. When a parent lives into old age, has accomplished much, and has lived "a good life," it feels like there is less to grieve because less has been lost. Their terrestrial life is, we might say, as good as we could have expected. In fact, we are more inclined to celebrate their lives even as we feel their loss. This fact is surely relevant for considering heavenly grief, given the Christian view that human beings have been presented by God with the possibility of something that is *vast*, a good far greater than a long terrestrial life lived well. And this astonishing possibility would be something the blessed experience not merely as a hope of faith but as a lived reality: eternal life in loving union with God and the blessed. The damned or annihilated have lost *that*: something infinitely greater than the terrestrial losses of a child who has died too soon. The grief we feel at a child's death may,

---

48. Wolterstorff, *Lament for a Son*, 55.

at least on this measure, be the best guide to how the blessed would feel towards the lost.

Another factor shaping why we grieve more when our children die is the nature of the relationship. As Wolterstorff notes, from the moment a child enters the world, vulnerable and helpless, those of us who are parents "give of ourselves to the formation of this other, from helplessness to independence, trying our best to match our mode of giving to the maturing of the child."[49] This becomes an *investment* in the child's future:

> Our plans and hopes and fears are plans and hopes and fears for it. Along the way we experience the delights and disappointments of watching that future take shape, from babbling to oratory, from flounderings to climbing, from dependence to equality.[50]

Parents who love and care for their children invest themselves in their children's continued existence and in the development of their potential, of what they might become. In infancy there is almost nothing *but* potential. In every milestone we see the trajectory. We become accustomed to picturing their future, imagining where they might go, wishing for them all good things: joy, moral character, meaningful relationships, and fulfilling projects. And when we release them into the world, we envision them building on the lives they started in our care.

When I envision my grandparents still going on their walks in the Østmark woods, I envision the lives of people I first knew as fully actualized adults and who, when they died, had lived earthly lives as good and rich as one could hope for. Partly, this means there is less to grieve, when considering things in purely terrestrial terms. But it also means I am less profoundly invested in their very existence and their futures. And this means that when I pretend that they are still there in Norway living their lives, there is less at stake in the comforting image being real. The fantasy is enough to settle any tremors the reality of absence might cause.

But if it were one of my children, my whole self would cry out for more than a fantasy. If we want to understand what a morally perfect grief flowing from a morally perfect love would look like, we need to dwell on, or dwell in, a love like this, in which the level of investment in the continued existence of the lost is so great that the deepest places in

---

49. Wolterstorff, *Lament for a Son*, 57.
50. Wolterstorff, *Lament for a Son*, 58.

the heart cry out against mere pretense. Or we need to imagine conditions that preclude the very possibility of pretense.

Mark Doty invites us into such a space. It is a space in which life goes on because it must. But it is a life transformed. "The possibility of consolation," he says, "of joy even, does not dispel the sorrow." Instead, sorrow has become the defining reality in which life's possibilities are housed:

> Sorrow is the cathedral, the immense architecture; in its interior there's room for almost everything: for desire, for flashes of happiness, for making plans for the future. And for watching all those evidences of ongoing life crumble in the flash of remembering, in the recurring wave of fresh grief.[51]

Wolterstorff expresses a remarkably similar sentiment. "Sometimes I think happiness is over for me," he says, but then notes he can still laugh. "Perhaps what is over for me," he says instead, "is happiness as the fundamental tone of my existence. Now sorrow is that." And in a metaphor strikingly like Doty's, he concludes, "Sorrow is no longer the islands but the sea."[52]

Doty is a deeply spiritual agnostic, Wolterstorff a man of deep Christian faith. Both, confronting profound loss, find themselves *inhabiting* sorrow even as other emotions come and go. Wolterstorff is convinced that, until the fruition of God's redemptive work, it would be a mistake to *stop* inhabiting it. After reading books on grief, he is troubled by the way they encourage looking away from death, often by focusing instead on the "grief process" itself: "I will not have it so. I will not look away. I will indeed remind myself that there's more to life than pain. I will accept joy. But I will not look away from Eric dead. Its demonic awfulness I will not ignore. I owe that—to him and to God."[53]

We ought to resist the urge to let grief abate through the forgetfulness that familiarity allows or the pretense that distance permits. Wolterstorff explains why in a reflection on the beatitude that declares mourners blessed (Matt 5:4). He notes that the other beatitudes mention qualities—thirst for righteousness, mercy, peacemaking—that "belong

---

51. Doty, *Heaven's Coast*, 62.
52. Wolterstorff, *Lament for a Son*, 47.
53. Wolterstorff, *Lament for a Son*, 54.

to the life of the kingdom. But why does he hail the mourners of the world?"[54] Wolterstorff answers:

> The mourners are those who have caught a glimpse of God's new day, who ache with all their being for that day's coming, and who break out into tears when confronted with its absence. . . . They are the ones who realize that in God's realm of peace there is neither death nor tears and who ache whenever they see someone crying tears over death. The mourners are aching visionaries.
>
> Such people Jesus blesses. . . . And he gives them the promise that the new day for whose absence they ache will come. They will be comforted.[55]

From the resources of his faith, Wolterstorff extracts a way to inhabit sorrow's cathedral: "Be open to the wounds of the world," he says. "Mourn humanity's mourning, weep over humanity's weeping, be wounded by humanity's wounds, be in agony over humanity's agony. But do so in the good cheer that a day of peace is coming."[56]

The cathedral of sorrow has a door, and there will come a day when that door will swing wide and we will step out into the sunlight.

Unless, of course, the doctrine of limited salvation is true. In that case, some will not walk into the sunlight. And those who do will carry into that light the sorrow for lives cut short, potential eternally unfulfilled, and severed relationships never healed. They will carry these things because, as morally sanctified children of God, there will be no room for the forgetfulness or pretense that allows us to function as if all is well when some of those we love are lost.

SELF-DESTRUCTION AND GRIEF

At least according to the broadly Arminian version of limited salvation, the lost will be those who *brought it on themselves*. God gave them all they needed for salvation except their freely chosen response. What they could have been will never be, but that's *their own fault*. In Jerry Walls's terminology, the ranks of the damned are restricted to those who have

---

54. Wolterstorff, *Lament for a Son*, 84–85.
55. Wolterstorff, *Lament for a Son*, 85–86.
56. Wolterstorff, *Lament for a Son*, 86.

made "a decisive choice for evil"[57] even in the face of God's bestowal of "optimal grace."[58] Why think the eternal loss of such people should be a cause for grief?

At least in part, this question about why we should grieve them is really about why we should *love* them—and that is a question with answers in the Christian tradition, answers we'll consider in detail in chapter 4. But maybe the question is more about *how* we love them. The sort of love that desires the loved one's being and welfare, and that longs for a healthy mutual relationship, is a love that makes us *vulnerable*—especially if they're on a self-destructive path. Self-protection might counsel an emotionally distanced love. Not a complete severing of concern (we might still pity them as they tumble into hell or oblivion), but an untethering of the emotional ties that trigger grief.

But does love even work like that? *Should* it?

Here again, Mark Doty's remarkable memoir offers lessons. Although the memoir focuses on the loss of Wally, this period of Doty's life was also wracked by another loss: his close friend, Lynda, whose death from a car crash was the culmination of a pattern of addiction and reckless disregard for her life.

"I'm stricken and horrified and half-numb," Doty writes. "I am full of confusion, because my grief is so inextricable from my fury and my fear, conflicting feelings tumbling together like the slap of wave on wave." His fear is about how he'll endure another death, but the fury is about Lynda's self-destructiveness: "And how could I face the bitter sense that she'd tossed her own life away, with all her extraordinary gifts, that she's spun out of control in a long skid she could have prevented?" Her dismissive remark—about all "the beautiful elegies" her friends would write if she died—horrifies him: "I couldn't abide the romanticization of harm, that weird combination of self-aggrandizement and willful disregard of the gifts of one's own life."[59]

The last time Doty meets her, coming drunk out of an AA meeting, he confronts a hard truth: "My friend, whom I've loved for years, my adventurer, wonderful poet, survivor, heroine, role model, flash girl, paragon of style and endurance—well, I find I just don't like her at all."[60] After her death, his grief is wedded to anger at what might have been, at

57. Walls, *Hell*, 115–17.
58. Walls, *Hell*, 88–90.
59. Doty, *Heaven's Coast*, 94.
60. Doty, *Heaven's Coast*, 95.

the magnified tragedy of a life ended at the bottom of a self-destructive spiral. His anger "is so big that it almost obscures grief,"[61] a rage intensified by the contrast with Wally's death: "How vain and self-indulgent self-destructiveness looks in the face of AIDS! The virus in its predatory destruction seems to underline the responsibility of the living; life's an unlikely miracle, an occasion of strangeness and surprise, and isn't it appalling to dismiss it, to discard this gift?"[62]

In the midst of this, he recognizes that addiction is an illness. And so his anger collides with contrary impulses: "My friend must have wrestled so terribly, and who am I to say that her disease was any less relentless than Wally's? Partly my rage is just anger that she's left me, too. And partly my rage is at the world, at God, at the blind bone-breaking ugly design of things."[63]

The failure of loved ones to live up to their potential does not erase grief over their passing but layers it with anger at their misbegotten choices—and additional grief about the squandered potential, the un-actualized possibilities. When facing the deaths of loved ones who made ruinous choices, how can we help but cry out for the *what-might-have-beens*?

In my grief over my father's passing, there is a milder version of these things. Like all terrestrial relationships, ours was incomplete. We bonded intellectually, pursuing joint projects, partly to make up for deficits in emotional connection. We exhibited the all-too-common failures among men in our culture to show and nurture our feelings, to express and thereby deepen the truth about what we meant to each other.

When I bought a plane ticket to see him one last time, days after the news that the cancer had resurfaced, I was determined to sit by his bed and say the things I hadn't said. When my sister feared his death was imminent, I changed the ticket to the next available flight because I needed to look him in the eye and say what both of us were so inept at voicing.

I didn't get the chance, and I still long for it. Like Wolterstorff, I yearn for the "Great Day" that love needs. It isn't just something those filled with regret need: it isn't just *Lynda* who needs it. Doty needs it too. It isn't just a day when we can say, "I'm sorry," but a day when we can hear it. A day when love can blossom free of the constraints of sin and death.

If we love, how can we *stop* longing for a day when *love* has the final word rather than sin and death? If we love as the blessed are supposed to

61. Doty, *Heaven's Coast*, 107.
62. Doty, *Heaven's Coast*, 108.
63. Doty, *Heaven's Coast*, 108.

love, how can we not be Wolterstorff's "aching visionaries" who see what God's kingdom is supposed to be and "break out into tears when confronted with its absence"? How could Doty not see Lynda's fate, should it prove to be the final word in her story, as anything but the *eternal* not-yet of God's kingdom?

CONSOLATION WITH LIMITS?

Salvation is not just a promise of death transcended but of *sin* transcended. It promises not only joy but *sanctification*—including the sanctification of our relationships. Heaven is a community in which no relationships are left incomplete by sin or by running out of time. This is an extraordinary promise and consolation in the face of grief and the regrets that weave through loss—a consolation that, according to the doctrine of limited salvation, has limits.

It is easy to trivialize the loss of those we typically imagine fall outside these limits: the Hitlers of the world, or those portrayed in C. S. Lewis's *The Great Divorce* who reject heaven's blessings for any number of petty, self-absorbed reasons. If all of this loss is their own fault, it is easy to think "good riddance." But what *makes* it easy is that we fall short of Jesus' radically inclusive love. It is hard for us to truly inhabit the emotional place of the blessed, those who have attained such love, as *they* consider the eternal loss of any bearer of God's image, born with the potential to live eternally in a state of love and joy but falling infinitely short of that potential.

But there may be an emotional space easier for me to inhabit that comes closer to what the blessed must feel for the lost. One of the most terrifying experiences I've had as a parent occurred when one of my kids, as a toddler, tore free of my hand and ran headlong into a busy parking lot. Brakes squealed; my wife ran—faster than me—to reclaim our errant child, seizing up that precious little body with terror, fury, and relief.

That this terrifying moment was one of willful toddler rebellion, fueled by immature impulses and emotional excess, would have in no way mitigated my grief had my child died. But all the lost possibilities that flashed before my eyes—all the imagined activities and relationships and milestones, symbols of everything my child might do and become—would surely have magnified the grief.

When faced with choices that can seal our eternal fates for good or ill, are we wiser than toddlers faced with life-and-death choices? And if the blessed in heaven love in anything like the way our Heavenly Parent loves, wouldn't they measure the eternal loss of anyone against the life they could have enjoyed had they made choices less willfully defiant, less defined by immature impulse or emotional excess?

Perhaps, in the grip of imperfect emotions, I imagine things poorly. Perhaps I'm wrong to think the blessed feel towards the lost the way a parent would feel about their toddler who, in a tantrum against parental rules, flung themselves into traffic and died.

If so, intellectual engagement with these questions may expose the errors of this emotional starting point. But intellectual engagement *without* such a starting point risks the "cold" and "callous" abstraction from feelings that Marilyn McCord Adams so eloquently warns against. And so I start with human feelings, with meditations on grief from my own life and from the vivid narrative accounts of some of our most observant and eloquent writers. Looking at the doctrine of limited salvation from this starting place, I see a blessedness eternally marred by grief over loss, by anger at the self-destructive choices that produced such loss, and by the anguished, heart-breaking fury at the bone-breaking ugly design of a world that keeps God's family eternally apart.

3

Sympathy for the Damned

INCOMPATIBILITY ARGUMENTS: HEAVENLY GRIEF AND SYMPATHY

THE IDEA THAT THE fate of the lost might trouble the bliss of the saved has been discussed to some extent at least since St. Thomas Aquinas, who considered the possibility only to dismiss it with a few brief words.[1] To my knowledge, the first Christian scholar to invoke this idea to *challenge* limited salvation was the nineteenth-century Protestant theologian, Friedrich Schleiermacher. In more recent times, contemporary philosophers of religion such as Thomas Talbott, Nicole Hassoun, and myself have advanced arguments along the same lines.

But to the extent that such arguments have been developed and critiqued, the focus has typically been on a version that challenges the doctrine of hell rather than *any* version of limited salvation. And rather than focusing on grief, these arguments have invoked more generally the negative emotional impact of being aware of loved ones' eternal suffering. When a single negative emotion is identified, it is typically *sympathy* for the damned. Since sympathy for those who suffer finite pain disturbs the joy of good people in this life, wouldn't sympathy for those who suffer eternal torment perturb heavenly bliss?

A recent exception to this emphasis on heavenly sympathy is James Spiegel in his book-length defense of annihilationism, *Hell and Divine Goodness*, in which he explicitly addresses the problem of heavenly grief.

---

1. Aquinas, *Summa Theologica*, Suppl., Q. 94, Art. 2.

That an annihilationist would focus on *grief* is unsurprising. At the death of loved ones afflicted by painful illnesses, we often feel *relief* that their suffering is over. But while the pains of sympathy end, grief does not, since the loved one is now *gone*. A similar dynamic would arguably prevail among the blessed were annihilationism true.

Of course, given the doctrine of hell, *both* grief *and* sympathy are potential disturbers of heavenly bliss—because the blessed might grieve both their separation from the damned and the losses the damned endure. Nevertheless, when we consider blessedness in light of the doctrine of hell, it is natural for the dominant question to be, "How can I be perfectly happy if my loved one is suffering forever?" This question inspires us to reflect more on sympathy than on grief. Furthermore, if the damnation of loved ones would produce negative emotions that diminish heavenly joy, this would be a problem regardless of *which* and *how many* negative emotions contribute to this effect. When the focus is on hell, then, and given the obvious potential for sympathy for the damned to disturb bliss, there may be little need to tease out grief's distinct contribution to that disturbance.

It is useful, then, to distinguish *the argument from heavenly grief* from *the argument from heavenly sympathy*, where the latter specifically targets the doctrine of hell and does so by invoking the negative emotions the blessed would feel about the damned, with an emphasis on sympathy. Since both arguments purport to show an incompatibility between the doctrine of perfect blessedness and some version of non-universalism, both are species of a broader kind of argument. Let us call any such argument an *incompatibility argument*.

In this chapter I set the stage for developing my preferred version of the argument from heavenly grief by reviewing earlier incompatibility arguments, which have tended to be arguments from heavenly sympathy. A review of them is instructive, first, because there are important similarities between the disturbances posed by sympathy and grief. Second, these other arguments can be read in ways that *encompass* grief and so have bearing on this book's focus, even if they emphasize sympathy. Third, most of the purported *solutions* to the problem of heavenly grief, which I will consider in chapters 6 and 7, were initially formulated as solutions to the parallel problem of heavenly sympathy. While I will adapt them to the problem of heavenly grief, an awareness of their original context is helpful.

Finally, a review of arguments from heavenly sympathy will expose issues and distinctions that apply in parallel fashion to the argument from heavenly grief. Notably, while some versions of the argument from heavenly sympathy focus on how *anyone's* damnation would diminish the blessedness of *all* the saved, others focus on how it would affect the blessedness of those among the saved who personally loved some of the damned in this life. The argument from heavenly grief admits of a parallel distinction. In both cases, we can distinguish between "universal" and "personal" versions of the argument, as well as a synthesis of the two.

THE UNIVERSAL VERSION OF THE ARGUMENT FROM HEAVENLY SYMPATHY

Towards the end of *The Christian Faith*, Schleiermacher levels the following short argument against the doctrine of hell:

> If we now consider eternal damnation as it is related to eternal bliss, it is easy to see that once the former exists, the latter can exist no longer. Even if externally the two realms were quite separate, yet so high a degree of bliss is not as such compatible with entire ignorance of others' misery, the more so if the separation itself is the result purely of a general judgment, at which both sides were present, which means conscious each of the other. Now if we attribute to the blessed a knowledge of the state of the damned, it cannot be a knowledge unmixed with sympathy. If the perfecting of our natures is not to move backwards, sympathy must be such as to embrace the whole human race, and when extended to the damned must of necessity be a disturbing element in bliss, all the more that, unlike similar feelings in this life, it is untouched by hope.[2]

Schleiermacher here assumes, with most Christians, that the saved enjoy both perfect joy and sanctification ("the perfecting of our natures"). He thinks the latter entails sympathy for all humanity and hence the damned. But those with such sympathy would, if aware of the damned's suffering, be pained by it—especially if the sympathy "is untouched by hope," by which he presumably means the hope that the suffering will end through redemption.

This last point warrants attention. If I know you are suffering but also *know* it is short-lived and will be redeemed, I may feel no sympathetic pain

2. Schleiermacher, *Christian Faith*, 721.

at all. Suppose you have been separated from your spouse for months, but the separation is ending earlier than expected: your spouse is back in town, intending to surprise you at an upcoming gathering . . . and I'm in on the surprise. It's my job to drive you to the gathering. On the way, you confess that you aren't looking forward to it: events where your spouse would ordinarily be present just intensify your sense of their absence. Given my knowledge of what's to come, I might not feel *any* sympathetic suffering. I might even have to repress a surprise-ruining smile.

Another important element of Schleiermacher's argument is this: he recognizes that the propensity of the blessed to sympathize with the suffering of others does not *by itself* imply that infernal suffering would diminish heavenly joy. It would do so only if the blessed *knew* some were damned. But he is convinced the blessed state "is not as such compatible with entire ignorance of others' misery," and based on this concludes that the salvation of any requires the salvation of all.

More recently, Thomas Talbott has similarly argued that "the eternal damnation of a single person would undermine the salvation of all others; so an optimal balance between saved and unsaved could not possibly include any who are unsaved."[3] Like Schleiermacher, he thinks blessedness involves not just supreme happiness but moral sanctification—which for Talbott means the saved are "filled with love for others" such that they desire "the good for all other created persons."[4] Also like Schleiermacher, Talbott thinks anyone who truly loves some person S "cannot be happy knowing that S will be forever miserable."[5] Hence, the saved will not be perfectly happy if they know that some are damned.

However, Talbott does not claim directly, as Schleiermacher does, that the blessed could not be ignorant of the state of the damned. Instead, he claims that "salvation brings not only happiness, but the kind of happiness that could survive a full disclosure of the facts; the blessedness of those in heaven is not merely, in other words, a blissful kind of ignorance."[6]

To be clear, Talbott is not saying that the joy of the blessed is so callous it could *resist* a full disclosure of the facts, even tragic ones. His point, rather, is that the happiness of the blessed will be suited to the actual facts and not merely a mistaken understanding of them. Talbott

---

3. Talbott, "Providence, Freedom, and Human Destiny," 240.
4. Talbott, "Providence, Freedom, and Human Destiny," 239.
5. Talbott, "Providence, Freedom, and Human Destiny," 240.
6. Talbott, "Providence, Freedom, and Human Destiny," 239–40.

captures this idea by saying that the happiness of the saved would not just be supreme in subjective quality but *supremely worthwhile*—and happiness that depends on ignorance of unpleasant truths is *not* supremely worthwhile.

The idea is this: in good people, emotions track the state of things such that positive emotions are a response to good states and negative emotions a response to bad ones. And good people *want* their emotions to track the way things really are. They don't want ignorance shielding them from painful truths. What they want is an end to the evils that properly *occasion* negative emotions.

Good people will be *perfectly* happy only if they believe *all is well*; and if such happiness is based on a mistake—all is *not* well—then it is *defective*. To be saved, according to Talbott, is to be free of all such *defective* emotional states. If all is *not* well, the happiness of the saved will thus admit of one of two defects: either it will fit reality and so fall short of perfect happiness, or it will be out of touch with reality. Either way, the saved are less than perfectly blessed.

In short, both Schleiermacher and Talbott argue that anyone *aware* that some are eternally damned would lack perfect blessedness. Where Schleiermacher goes on to insist that were any damned, the saved *would* be aware of it and hence be less than perfectly happy, Talbott holds that were anyone damned and the blessed *weren't* aware of it, their happiness would be out of touch with reality and hence defective.

But these may be different ways of making essentially the same point. Talbott's view, essentially, is that a supreme happiness that depends for its persistence on ignorance is a sham happiness, like someone celebrating their son's college graduation when, in fact, their son flunked out and lied about it. The blessed experience perfect joy because they believe the circumstances warrant it. If the circumstances *don't* warrant it, being unaware of this is not trivial, since the effect of such unawareness is to produce *an emotional response to the world that fails to fit reality*.

Talbott's view, then, amounts essentially to the view that such an error-riddled state cannot be properly called "perfect blessedness." Arguably, this is exactly why Schleiermacher claims that "so high a degree of bliss is not as such compatible with entire ignorance of others' misery." To experience perfect blessedness entails, if not omniscience, at least freedom from the kind of ignorance that leads to *errors*. This is especially true if the errors touch on the moral domain, leading the blessed to adopt attitudes, emotions, and behaviors *that they would judge morally unfitting if they knew the truth*. As such, moral sanctification cannot be severed from a refinement of our *epistemic* faculties—a refinement of our capacity for knowing the truth that guards us against error.

These are issues I will return to in chapter 6. For now, it is enough to note that Schleiermacher's and Talbott's perspectives converge on the idea that a perfectly blessed state is characterized not only by moral sanctification and supreme happiness, but also by *freedom from error*. If I love you and you are eternally damned, I cannot be perfectly happy unless I am oblivious to (ignorant or unaware of) your fate. But unlike some kinds of obliviousness, which just mean there are things outside the scope of what I consciously know, obliviousness to the fate of the damned would lead me into *error*, at least if I were enjoying a perfect happiness that depends on remaining oblivious. *Such* obliviousness is incompatible with perfect blessedness.

While Schleiermacher and Talbott identify the sympathetic pain the saved would feel (were they aware of the truth) as the main reason the blessedness of the saved would be marred were any damned, their thinking does not exclude other reasons, such as grief. In fact, it is natural to suppose that, if the blessed love the damned, their sympathy would be accompanied by grief over all the losses damnation entails.

And there are further potential disturbers of happiness. Schleiermacher argues that "our sympathy cannot fail to be attended by the bitter feeling always present when we see a real connexion between our own gain and another's loss."[7] In a clear reflection of his Reformed heritage, he thinks this bitter feeling would come from knowing that "the circumstances of our having enjoyed helpful dispensations was due to the very same disposition of things as insured that such help should not reach [the damned]."[8] When he notes that the blessed will have memories of their earthly lives in which "some of us were associated with some of them," it is not to highlight the personal love relationships that would be a source of grief but to highlight the blessed realization that "there was a point when we were as little regenerate as they."[9] This would prompt an additional disturbance to heavenly bliss, akin to survivor's guilt.

But given Schleiermacher's seminal focus on sympathy for the damned, it is worth thinking a bit more about sympathy itself before

---

7. Schleiermacher, *Christian Faith*, 721–22.
8. Schleiermacher, *Christian Faith*, 721.
9. Schleiermacher, *Christian Faith*, 721.

closing out this section. In particular, I think it is helpful to distinguish sympathy from a related concept, namely empathy.

In actual usage, "sympathy" and "empathy" are often used in overlapping ways, and there is reason to think their meanings have shifted over time—such that, for example, what Hume meant by "sympathy" is closer to what we mean today by "empathy."[10] In current usage, however—and in terms of unpacking the argument from heavenly sympathy—I think sympathy is best understood as an emotion. I will say more in chapter 5 about my understanding of emotions, but for now I'll note that emotions have an intentional object, a distinctive way they feel (their "affect"), the potential to motivate action, and a correlation to a value judgment (even if we might resist making that judgment). Sympathy fits this characterization: its object is others' suffering; it has a distinct feeling to it, a negative one a bit like an ache; it has the potential to motivate action to alleviate the suffering of others; and it is correlated with the judgment that the suffering in question is bad.

While empathy is variously understood and defined,[11] I think it can be helpful to use the term "empathy" to call our attention, not to a distinct emotion, but to a perspective-taking process in which we imaginatively put ourselves into the experiential position of another, in effect imaginatively mirroring (to some extent or in some respects, and perhaps inaccurately) what they are feeling. Shannon Spaulding defines empathy in the way I have in mind, when she says that "to empathize is to (try to) imaginatively adopt a target's mental states and, as a result, come to share the target's affect."[12] Peter Rosan offers a phenomenological account of empathy conceived along these lines, in which he describes it as a "resonance with the other" that "ultimately subserves the cognitive aim of knowing another person," but which does so by passing through "a middle phase involving the subject as a participant in the other's disclosure of him/herself."[13] This middle phase involves a "co-experience" that features an increasingly "explicit and differentiated unfolding of the subject's attunement to the other."[14]

Empathy sometimes happens rather easily—so easily that, even though it is something we *do*, it may involve little or no conscious

---

10. Rosan, "Varieties of Ethical Experience," 160–61.
11. See, for example, Batson, "These Things Called Empathy."
12. Spaulding, "Motivating Empathy," 2.
13. Rosan, "Varieties of Ethical Experience," 163–64.
14. Rosan, "Varieties of Ethical Experience," 168.

deliberation. For most of us, those we are spontaneously inclined to empathize with constitute a small subset of the human population. For those falling outside this subset, empathy may not come naturally and may take work. As Spaulding puts it, "Each one of us is inclined to empathize with some people in some situations some of the time, but not others in other situations at other times."[15] A range of problematic motives, especially apathy and tribalism, can limit our empathy for others.[16]

But what about the blessed? Presumably, their disposition to empathize would be perfected, operating in accord with perfect love, meaning it would not be limited by apathy or tribalism or other morally problematic motives. Also, when they imaginatively feel what others feel, they wouldn't get it wrong. But would such perfection of their empathetic capacities also mean they would empathize *indefinitely* with the damned? Perhaps not, since empathy might reasonably be construed as a *purpose-driven activity*, its purpose being to understand what it is like to be in another's circumstances, to see the world through their perspective and grasp how they feel. Once we achieve such understanding, continuing to "inhabit" their experiential place may be uncalled for. On this view, then, perfected empathy for the damned would not require living permanently in their experiential position. If it did, the damnation of anyone would entail the damnation of all—since the blessed would by their moral perfection permanently inhabit the experiential position of the damned, experiencing eternal damnation along with them.

It is perhaps better, then, to suppose that the blessed's perfected empathy would mean stepping into the position of the damned long enough to apprehend what the damned are going through and appreciate how terrible it is for them. Sympathy can, I think, be usefully understood as the enduring *effect* of such empathy: the emotional product of the act of empathizing with those who suffer. In short, the blessed would empathize with the damned by envisioning themselves in the experiential place of their afflicted neighbors. They would feel what damnation is like: its staggering magnitude, a suffering of unthinkable extremity. Even if they didn't remain forever in that experiential place, the journey there would produce a sympathetic emotional response. Given the magnitude of the suffering, their sympathy would feature a powerfully negative affect that

---

15. Spaulding, "Motivating Empathy," 5.
16. Spaulding, "Motivating Empathy," 12.

persisted in the blessed for as long as the suffering persisted—which, on the traditional doctrine of hell, would be forever.

THE PERSONAL ARGUMENT FROM HEAVENLY SYMPATHY

In his book *Destined for Joy*, Father Alvin Kimel shares the tragic story of his son's death by suicide. For Kimel, that loss destroyed any credibility he had previously found in C. S. Lewis's idea (which we will look at in chapter 7) that sympathy for the damned amounts to inappropriately allowing the damned to hold the blessed hostage emotionally. As Kimel puts it,

> If we love someone, then of course we will be held hostage to their infernal misery. Their suffering must become ours; otherwise, love is not love. At Aaron's funeral a week later, I cried out from the pulpit with all of my being: I will not be saved without my Aaron! There can be no heaven for me without my son. My love for him is too great. He is too much a part of my life, my identity. We will be saved together in Christ. God will make it so.[17]

Kimel's words reflect ones Nicole Hassoun found written on the walls of Nonberg Abbey: "Neither of us can go to heaven unless the other gets in."[18]

These anonymous words, and Kimel's impassioned cry, gesture to a much more intimately personal version of the kind of argument we've been looking at. Schleiermacher also acknowledges personal reasons why someone's damnation could disturb the blessedness of others, even if his main focus is the impact the damnation of anyone would have on all the saved. But the personal reasons he identifies—the way prior acquaintance drives home how little separates the blessed from the damned—are quite different from those of Kimel. And Kimel's reasons are, I suspect, more intuitively obvious: the personal, affectional love for a parent or child or spouse makes the prospect of their eternal misery a source of personal pain.

Even though Talbott emphasizes that salvation involves being "filled with love for others" and so desiring "the good for all other created

---

17. Kimel, *Destined for Joy*, 351–52.
18. Hassoun, "Eternally Separated Lovers," 633.

persons,"[19] he weaves more personal considerations into his argument. Arguably, the most powerful formulation of his argument focuses on what damnation would mean were it his own daughter who was damned:

> If I truly love my own daughter . . . and love her even as I love myself, then I simply cannot be happy knowing that she is suffering or that she is otherwise miserable—unless, of course, I can somehow believe that, in the end, all will be well for her. But if I cannot believe this, if I were to believe instead that she has been lost to me forever—even if I were to believe that, by her own will, she has made herself intolerably evil—my own happiness could never be complete, not so long as I continued to love her. . . . For I would always know what could have been, and I would always experience that as a terrible tragedy and an unacceptable loss, one for which no compensation is even conceivable.[20]

Even when formulating his universal version of the argument, he pairs it with this more personal dimension:

> Either I will love my child even as I love myself, or I will not. If, on the one hand, I do so love her, then her being lost to me forever would be the kind of evil for which there could be no conceivable compensation; I cannot both love my child as myself and be happy knowing that she will be forever miserable. If, on the other hand, I do not so love her, if I am, or become, so calloused that I do not experience her loss as my own loss, then two things follow: first, that I have a serious moral defect myself, and second, that I therefore have no capacity for the kind of happiness that is supremely worthwhile.[21]

Talbott concludes that his daughter's eternal damnation would do irreparable harm to him: God must either allow him to be mired in sinful callousness or allow him to remain forever miserable, either of which is incompatible with his welfare. He sees only one way to avoid this outcome: God could deceive him concerning his daughter's fate, producing a blissful ignorance. But Talbott sees this way out as incompatible with the Christian conception of God, which entails that "God is incapable of such immoral deception."[22]

---

19. Talbott, "Providence, Freedom, and Human Destiny," 239.
20. Talbott, *Inescapable Love of God*, 126–27.
21. Talbott, "Providence, Freedom, and Human Destiny," 238.
22. Talbott, "Providence, Freedom, and Human Destiny," 238.

It is interesting to note here that on this personal version of the argument, Talbott takes it for granted that, were his daughter damned, he would know about her fate absent divine deception—even though, as we've seen, a comparable assumption does not feature into the universal version of his argument. The difference here tracks a difference we find in this life: if I am oblivious to the suffering of strangers, this does not require an explanation in terms of deception. We do not *expect* people with finite knowledge to know everyone's condition. But unless I am a bad father, I will *want* to know how my kids are doing, and I will *notice* if they are not around. If I am in heaven and never see my children or experience a joyful reunion with them, how could I fail to suspect they are not among the saved? Unless, of course, God deliberately obscures the truth.

Furthermore, were I longing for reunion that never came, this would pain me even if I never learned they were eternally damned. Grief over their absence would be enough to mar my bliss, even absent sympathy for their suffering. This point calls attention to another element of Talbott's argument: when the focus turns to the damnation of those close to us, it is hard to imagine sympathy as the *only* source of pain. When Talbott pictures his daughter's damnation, he speaks not just of sympathy but also the pain of her "being lost to me forever" and of knowing "what could have been," counting these things as "a tragedy and an unacceptable loss."[23] This is the pain of *grief*. In the personal version of the argument, it becomes almost impossible to avoid imagining that the blessed would grieve. And so, when Talbott brings the personal into his argument, grief is vividly interlaced with other sources of pain.

Talbott draws a further conclusion from this more personal formulation of the argument: if God had done less than God could have done to save his daughter, that would undercut Talbott's love for *God*:

> I cannot *both* love my daughter as myself *and* love (or worship wholeheartedly) a God whom I believe to have done less than he could to save her from a life of misery and torment. For necessarily, if I truly love my daughter, then I will disapprove of any God whom I believe to have done less than his best for her, less than I would have done if I should have had the power; and necessarily, if I disapprove of God, then I do not truly love him.[24]

---

23. Talbott, *Inescapable Love of God*, 127.
24. Talbott, "Providence, Freedom, and Human Destiny," 239.

The point is not merely that Talbott *would* find it harder to love God under these conditions. The point is that he *should*. If his love were the kind a father should have, it would interfere with love for a God who, although able to do more to save his daughter from eternal misery, chooses not to.

Presumably, however, this is not quite what Talbott means to say. Suppose someone had the power to save my daughter from a dire fate but could do so only by committing a grievous moral wrong. If this potential savior failed to save my daughter, it isn't obvious that my love for my daughter would preclude loving this failed savior. Similarly, if God's only way to save Talbott's daughter were one that no *good* person could avail themselves of, it is less clear that God's failure would undercut Talbott's love for God.

Furthermore, there are different senses of "love," and in one important Christian sense, it is clearly possible to love those who sinfully fail us. It is the kind of love God has for us while yet we are sinners, the "agape" that embraces even those mired in wickedness, even enemies. But when we are called to love God, the sort of love we can have for sinners who let us down cannot exhaust the scope of that call. When we are called to love God with all our heart, soul, and mind, we are called to attend to and value God's infinite worth and goodness. This is a love that culminates in worship—and worship is never a proper expression of the love we have for sinners. Perhaps this is why Talbott parenthetically notes that the problem lies in his capacity to *worship* a God who would let his daughter be damned.

What these observations call for is a refinement of Talbott's point. A God who could save my daughter *without doing anything wrong*, but chooses instead to let her fall into *eternal suffering*, would be a God I could not *love in a manner whose fitting expression is worship*—at least not if I love my daughter as a father should. Thus modified, Talbott's corollary argument has important bearing on any version of Christian theism holding that God can, without doing anything wrong, bestow "efficacious grace" on anyone or everyone. Efficacious grace is a grace sufficient by itself to transform the hearts of the unrepentant and inspire a conversion of their wills such that they meet every condition necessary for salvation and are saved. It is the kind of grace Calvinists think God bestows on all of the elect and on none of the damned.

Not all Christians believe God can bestow such grace without doing anything wrong. Arminians might argue that such grace violates a moral requirement to respect creaturely freedom, while Calvinists might argue that bestowing it on everyone would violate a moral requirement to manifest justice through the infliction of eternal torment on *some* of those who deserve such a fate. But for those Christians who do believe God can bestow efficacious grace without doing anything wrong, Talbott's corollary argument here is significant. If God does less than God could have morally done to spare our loved ones from eternal torment, the kind of love we would expect good people to have for their own children and spouses appears incompatible with loving God in a way that fittingly expresses itself in worship. These two loves are thus pitted against each other, meaning the blessed would have to fall short with respect to one or the other. If one supposes that neither kind of love can be relinquished without a loss of moral character, what we arrive at is a different way in which non-universalism threatens perfect blessedness: not by making perfect joy impossible, but by making moral sanctification impossible.

I will not critically assess this argument any further here, but it deserved mention not only because it is tied so closely to Talbott's personal version of the argument from heavenly sympathy, but also because of how it reveals the potential scope of the problems non-universalism poses. In addition to the concerns that are the focus of this book, there are other worries about the impact limited salvation would have on the moral sanctification of the blessed.

THE DISTINCTNESS OF THE PERSONAL VERSION

One advantage of the personal version of the argument from heavenly sympathy is how well it taps our moral intuitions about how love affects our emotions. The universal argument is a philosophical abstraction. The damned are faceless, anonymous. With such hypothetical people, it is easier to fall into that cold intellectual place Marilyn McCord Adams warns against—and so imagine that love for the damned could take the form of nothing but dispassionate pity. But if *my beloved daughter* suffers eternal torment, the dispassionate pity that says, "Poor thing, but she brought it on herself," looks like a radically deficient love.

Even so, this personal version is not merely the universal version brought alive by imagining our loved ones among the damned. It is its own distinct argument. Nicole Hassoun makes this clear when she formulates her variant of it, what she calls "the Argument from Love," and contrasts it with both Schleiermacher's and my formulations. As she puts it, "the Argument from Love starts from weaker premises" in that "it does not assume that the blessed love or have sympathy with everyone."[25]

Her argument's conclusion is also more modest. The universal version purports to show that if *anyone* is damned, *no one* can experience perfect blessedness. But Hassoun says her version of the argument simply "challenges the idea that those who love others can be in heaven while their beloveds are in hell."[26] In fact, however, I think her argument does more than this: if it works, it entails that there is an incoherence within traditional Christian thought. It is true that Hassoun does not indicate which Christian teaching should be jettisoned in order to eliminate the incoherence. Still, the success of her argument would require that *something* Christians typically believe be jettisoned. In this sense, her argument is like other incompatibility arguments: it poses a problem for traditional Christian belief in the form of an apparent conflict between non-universalism and what it means to be saved.

Like others who formulate a problem of this kind, she understands "being in heaven" to involve "being perfectly happy—or at least free from all suffering."[27] She develops the argument by noting that, if we "think of love in a standard way," then "one could not be perfectly happy, or free from all suffering, if one knows that one's beloved is suffering."[28]

Hassoun formalizes her argument as follows:

1. No one who loves another can be perfectly happy or free from suffering if they know that their beloved is suffering.

2. Anyone in hell suffers (at least as long as they are in hell).

3. Anyone in heaven is perfectly happy or at least free from suffering.

4. There can be no one in heaven who is aware of the fact that his or her beloved is in hell. (1, 2, and 3)[29]

Premises 2 and 3 are traditional Christian beliefs (3 being an implication of the doctrine of perfect blessedness), and premise 1 strikes Hassoun as so plausible based on our usual understanding of love that it is hard to deny. Thus, she thinks traditional Christians should accept her

25. Hassoun, "Eternally Separated Lovers," 636.
26. Hassoun, "Eternally Separated Lovers," 636.
27. Hassoun, "Eternally Separated Lovers," 633.
28. Hassoun, "Eternally Separated Lovers," 634.
29. Hassoun, "Eternally Separated Lovers," 635.

conclusion. But this conclusion can, she thinks, be restated as follows: "Either (a) no one is in heaven, or (b) no one is in hell, or (c) no one in heaven loves any person in hell, or (d) no one in heaven knows that his or her beloved is suffering in hell."[30]

Formulated in this way, the conclusion allows her to draw the implication that something is amiss with traditional Christian belief (although she abstains from specifying what). Both (a) and (b) are at odds with traditional Christian teachings, so traditional Christians must endorse either (c) or (d) in order to preserve the entire package of traditional Christian doctrine. But both (c) and (d) strike her as untenable. She dismisses (d) because, if true, "God would have to be a deceiver."[31] She dismisses (c) for two reasons, even while granting that "God could make everyone in heaven simply stop loving anyone who goes to hell."[32] First, "the loss of love would, presumably, cause great suffering." Second, "those who embrace the traditional Christian doctrine think that love is a good thing," which means "it would be better if heaven had everyone's love in it."[33]

Let's consider the first of these points. Is loss of love (as opposed to loss of a loved one) always painful? Generally, there is pain involved when we stop loving someone we used to love. But is this pain intrinsic to the loss of love itself, or does it merely *attend* lost love because of other factors (such as the pain of disentangling our lives from those who used to feature importantly into it)? While it strikes me as plausible that loss of love is intrinsically painful, is it a pain that would fittingly *endure*? If it's only a passing pain, it would at worst preclude perfect joy temporarily.

This last question is closely tied to issues I will take up in chapter 7, relating to whether grief over the loss of a loved one should endure. If the loss of *a loved one* is a proper cause for enduring grief, then arguably so is the loss of *the love*. But since I cannot take up these issues fully here, and since Hassoun's second point is stronger than the first, I will set her first point aside to focus on the second. This second point suggests an argument along the following lines: Love is good. Heaven preserves what is good. Hence, if a condition for being in heaven is having one's love destroyed, there is something unheavenly about heaven.

---

30. Hassoun, "Eternally Separated Lovers," 635.
31. Hassoun, "Eternally Separated Lovers," 638.
32. Hassoun, "Eternally Separated Lovers," 637.
33. Hassoun, "Eternally Separated Lovers," 638.

This thinking is connected to the traditional view that blessedness involves the perfecting of our characters. Even if Hassoun does not assume that moral sanctification broadens our love to include all rational creatures, surely the *extinguishing* of the love we feel for others would be at odds with the cultivation of the good that heaven represents. These considerations lead Hassoun to conclude that we should not accept (c) or (d), even though we must accept at least one of (a)-(d) given the Argument from Love. But if we shouldn't endorse (c) or (d), that means that if we accept the premises of the Argument from Love, we will have to endorse either (a) that no one is in heaven or (b) that no one is in hell—claims traditional Christians reject. This is why Hassoun's argument calls into questions the coherence of traditional Christian doctrine, even if it doesn't specify how traditional Christians should modify their teachings.[34]

What Talbott and Hassoun agree on is this: perfect blessedness of the sort traditionally attributed to the saved is incompatible with the eternal damnation of a loved one, because anyone who is perfectly blessed would know about the beloved's fate and continue to love them, and because ongoing love for someone in a state of eternal suffering precludes perfect happiness.

THE PERSONAL ARGUMENT AND THE CALL TO LOVE

If we accept the personal argument but not the universal one, perfect blessedness will be reserved for those lucky enough never to have loved any of the damned. If universalism is true, then *all* are so lucky. But if the doctrine of hell is true, it certainly seems as if some will be eternally deprived of perfect blessedness, not because of their refusal to repent for their sins or their lack of faith or their resistance to divine grace, but because they have the misfortune of loving someone who ended up in hell.

What seems to follow is a distinction among the saved or, if you will, two tiers of the blessed: those who didn't love any of the damned during their earthly lives, and those who did. The latter will be afflicted by a suffering the former are spared, even if both will presumably still enjoy

---

34. James Spiegel suggests a possibility Hassoun overlooks: perhaps some are eternally lost but none of the lost are among those loved by any of the blessed. See Spiegel, *Hell and Divine Goodness*, 119–22. If this is a real possibility, Hassoun's argument fails because traditional Christians could endorse (c) without holding that the blessed *stop* loving anyone. I will critically assess Spiegel's proposal in chapter 6.

the blessings of moral sanctification and a range of other goods denied the damned. Whether the former might still experience perfect blessedness depends on a range of other issues—such as whether they would be pained by sympathy for the less fortunate among the blessed, and whether the universal version of the argument has merit. This personal version of the argument is thus at least *potentially* narrower in scope than the universal version. Rather than diminishing the blessedness of *all* the saved, it *may* only diminish the blessedness of some—since some of the blessed may have been lucky enough to count none of the damned among their loved ones. But it is hard to imagine that all of the blessed fall into that category. Thus, even if this personal version of the argument doesn't imply that all the saved experience imperfect joy, it probably implies this with respect to most and surely to some.[35]

But even if it implies this for only a few of the saved, that would be enough to generate serious difficulties. First, it would mean that each of us is *vulnerable* to having our heavenly joy diminished by whom we love. Suppose God bestows resistible grace on all and, given this, the choice not to resist God's grace is sufficient for salvation. If the personal version of the argument from heavenly sympathy is sound, then such non-resistance would be sufficient only for a second-rate blessedness marred by suffering. To have perfect blessedness, not only would I need to display such nonresistance myself, but so must all my loved ones.

This problem leads directly to another one: it appears we would risk the quality of our blessedness by cultivating close relationships with the "wrong" sorts of people, those we judge less likely to be saved because they are on a suspect life trajectory. This could be a powerful motive to withhold from them the very thing that would increase their chances of salvation: genuine human connection with someone in a right relationship we God. But how can we claim *to be* in a right relationship with God if we withhold our love from those who need it most?

This shows that the personal version of the problem is every bit as serious as the universal version, even if it does not necessarily extend to all the saved. If I set out to avoid loving anyone I fear might end up among the damned, I put myself on a trajectory *away from* the God of love and away from living out the law of love—in order to secure a more joyful afterlife. Surely, such a scheme could not *succeed*. Surely, the heavenly

---

35. Again, Spiegel denies this, but I will put off critiquing his reasons until chapter 6.

state is not organized such that those who limit the scope of their love for personal gain have a *better shot* at perfect blessedness.

On the contrary, the joys of heaven appear to be intrinsically linked to the cultivation of our capacity for love. Hence, if non-universalism is true, the very thing we must cultivate in order to be the kind of people who can experience the full riches of blessedness is that which makes our blessedness vulnerable to being marred by the suffering of the damned.

SYMPATHY AND GRIEF, HELL AND ANNIHILATION

In this chapter, we have been considering a version of the incompatibility argument that focuses on the sympathy that some or all of the saved would feel for some or all of the damned. We have seen a universal version, which posits that the blessed would be perfected in love and so would sympathize with all the damned—meaning all the blessed would have their heavenly joy diminished if any were damned. We have also looked at a more personal version, which posits that if any are damned there will be those among the saved who class these afflicted persons among their loved ones. Since the saved will not lose their love for these damned persons, they will sympathetically suffer. Thus, at least some of the saved will have their blessedness diminished, and everyone will be at risk of it. In fact, the more we strive to follow Christ in this life, loving as he loved, the more at risk we are.

Correlated with these arguments is a *problem* of heavenly sympathy with both a universal and personal dimension. It is the problem, faced by traditionalists, of accounting for how the promise of perfect blessedness for the saved can be sustained given allegiance to the traditional doctrine of hell.

While much of the critical discussion that follows will apply to this problem of heavenly sympathy, my main focus is on the related problem of heavenly grief. As noted at the start of this chapter, the reason to focus on the latter problem is that it applies to all forms of non-universalism. Arguably, annihilationism escapes the problem of heavenly sympathy. But all non-universalist doctrines face the reality of loss. Insofar as this is true of the traditional doctrine of hell, it is unsurprising that formulations of the argument from heavenly sympathy often encompass the grief associated with loss. In that sense, there is a problem of heavenly grief *folded into* the problem of heavenly sympathy.

But in the next pair of chapters I want to tease the former free of the latter, exploring how love is related to grief by focusing on two core issues: first, the kind of love the blessed would possess given what Christian ethics teaches about the command to love our neighbors as ourselves; second, the implications such love has for our emotional lives, especially our disposition towards grief. Based on this exploration, I will formulate what I take to be the strongest version of the argument from heavenly grief—one that, in accord with the distinction drawn in this chapter, recognizes that heavenly grief can have *both* universal *and* personal sources.

4

The Love of the Blessed

NON-UNIVERSALISM AND POTENTIAL SOURCES OF GRIEF

WHAT WOULD THE SAVED feel were non-universalism true? Given that the blessed are, on Christian teachings, morally perfected, this amounts to an ethical question about the emotions one ought to feel and the emotional dispositions associated with a good moral character. The blessed would have morally perfected emotional responses to the losses they would face were non-universalism true.

But before we begin to explore what such morally perfected emotional responses would look like, there may be value in thinking just a bit more fully about the range of losses in question. Were non-universalism true, what losses would the blessed have morally perfected emotional responses *to*?

It is important here to distinguish two senses of "loss." There is a narrow sense, which refers to some good *once present* that is now gone—such as all those routines and activities Lewis shared with his wife, which her death stole away. But there is also a broader sense of "loss." When a good that *should* have and *could* have obtained does not obtain, we count that as a loss. Consider parents who watch a child squander their potential and fall into addiction: never developing their talents, never forming meaningful relationships because every relationship becomes just a means of feeding their addiction. The parents will surely grieve, but they grieve not because their child developed talents and meaningful relationships and then lost them—not if their child fell into addiction before they ever had a chance to develop these things. They grieve on account of all the unrealized potential: every good that might have been. Typically, when a young person dies, loved ones grieve for both kinds of losses: the loss of everything the young person already was, but also the loss of all the goods that might have been.

Non-universalism entails not only losses in the narrow sense, insofar as people who were once in community with the blessed are now separated or annihilated. It also, and primarily, involves a range of losses in the broader sense: all the goods that might have been had the unsaved not been damned or annihilated. Children of God, made by God for a glorious end, tumble instead into the ash heap of eschatological history. They never have the eternal life, joy, and moral sanctification that God desired them to have, nor the loving relationships with God and the blessed.

Would the blessed in heaven grieve for all that unrealized potential?

This question has significance whether one thinks the goods of heaven are humanity's *natural* end—what our natures orient us towards—or a supernatural gift of God.[1] Obviously, on the former view, the final state of the unsaved is one in which their natural potential is permanently unrealized: what they were *designed* to be never *comes* to be. This gap between natural potential and reality represents a *vitiation* of their natures.

But even if heaven's blessings are a supernatural gift, traditional Christian theology holds that *sin* vitiates our natures—and the lost never receive the grace required to escape sin. Furthermore, even if we are naturally ordered only to finite goods that fall far short of the goods of heaven, God makes the latter goods available to all who respond to God in the right way. God *desires* that all respond in the right way. And so, these heavenly goods are ones the lost *would have enjoyed* had they made other choices—goods they thus had the potential to enjoy because of who God is and what God offers, if not because of their own natures.

This last point touches on the biblical teaching that God "desires everyone to be saved" (1 Tim 2:4), which points us to another major loss if non-universalism is true: the eternal thwarting of God's desires. Some may seek to soften the significance of this loss by invoking the distinction between God's antecedent and consequent desires, arguing that God

---

1. For a fuller characterization of this distinction and reasons to favor the view that human beings are naturally ordered to heaven's goods, see Kronen and Reitan, *God's Final Victory*, 74–79.

desires that all be saved only in the former sense. As we saw in chapter 1, God's antecedent desires are God's "all-else-being-equal" desires: what God would want were circumstances arranged to God's liking. God's consequent desires are God's "all-things-considered" desires: what God in fact desires given actual circumstances—circumstances in part determined by *our* choices.

Construed in this way, God's desire for the salvation of, say, Bob, is an antecedent desire. Whether it produces a consequent desire for Bob's salvation is *conditional* on whether Bob makes the right choices. But this does not mean God has *no* desire for Bob's salvation *absent* these choices. If God has no desire for Bob's salvation prior to Bob making the right choices, how could we meaningfully claim that God *has* a desire for Bob's salvation, even if only in the antecedent sense? In order to coherently say God *has* an antecedent desire for Bob's salvation and *would* have a consequent desire for it if only (say) Bob repented, we must hold that (a) God *conditionally* desires Bob's salvation, the condition being Bob's repentance, and (b) God *unconditionally* desires that Bob repent. In short, we can meaningfully say God has an antecedent desire for the salvation of all only if God *wants the conditions under which all would be saved to obtain*. If those conditions are never met for some people, *a divine desire is eternally thwarted*.

Thus, if God antecedently desires the salvation of all but non-universalism is true, God has eternally thwarted desires. Furthermore, everything God desires is *good*. For God's desire to be unfulfilled is for something good to go unrealized. If non-universalism is true but we accept the message of 1 Timothy 2:4, it follows that the final state of creation fails to exhibit a significant good God desired that it have. The blessed would presumably care about this loss, both because of the unrealized potential in creation and because they love God, whose significant desires are eternally thwarted.

What we have here, then, are a range of interrelated losses were non-universalism true. Would it be fitting for the blessed, confronting such losses, to be *perfectly* happy? Or would their happiness instead be diminished by grief? To answer this, we need to think more deeply about what it means to be morally sanctified.

THE CENTRALITY OF LOVE

In Scripture, both Jesus and Paul testify to the ethical centrality of love. When asked to name the greatest commandment, Jesus identifies two: "You shall love the Lord your God with all your heart, and with all your soul, and with all your mind," and "You shall love your neighbor as yourself" (Matt 22:37–38). Paul explicitly calls the latter "the fulfillment of the law," encompassing all earthly commandments, including those against adultery, murder, theft, and covetousness (Rom 13:9–10). Paul thus treats the command to love our neighbors as what moral philosophers would call a fundamental moral principle.

According to Jesus, this command to love our neighbors is "like" the command to love God, suggesting an intimate connection between the two. This is interesting—and *puzzling*—because the two commands not only have different objects (God and neighbor) but seem to call us to love in radically different *ways*. Paul Ramsey notes that the call to love your neighbor as yourself is a call to care about and pursue your neighbor's good whether your neighbor deserves it or not, since that is how you love yourself: "You naturally love yourself for your own sake. You wish your own good, and you do so even when you may have a certain distaste for the kind of person you are."[2] Since self-love "does not wait on worth," neither does Christian neighbor-love.[3] For this reason, Ramsey takes "disinterested regard for another person" to be "one of the primary meanings of 'Christian love.'"[4]

But love for God surely does not set aside all consideration of God's worth in the way neighbor-love sets aside considerations about our neighbors' worth. On the contrary, love for God essentially involves a *recognition* of and responsiveness to God's supreme value. Furthermore, while we can value God's greatness and honor it, nothing we do can *promote God's welfare*. But caring about and appropriately pursuing our neighbors' welfare is essential to neighbor-love. In short, while neighbor-love is about pursuing the neighbor's good without regard for the neighbor's worth, love of God has nothing to do with pursuing God's good and everything to do with showing a high regard for God's worth. Seen in this light, love for God and neighbor appear to be nothing alike—and yet Jesus says the one is like the other.

2. Ramsey, *Basic Christian Ethics*, 100.
3. Ramsey, *Basic Christian Ethics*, 100.
4. Ramsey, *Basic Christian Ethics*, 95–96.

First John offers a solution to this puzzle. Here we encounter not only the Christian idea that God *is* love but a rich exploration of the relation between this understanding of God and the Christian moral life, including the intimate connection between God's love for us and our love for each other. John tells us *God's love for us* should be the starting point for our understanding of love: "In this is love, not that we loved God but that he loved us and sent his Son to be the atoning sacrifice for our sins" (1 John 4:10). On account of this divine love for us, we are called to "love one another" (1 John 4:11). In obeying this call, God's love for us does more than offer the model for how we should treat one another. When we love one another, "God abides in us, and his love is perfected in us" (1 John 4:12).

In all of Scripture, no portrait of intimacy with God is more complete: when we allow God to make us instruments of divine love, God *abides* or *lives* in us. This leads John to understand our love for God *in terms of* our love for other people: "Those who say, 'I love God,' and hate a brother or sister are liars, for those who do not love a brother or sister, whom they have seen, cannot love God, whom they have not seen. The commandment we have from him is this: those who love God must love their brothers and sisters also" (1 John 4:20–21).

The idea appears to be this: we love God when we make ourselves into vessels of divine love, allowing that love to inhabit us and flow through us into the world. Loving God and loving neighbor become two sides of the same act: we submit ourselves to God, opening ourselves to the source of love and making ourselves its vessel; then we express that in relation to our neighbor. As such, we should expect the ethical life to be wholly comprehended in loving our neighbors—just as Paul declared. As Ramsey puts it, "God, who is Love, is the 'ground' from which real love for neighbor proceeds."[5] To love our neighbors is to attune our wills to God's will, to say, "Thy will be done," and thus allow God's love to flow through us.

THE NATURE OF CHRISTIAN LOVE: AGAPE

If all of this is right, we need to know who our neighbors are and what neighbor-love looks like. When asked about the former, Jesus tells the parable of the good Samaritan. Paul Ramsey notes that by responding in

---

5. Ramsey, *Basic Christian Ethics*, 118.

this way, Jesus *challenges* those who ask, "Who is my neighbor?" No one has to pass a *test* to qualify as an object of love. The questioner should "revise entirely his point of view, reformulating the question first asked so as to require neighborliness of himself rather than anything of his neighbor."[6] The Samaritan—a member of a marginalized and despised group—makes the injured victim on the road *into* a neighbor by caring for him in his time of need. We should do likewise.

The Lutheran theologian Anders Nygren reaches a similar conclusion by focusing on Jesus' call to love our enemies.[7] If Christian love extends even to enemies, that tells us something essential about its nature: it does not discriminate based on the neighbor's virtues or desirable qualities. Christian love thus turns everyone into a neighbor, even our enemy. It has a universal scope—but not, as Ramsey warns, in the sense that what I love is some generic humanity.[8] Christian love is universal in the sense that *each* person is its proper object.[9]

The fact that God is love, and that our love for one another channels God's love for us, provides another avenue for fleshing out the nature of Christian love: by looking at how God expresses divine love for us. For Christians, this means looking to the incarnation and atonement. Scripture affirms (John 3:16) that this pivotal divine intervention in human history springs from God's love for the world. And in 1 John, the divine act of God giving Jesus as "the atoning sacrifice for our sins" is held up as the paradigm of what love is (1 John 4:10). Love is seen to be a *giving of the self* for the other's sake, without regard for whether they deserve it.

What the cross reveals is also revealed in creation, which Gustav Aulen describes as "primarily the life-giving work of sovereign divine love."[10] Creation bestows the good of existence, the precondition for all other goods. Like Christ's atoning sacrifice, creation represents a divine love that gives freely for the other's sake. As Stanley Grenz puts it, "Because God is love, God is self-giving. Because God is self-giving, God willingly creates the world."[11] Karl Barth sums up his understanding of Christian love in similar terms: "Love is a free action: the self-giving of

---

6. Ramsey, *Basic Christian Ethics*, 93.

7. Nygren, *Agape and Eros*, 66.

8. Ramsey, *Basic Christian Ethics*, 94–95.

9. Ramsey, *Basic Christian Ethics*, 95.

10. Aulen, *Faith of the Christian Church*, 181.

11. Grenz, *Theology for the Community of God*, 101. See also Aquinas, *Summa Theologica* I, Q. 20, Art. 2.

one to another without interest, intention or goal; the spontaneous self-giving of the one to the other just because the other is there and confronts him."[12]

Christian love gives for the neighbor's sake, meaning it focuses on the neighbor's *good*, and does so without expecting *reciprocation*. It is free of self-seeking motives. Such *giving*-love needs to be distinguished from the love Scrooge has for his money: the covetous desire to possess. Anders Nygren uses two ancient Greek terms to distinguish these kinds of love: *eros* and *agape*. *Eros* names the desiring love that longs to possess an object (or a person, who is thereby objectified), whereas *agape* names the self-giving Christian love described above.

Like Nygren (and Ramsey), Martin Luther King Jr. captures the essence of Christian love by distinguishing kinds of love in relation to distinct Greek terms:

> There are three words for love in the Greek New Testament. First, there is *eros*. In Platonic philosophy *eros* meant yearning of the soul for the realm of the divine. It has come now to mean a sort of aesthetic or romantic love. Second, there is *philia*. It meant intimate affectionateness between friends. *Philia* denotes a sort of reciprocal love: the person loves because he is loved. When we speak of loving those who oppose us we refer to neither *eros* nor *philia*; we speak of a love which is expressed in the Greek word *agape*. *Agape* means nothing sentimental or basically affectionate; it means understanding, redeeming good will for all men, an overflowing love which seeks nothing in return. It is the love of God working in the lives of men. When we love on the *agape* level we love men not because we like them, not because their attitudes and ways appeal to us, but because God loves them.[13]

King identifies Christian love with agape: a love that extends even to enemies and evildoers, that does not depend on *liking* or having affectionate feelings for them, and that expects nothing in return: it is self-giving for the neighbor's sake.

---

12. Barth, *Church Dogmatics* 4.2, §68, 752.
13. King, "Nonviolence and Racial Justice," 8–9.

CHRISTIAN LOVE AND INHERENT WORTH

Despite King's clear indebtedness to Nygren and Ramsey, there are important ways in which King modifies their understanding of Christian love, a modification rooted in his personalist commitments and his own experience as an activist for social justice and a target of racist discrimination.

Nygren claims that God's agape "does not recognize value, but creates it. Agape loves and imparts value by loving. The man who is loved by God has no value in himself; what gives him value is precisely the fact that God loves him."[14] This is why Nygren holds that Christian love, mirroring God's love, is "unmotivated" and "indifferent to value."[15] Ramsey reflects this view, saying that Christian love does not discriminate "between worthy and unworthy people according to the qualities they possess."[16]

In articulating the theological underpinnings of the civil rights campaign, Martin Luther King borrows heavily from Ramsey's characterization of agape, calling it a "disinterested" love that "does not begin by discrimination between worthy and unworthy people," and hence "makes no distinction between friend and enemy."[17] But as someone who experienced social messages of worthlessness, King resists the idea that human beings have no inherent worth or that Christian love is in *no* way responsive to that worth. Instead, King promulgates the idea that human persons have inherent worth and we fail to love properly if we do not honor the "sacredness of human personality" and "the inherent dignity of man."[18]

King is drawing here on convictions he learned from the Boston personalists, who not only took personality to be at the heart of reality—in God's personhood—but saw the creation of humans as a divine act of imparting this fundamental reality to the world.[19] Our personhood *is* the image of God within us, imbuing us with sacred value. King expresses his experiential grasp of racism's evil in terms of this personalism: racism fails to recognize and respond properly to the inherent worth of the personhood residing in each human being, regardless of race or other

---

14. Nygren, *Agape and Eros*, 78.
15. Nygren, *Agape and Eros*, 66.
16. Ramsey, *Basic Christian Ethics*, 93.
17. King, "Nonviolence and Racial Justice," 8–9.
18. King, "Ethical Demands of Integration," 119.
19. For a discussion of King's indebtedness to the personalist tradition, see Hackett, "Martin Luther King, Jr."

category: "There is no graded scale of essential worth; there is no divine right of one race which differs from the divine right of another. Every human being has etched in his personality the indelible stamp of the Creator."[20] Based on this view, King insists that "man is not a thing" and should never be treated as an "animated tool" but always "as a person sacred in himself." To do otherwise is to "depersonalize" and "desecrate what he is."[21]

Drawing on this perspective, King departs from Ramsey's view that there is no place for self-love in the Christian love ethic. Where Ramsey sees Christian agape as the "inversion" of self-love, directing the love we have for ourselves to our neighbor *instead* of ourselves,[22] King knows that oppressed peoples *need* to love themselves—in the form of a self-respect that demands respect from others in defiance of contrary social messages.[23] It is only by overcoming oppression that God's image can be reclaimed by oppressed and oppressors alike:

> So long as the Negro . . . is seen as anything less than a person of sacred worth, the image of God is abused in him and consequently and proportionately lost by those who inflict the abuse. Only by establishing a truly integrated society can we return to the Negro the quality of "thouness" which is his due because of the nature of his being.[24]

What emerges here is a view of Christian love as essentially *responsive* to the inherent worth of every person. Self-love in this sense is not selfishness but the expression of a love that acknowledges the inherent worth of persons—including ourselves.

Furthermore, responsiveness to the inherent worth of persons can and does ground a love that extends to all people—friend or enemy, self or other—regardless of their moral character, our relationship with them, or how useful they are to us. Hence, we needn't posit an indifference to worth *in every sense* in order to construe agape as a love that extends to every neighbor. In this way, King's personalism preserves a tradition in Christian ethics with deep roots. Augustine, for example, posits a hierarchy of objective values among existing things, wherein the value

---

20. King, "Ethical Demands of Integration," 119.
21. King, "Ethical Demands of Integration," 119.
22. Ramsey, *Basic Christian Ethics*, 100.
23. King, "Facing the Challenge," 137. See also King, "Rising Tide," 145–46.
24. King, "Ethical Demands of Integration," 119.

something has *in itself* or inherently does not depend on its utility and is distinct from the subjective value people attach to things:

> Thus the reason of one contemplating nature prompts very different judgments from those dictated by the necessity of the needy, or the desire of the voluptuous; for the former considers what value a thing in itself has in the scale of creation, while necessity considers how it meets its need; reason looks for what the mental light will judge to be true, while pleasure looks for what pleasantly titillates the bodily sense.[25]

Aquinas expresses similar ideas. As he puts it, "All things are good, inasmuch as they have being."[26] Furthermore, even though all finite beings depend on God and only exist because of God, they still have *their own value*. In Aquinas's words, "everything is called good by reason of the similitude of the divine goodness belonging to it, which is formally its own goodness, whereby it is denominated good."[27]

Nygren's view—that agape "does not recognize value but creates it"—get its impetus from conceiving of God's creative activity as *the* paradigmatic act of love. According to Nygren, "the man who is loved by God has no value in himself" but acquires value purely as a consequence of being loved by God.[28] This idea makes some sense in relation to the divine act of creation as an expression of love: God's creation of a person *cannot* be motivated by respect for the person's inherent value, since prior to creation the person doesn't exist, and non-existent things don't have inherent value.

But there are three difficulties with drawing from this fact the conclusion that Christian love is not responsive to inherent value. First, even if humans do not exist prior to God creating them, God might still have the motivating desire to *bring inherently valuable beings into existence*. Creating a person increases the representation in the world of a person's distinct kind of inherent value. Hence, even if responsiveness to a not-yet-existent person's inherent worth cannot motivate God to create them, respect for what is inherently valuable—persons—could still be a motive for God to bring persons into being. And once a person has been created,

25. Augustine, *City of God*, 11.16.1.
26. Aquinas, *Summa Theologica* I, Q. 6, Art. 4.
27. Aquinas, *Summa Theologica* I, Q. 6, Art. 4. Like Augustine, Aquinas also recognizes a hierarchy of being in which some things possess more being than others and hence more value. See Aquinas, *Summa Theologica* I, Q. 78, Art. 1; I, Q. 96, Art. 2.
28. Nygren, *Agape and Eros*, 78.

the inherent worth they then possess is something God—a valuer of what is good—would respect. To do otherwise would, in King's terms, depersonalize and desecrate a person's sacred dignity, something God would never do.

Second, unlike God, humans do not create the neighbors they are called to love. When Nygren speaks of human agape, he skirts the significance of this by claiming that human agape does not respond to fellowship but creates it.[29] While this *is* an important way human love can be creative, we are called to love our *neighbors*, not merely or primarily the *fellowship* our love for them helps create. While God's love creates the very object of love, every human act of love targets a neighbor who already exists and already possesses inherent value.

Third, Jesus calls us to love our *neighbors*, not Norwegian sweaters or bowls of goulash. And part of the reason, surely, is that our neighbors have an inherent value inanimate things lack. Our neighbors bear God's image. Sweaters do not. Likewise, the incarnation and atonement were acts of divine love aimed at the eternal good of human beings. God did not become flesh and dwell among us, suffer death, and rise again for the salvation of goulash.

Of course, human beings can suffer or flourish, stagnate or grow, fall into vice or cultivate virtue in ways goulash cannot. Thus, humans *have* a good, a welfare, that both we and God can pursue. Is it this fact about humans, rather than any inherent worth, that singles them out as proper objects of agape? Should we love human beings without *any* regard for their value, motivated only by the fact that they can benefit or be harmed by how we treat them?

There are several problems with such thinking. First off, this idea that people (and other living things) are objects of moral concern only because they can be benefited or harmed by our actions is a key element of utilitarian thinking, and in that guise has been criticized for reducing people (and other living things) to mere vessels or containers of happiness or welfare. But surely human welfare matters because human beings matter, not the other way around. Furthermore, so much of what comprises our "welfare" is about what we need to keep on living—but why care about keeping persons alive if their existence has no value in itself? More significantly, it is because we are finite *persons*, capable by nature of more or less fully actualizing our potential, that some things are

---

29. Nygren, *Agape and Eros*, 102.

good for us in a sense more profound than merely contributing to survival—things like authentic fellowship, moral virtue, and excellence in the exercise of our talents. But this surely presupposes that there is value in us fully *becoming* what our nature suits us to *be*—meaning the value of our welfare cannot be separated easily from the value of our being.

A final reason we cannot cleanly disentangle what is good for us from what makes us inherently valuable is this: failure to honor the dignity of persons is one of the most profound ways we harm them. King knew this firsthand: it is not good for people to be treated like mere things. How, then, can we promote the good of our neighbors unless we respect the inherent value they possess?

Nygren elegantly captures the gift-like character of Christian love, its universal scope, and how it mirrors God's creative love. But in saying that "the man who is loved by God has no value in himself," he risks misplacing an important theme of Christian thought that emphasizes responsiveness to inherent worth as a key feature of the moral life. Furthermore, he risks forgetting how the failure to honor the inherent worth of persons harms them—arguably the most distinctive harm of oppressive systems. King, by holding fast to his personalism while appropriating Nygren's and Ramsey's insights, frames an understanding of Christian agape that encompasses all persons without losing sight of their inherent value. As such, his understanding retains the insights of such towering figures in Christian thought as Augustine and Aquinas and affirms the experiential insight—most vividly apparent to oppressed people—that concern for the welfare of our neighbors requires affirming their inherent dignity and worth.

Before moving on, I want to explore more deeply a point made above, namely that the most important human goods are tied to the fact that we can more or less fully actualize the potential found in our nature. The idea here is that human welfare cannot be separated from the actualization of human potential, and that this is especially true with respect to moral sanctification. Sin *vitiates* us—diminishing what we are meant to be according to God's original design plan for humanity. Moral sanctification, by contrast, actualizes our potential: we become more fully and truly human, living up to and into our original natures.

Those who do so flourish in a way those who fail to do so can't. Thus, the Christian understanding of human flourishing is inseparable from moral sanctification: happiness is not just a reward for being good. Being good *is* the reward. More precisely, being morally sanctified is a constitutive element of a truly happy human existence that features loving relationships with God and the blessed (impossible absent such sanctification).[30]

But this idea, that humans by their nature have a potential that can be actualized or not, implies something else relevant to our discussion here. Those who actualize their potential through moral sanctification more fully express the value inherent in personhood than those who fail to do so. And there is a crucial difference between *being a person* but failing to fully express the worth of a person and fully expressing the worth of the kind of being you are when the kind of being you are is one of lesser value than a person. The former represents *unrealized potential*: something of value is missing that, in an important sense, *ought to be there*. This absence is a *loss* in what I have called the broader sense: a good that *should* and *could* have been part of the world is missing from it.

When we love someone, we value not just who they are but *who they have the potential to become*. This is why we grieve more deeply over the death of children than over the death of those who have lived full lives. It is also why those who love themselves *well* desire their own growth and maturation and moral improvement. And when Jesus calls us to love our neighbors as ourselves, he surely means we should love them as we love ourselves when we do so *well*. Such love values not only the inherent worth of persons but the actualization of the potential persons possess and the overcoming of what vitiates or diminishes them.

MUTUAL LOVE AND FELLOWSHIP

The call to love our enemies makes it clear that as Christians, we are to love our neighbors whether or not they love us back. Martin Luther King Jr. distinguishes agape from *philia*—the love of mutual affection and care found in healthy human relationships—and identifies Christian love with agape. Similarly, Ramsey warns that "the prospect of requital in the not far distant future produces such an effect that one cannot definitely see what is Christian love and what is enlightened selfishness."[31] In other words, a love that is motivated by the hope of reciprocity is not genuinely Christian love.

---

30. For more on this, see Kronen and Reitan, *God's Final Victory*, 29.
31. Ramsey, *Basic Christian Ethics*, 99.

But that doesn't mean Christian love shouldn't inspire us to *pursue* relationships that feature mutual affection and care. A key dimension of God's agapic love for us lies in God's active pursuit of loving union with us. *Mutual* love is essential for real union or fellowship, and such union—among humans as well as between humans and God—is vital for human welfare. Miroslav Volf thus insists that "the *goal* of self-giving love is mutuality of perfect love."[32] Similarly, even though King identifies Christian love with agape, his moral vision is shaped by the image of the "beloved community,"[33] an image that inspired him to seek integration, not mere desegregation, because only integration—replacing division with community—can properly reflect "the solidarity of the human family."[34]

The Christian conception of heaven features just this kind of community of mutual love or fellowship. Heaven is not a place of unrequited love but of mutuality, where God and creatures are bonded through reciprocal love. This is so precisely because loving fellowship is a key constituent of human welfare. As such, it is one of the greatest gifts we can offer—the kind of gift agapic love *would* offer (even if it cannot be forced).

In authentic fellowship, we both give and receive. As we give compassionate attention, we receive the gift of another self: their experiences, feelings, convictions. As we share ourselves, we receive the gift of attention. We bridge the gap between self and other while preserving the integrity of each. On classical Christian theology, God's very essence embodies such unity in diversity. God's nature is not just love, but *mutual* love. In the Trinity, there is loving *fellowship*. Arguably, when human self-giving love becomes mutual, God inhabits the entire relationship, bringing persons together in a way that reflects God's triune nature.

We can't produce such reciprocal love alone. But we can work to inspire it. When Nygren says agape creates fellowship where it is absent, he hits on the key to inspiring fellowship. As King puts it,

> Love is the only force capable of transforming an enemy into a friend. We never get rid of an enemy by meeting hate with hate; we get rid of an enemy by getting rid of enmity. By its very nature, hate destroys and tears down; by its very nature, love creates and builds up. Love transforms with redemptive power.[35]

32. Volf, *Exclusion and Embrace*, 190.
33. See King, "Advice for Living," 106.
34. King, "Ethical Demands of Integration," 121.
35. King, *Strength to Love*, 54.

Agapic love, while distinct from the mutual love that constitutes fellowship, is nevertheless oriented towards authentic fellowship. When we love in the agapic sense, we value fellowship where it exists, are open to it where it is absent, plant seeds of fellowship where we can, and nurture those seeds as we are able.

Let me be clear: being open to fellowship does not mean submitting to abusive or exploitative relationships. Such relationships are not fellowship. I can be open to fellowship while not being open to *that*. I can be realistic enough to know when something dysfunctional is all I am likely to get, and since I can only cultivate a finite number of relationships, my openness to fellowship may orient me, all else being equal, to cases where my efforts are more likely to bear fruit.[36] Furthermore, imposing conditions on a relationship can be an expression of love, such as when loving parents impose rehab as a condition for welcoming home a drug-addicted child. It is not their *love* that is conditional, since unconditional love might be the very thing motivating the condition.

The point is this: if I am perfected in agapic love, my openness to fellowship with you will be conditional only if and to the extent that the conditions themselves spring from agapic love—for you, for myself, and for others. They will be conditions the meeting of which will *advance* mutual fellowship. And this means I will never shut you off from fellowship by imposing conditions you can't meet or conditions the meeting of which are not conducive to the aims of love. For example, while I might insist as a condition of fellowship that an alcoholic maintain sobriety with the help of a program like AA, I will not make it a condition of fellowship that they have never in their lives been an active alcoholic.

THE EMERGENT PICTURE OF CHRISTIAN LOVE

In his recent book, *Love Divine*, Jordan Wessling argues that "reflection upon ideal human love can significantly inform how we ought to conceive of God's love."[37] Put another way, we have an experience of love's nature

---

36. I say "all else being equal" because agape is also concerned with the neighbor's good, and some neighbors are more desperately in need of fellowship than others. Those in greatest need may also be those with whom pursuing fellowship is fraught with risk. In rare cases, I may be uniquely positioned to nurture fellowship with such a person with limited risk of harm—in which case doing so may be exactly what agapic love calls for.

37. Wessling, *Love Divine*, 9.

in our lives, and this experience points us beyond our flawed human love relationships towards love at its best. Our experience of human love is thus revelatory, telling us about the nature of God's love—at least when we use standards of philosophical coherence and consistency with Scripture to guide our reflection on that experience, as Wessling does. The implication, for Wessling, is that even though God and God's wisdom are so far beyond us that we are often "in the dark about how God will *act* in love," we are not similarly "in the dark about the *nature* of God's love."[38]

Following this approach, Wessling articulates what he calls the "value account" of love. On this account, to love someone in an ideal way is "to perceive that individual's intrinsic worth . . . and to respond to that individual by valuing her existence, her flourishing, and union with her."[39] Wessling explains what valuing union means in terms of his "union thesis," which holds that "X values union with Y only if X values (i) mentally attending to Y (ii) intimately knowing Y, and (iii) Y's loving X."[40]

This picture of love functions as a kind of distillation of three key themes about love that I have been developing here. First, while not conditional on the usefulness or moral character of the neighbor, Christian love cares about and responds to the inherent worth that resides in each neighbor as a person created in God's image. One cannot value that worth while being indifferent to whether its bearer is annihilated. To value someone's inherent worth is, then, to value their continued existence.

Second, Christian love is directed towards the neighbor's good for the neighbor's sake. This is vividly modeled in the parable of the good Samaritan: I love my neighbor by responding to their need, by helping the robbery victim on the Jericho road rather than hurrying by. But while the good Samaritan was focused on immediate physical needs, agape is not limited to this. Notably, my desire for your good must include a desire that you be freed from bondage to sin. Only through moral sanctification will you flourish in the sense of actualizing your potential. Thus, even though agape cares nothing about the neighbor's moral character as a *condition* for loving them, it cares deeply about the neighbor's moral character *as an end of love*. Christian love values the neighbor's welfare in a way that includes their moral improvement.

---

38. Wessling, *Love Divine*, 27.
39. Wessling, *Love Divine*, 64.
40. Wessling, *Love Divine*, 58.

Finally, even if Christian love is distinct from *philia* and so is not conditional on reciprocity, such love values fellowship with the neighbor as an end, and so values reciprocity as an end. That is, Christian love values a relationship with the neighbor in which we not only value each other's existence and welfare but also *union*: an authentic sharing of selves where each sees and is seen, knows, and is known. For God, who is without limits, valuing union would express itself as actively pursuing union with each created person (the achievement of which might depend on their response). In our case, given our limits, valuing union expresses itself in the kind of openness to fellowship described above. Such openness would be to fellowship of varying degrees, with the most intimate fellowship reserved for a relatively small circle of loved ones. But even if most persons will not be ones I pursue active fellowship with, and even fewer ones I cultivate deep intimacy with, there will be a positive attitude towards fellowship and, by implication, a negative stance towards *barriers* to fellowship—including, notably, the kinds of barriers imposed by sin and death.

If all of this is right, we now have a core piece of our answer to what the moral sanctification of the blessed consists in. It means being perfected in agapic love, a love that extends without distinction to every neighbor, including the enemy-neighbor and especially the neighbor in need. The blessed in heaven, then, would love not only the saved but the unsaved, valuing their existence, their welfare, and fellowship or union with them. The eternal damnation or annihilation of anyone would, based on these values, be tragic.

UNEMOTIONAL LOVE?

Even granting all of the above, one might think that being perfected in agapic love would have no implications for how the blessed *feel* about the lost, on the grounds that agape is not *emotional*. King, for example, stresses that when he calls for "projecting the ethics of love to the center of our lives," he does not mean "some sentimental emotion" since it "would be nonsense to urge men to love their oppressors in an affectionate sense."[41] King is here mirroring Kant, who famously distinguishes between practical and pathological love, claiming that only the former can be commanded:

41. King, "Nonviolence and Racial Justice," 8.

> It is in this manner, undoubtedly, that we are to understand those passages of Scripture also in which we are commanded to love our neighbor, even our enemy. For love, as an affection, cannot be commanded, but beneficence for duty's sake may, even though we are not impelled to it by any inclination—nay, are even repelled by a natural and unconquerable aversion. This is *practical* love, and not *pathological*—a love which is seated in the will, and not in the propensations of sense—in principles of action and not of tender sympathy; and it is this love alone which can be commanded.[42]

If the blessed were perfected in this practical love—a love "seated in the will" that is about obedience to "principles of action" rather than "tender sympathy"—then, arguably, they could love the damned or annihilated without feeling any negative emotions over their tragic fate. But is this Kantian portrait of love—an emotionless determination of the will—the best account of what Christ's command to love our neighbors calls for?

There are several concerns. First, Kant's argument relies on the premise that this is the only kind of love that can be *commanded*. But this premise is false. While we cannot simply adopt any emotion on command, emotional dispositions *can* be cultivated through at least two kinds of character-development practices: habituation and attention. The former is central to Aristotle's virtue ethics, focused as it is on cultivating states of character through like activities, that is, through a process of habituation.[43] But emotions can also be affected by what we pay attention to, meaning we can regulate emotions through practices of attention and cultivate emotional dispositions by habituating mindful attention to relevant features of our environment.[44] The command to love might thus be construed as a command to cultivate emotional dispositions in these ways.

Second, even if agape is not *affectionate* or sentimental, this does not mean it is not emotional. Much hinges here on what we take an emotion to be, of course—something I will say more about in the next chapter. For now it is enough to note that unlike moods or sensations, emotions not only feature an *affect* (a way they feel, positive or negative) but have a cognitive dimension: they are *about* something; they have an intentional

---

42. Kant, *Fundamental Principles*, 17.
43. Aristotle, *Nicomachean Ethics* 1103b.
44. See Wadlinger and Isaacowitz, "Fixing Our Focus."

object and involve a value judgment. Anger feels a certain way, but it is also *about* something (the way one was treated, say) and involves a *judgment* about that object (that the treatment was wrong). As described here, agape clearly has an object—the neighbor—and involves value judgments about the neighbor (their existence and welfare are good, as is fellowship with them). So the question is whether agape has a distinctive affect, a way it feels, even if that feeling is not *affection* or *fondness*. Here, it may be worth reflecting on how parents at their best feel towards their children when the strains of parenting occlude all feelings of affection or fondness. Parents remain *devoted* to their children even then, and there may be a way such devotion feels.

Third, even were agape not *itself* an emotion, that doesn't mean it will have no implications for our emotions. Consider what Sara Ruddick says in *Maternal Thinking* about the "preservative love" that characterizes the practice of mothering. Ruddick notes that feelings are indispensable to preservative love, in that it is through her own and her child's feelings that a mother arrives at "the understanding that makes protection possible."[45] Even though these feelings are intense and indispensable for preservative love, they fluctuate greatly and are often ambivalent. Ruddick thus treats emotions as "at best the complex but sturdy instruments of work."[46] In other words, emotions are *tools* of preservative love:

> But the activity of preservative love, although intensely emotional, can never be reduced to the sum of its feelings. Although feelings and action are conceptually connected, to feel is not tantamount to acting. . . . Mothers' feelings towards their children vary from hour to hour, year to year. . . . Protective care itself can vary only within a narrow range. Preservative love cannot alternate evenly with violence or negligence without ceasing to be itself. Although imbued with intense, ambivalent, thought-provoking feelings, mothering is an activity governed by a commitment that perseveres through feeling and structures the activity.[47]

In short, Ruddick takes the preservative love at the center of maternal activity as emotional—indeed, intensely emotional—while denying that it can be reduced to emotion and while affirming that it can endure through the vicissitudes of emotional change on account of the

---

45. Ruddick, *Maternal Thinking*, 69.
46. Ruddick, *Maternal Thinking*, 70.
47. Ruddick, *Maternal Thinking*, 70.

commitment that perseveres through these changes. Likewise, we might suppose that agape is emotional even though it is not reducible to an emotion or identified with a specific emotion. Agape may be a *commitment* to the neighbor—a commitment to preserving their being and welfare while maintaining (properly conditioned) openness to fellowship. But being a commitment of the will does not rule out being emotional in the sense of expressing itself *through* emotions and featuring characteristic emotional dispositions and responses. A mother's love would not be maternal preservative love if, in the aftermath of failure to preserve the child's life, the mother didn't grieve.

A commitment of the will to promote the neighbor's existence and welfare, and to be properly open to fellowship, makes no sense unless we *value* these things. This is arguably why Wessling characterizes love in terms of this array of values and calls his account of love the "value account." But values are intimately bound up with emotions. We will look more deeply at this connection in the next chapter. For now it is enough to note the following: to subjectively value something is to desire that it persist or come to be, and there is a clear connection between what we want to be the case and our hopes, fears, joys, and sorrows. Thus, even if Kant is right that the essence of what the love command requires is a commitment of the will, it would be a mistake to conclude that faithfully living out the love command would have no implications for our emotional lives. Such a commitment involves aligning ourselves with certain *values*, and what we value impacts what emotions we are disposed to feel (at least when those values are sincere).

Finally, it is important to recall that the blessed will not only be perfected in agapic love. They will presumably also retain *intimate personal love* for those among the lost they were close to in their earthly lives. Such personal love, as we know from experience, is not just emotional in itself but disposes us to feel emotions such as sympathy when our loved ones suffer and grief when they are lost.

While it is hard to imagine that being morally perfected would involve the extinction of these terrestrial bonds of affection, I can imagine critics who would like to say exactly that. Hence, it may be worth saying a few words about why it is so implausible to suppose that moral sanctification involves the extinction of such personal love.

First, when we think about what it means to have personal love for someone, it becomes apparent that such love has what should now be a familiar form: it involves valuing their existence, their welfare, and fellowship with them. What distinguishes personal love from agape is that this valuation is tied to a personal history of interaction that has led us to pay attention to the loved one. The value we attach to the loved one flows out of interaction and attention that helps us to *know* the loved one. The affective dimension of personal love, the way it feels, is directly tied to this history and the intimate personal knowledge that results. When we have such a history of connection that binds us to someone, we *feel* the value of their existence, their welfare, and their fellowship in a way we don't feel the value of strangers or enemies.

But the latter is surely a limitation of our finite natures. The difference here appears to be the difference between loving someone in the abstract and loving them in their concrete particularity. It is the difference between knowing intellectually that someone has sacred worth and personally experiencing that worth. I may know *that* the stranger's existence is good, but I don't know them in the sense of personally experiencing them *as* inherently valuable. I haven't *felt* the sacred dignity rooted in their being the way a new parent, holding their baby and marveling at the life before them, is immediately personally aware of that sacred worth.

Likewise, the hostility between me and my enemy may interfere with my capacity to directly discern them as bearers of the divine image. I may be able to intellectually grasp that they have a sacred value, but a direct personal experience of that value is lost amidst the strong emotional aversion I have to their wicked *character* or to how they have hurt me or those I love. And so, I can acknowledge that they are persons with inherent value and commit myself to reflecting that in my subjective values, even cultivating an emotional recognition of that value—some presumably attenuated correlate of personal love. But I will not feel such love for them.

If someone is wicked, it is not their *character* towards which I or anyone else would or should feel the emotions of personal love. But many parents who have no *affection* for their child's *character* will nevertheless display an emotional love that reaches beyond character to the inherent worth that is the child's birthright, the divine stamp that the parents have become personally acquainted with by virtue of the intense level of attention they've paid to their child. Parents (often) see past their child's failures, past the ways their children have fallen short of their potential, to the sacred essence against which those failures are measured. It is because they know that their children's essence orients them to a good greater than what their children have become that loving parents are as deeply pained by their children's vices as they are.

Conceived in this way, personal love is what the command to love our neighbors would culminate in *were it not for human limits and the grim realities of sin*. The call to love in the agapic sense might thus fruitfully be construed as a concession to our finitude: we are called to love everyone, but we are incapable of knowing everyone in the intimately personal way that gives rise to personal love for all. This limitation would, it seems, apply to the blessed as well: while freed from sin, they are not freed from creaturely finitude. And this means that personal love for all will be impossible even for the blessed. But where personal love encounters limits rooted in human finitude, agape does not. It is not impossible for us to adopt a commitment to recognize and value the inherent worth of every person, and to cultivate a character—including emotional dispositions—that reflect this. This, at least, the blessed would do.

But if this is right, it makes no sense to suppose that the personal love of the blessed would be uprooted and discarded so they are left *only* with the kind of love we are called to as a concession to our finitude. If the worry here is that retaining such personal love leads to unjust bias in favor of loved ones, it is a worry born of a failure to appreciate what moral sanctification means. For the blessed, personal love would reflect an intimate and immediate awareness of truths that, while *acknowledged* in agapic love, are not as deeply felt. In the morally perfected, this difference would motivate *attribution* rather than bias: instead of playing favorites, the blessed would attribute to *all* what they know deeply and with feeling only in relation to *some*.

This same idea can be arrived at by reflecting on Ramsey's use of the self-love analogy for understanding Christian love. As Ramsey puts it, if you know how you love yourself, "you will know how a Christian should love his neighbor."[48] One significant truth about self-love is this: we *attend* to ourselves. We inhabit our own perspectives fully, immersed in what it is like to be ourselves. We experience our own being and have direct personal acquaintance with our subjectivity and agency—in short, our personhood.

What would it look like to attend to our neighbor in the same way we attend to ourselves? The problem here is that for finite beings, it is impossible—although we might come close to achieving it with a few loved

---

48. Ramsey, *Basic Christian Ethics*, 100.

ones. Parents who are committed to the parenting project as described by Sara Ruddick will, inevitably, pay deep attention to their child—and this attention brings them in touch with the personhood of the child in a way that, while not identical to our experience of ourselves, is so close that parents routinely *identify* with their children. Such identification is the source of an emotional connection that reaches deeper than the child's character or usefulness. The parent's emotional selves acknowledge the child's reality in a way that, arguably, we rarely do with others.

A recurring theme of Simone Weil's thought is that paying attention to someone is essential for love. In fact, at one point she claims that love for neighbors is "made of creative attention."[49] It is only when we pay attention that we really recognize their existence, which Weil equates with love: "Only the existence of those we love is fully recognized. Belief in the existence of other human beings as such is love."[50] Elsewhere, speaking on love, she says, "To know that this man who is hungry and thirsty exists as much as I do—that is enough, the rest follows by itself."[51] Sometimes other people become for us like figures on a movie screen, just phenomenal aspects of our own experience. The only reality we confer on them is their impact on us. Weil's point is that when we construe others in this way, we fail to truly recognize their existence. Our attention is on how they affect us rather than on them. To love them just *is* to attend to them in a way that brings the reality of their existence fully to life for us.

If their reality comes alive for us fully, it will come alive for us not just intellectually but emotionally. They will be real to us not merely in our heads, but in our hearts. While I suspect that agape includes such an emotional dimension, what we feel for strangers and enemies cannot have the depth of what parents feel for their children—perhaps not even among the blessed. But where the blessed *have* emotions that reflect such a profound experiential understanding of the *existence* of another person and its objective value, it makes little sense to suppose that their moral sanctification would include having that emotional connection snuffed out.

And, as noted above, one cannot sever a profound experiential understanding of another person's inherent worth from a desire to see the person's potential actualized. I cannot recognize the value of what you

---

49. Weil, "Forms of the Implicit Love of God," 149. See also Weil, *Gravity and Grace*, 112–13.

50. Weil, "Love," 271.

51. Weil, *Gravity and Grace*, 173.

essentially are, reflect that in my own values and desires, and yet fail to desire that you become what you are meant to be. And this means I will value your flourishing. It means I will value you coming to experience the network of healthy, reciprocal interpersonal relationships, including with God, that you were meant for—and by implication, that I will value such fellowship with you and desire that you make choices that make such fellowship possible.

In short, a profound experiential understanding of the inherent worth of a person and a full responsiveness to that worth, the kind achieved through immersive attention to that person, is the bedrock for all the dimensions of love we have so far discussed. Intimate personal love thus provides the crucible within which we learn the truth about human persons and their value and discover what it looks like to be responsive to that truth. Arguably, because of our finitude, we cannot extend such intimate personal love to all. Even so, with the help of divine sanctifying grace we can attribute the lessons of such love to each human being and cultivate a character that responds to the truths these lessons embody, not merely with respect to those we love personally, but to all persons, every bearer of the divine image, every beloved child of God.

The blessed, as recipients of God's sanctifying grace, will presumably love in just this way. The question, then, is what such love would imply with respect to the emotions they would feel were any created persons, bearers of God's image, permanently lost.

5

Moral Sanctification, Emotions, and Grief

EMOTIONS AND THEIR FITTINGNESS

WHAT ARE EMOTIONS? LINDA Zagzebski identifies four defining elements. First, unlike sensations and moods, emotions have an "intentional object." They are *about* something: "We fear something, hope for something, pity someone, love someone, feel indignation at some state of affairs, feel sympathy with someone's plight, feel angry at someone, and so on."[1] Second, they have "an affective component," that is, a distinctive way they feel: "It feels different to admire someone than it does to love her or to fear her or to be angry at her."[2] Third, they are "potentially motivating" in that they can "move us to respond by action or simply by expressing the emotion overtly."[3] Fourth, emotions represent their objects to us in a distinct way: "In a state of fear the object appears fearsome; in a state of pity the object appears pitiable."[4]

This last feature has important implications. As soon as any part of our world is *represented* in a given way, it makes sense to ask if this representation *fits* how things really are. One of the most important insights of Aristotle's ethical thought is tied to this point. For Aristotle, our

---

1. Zagzebski, *Exemplarist Moral Theory*, 32. Zagzebksi's wording here mirrors Magda Arnold's seminal expression of the same point: "We are afraid of something, we rejoice over something, we love someone, we are angry at something or someone. Emotions seem to have an object." See Arnold, *Emotion and Personality*, 170.

2. Zagzebski, *Exemplarist Moral Theory*, 33.

3. Zagzebski, *Exemplarist Moral Theory*, 33.

4. Zagzebski, *Exemplarist Moral Theory*, 33.

character is a function of our dispositions, especially emotional dispositions. And for any given emotional disposition, the difference between good and bad character, virtue and vice, lies with whether we are disposed to experience the emotion at the right time, in the right way, and to the right extent—rather than excessively or deficiently. Aristotle thus identifies virtue as lying in a mean between extremes.[5] But this "mean" is not some mathematical middle point. It is, instead, a matter of *fittingness*. As Zagzebski puts it, "in general, emotions can fit or not fit their objects, and we think that an emotion ought to fit its object."[6] The good person is disposed to experience emotions fittingly.

Consider anger. Among other things, I'm angered by social inequities that cause suffering, politicians who use fear-mongering to consolidate power, and people who deliberately hurt me or my loved ones. In each case, my anger correlates with a *judgment*: a negative moral judgment about unfairness, injustice, or wrongdoing.

But we need to qualify this. I can feel myself becoming angry about something and yet try to contain it *because I see my anger as unfounded*. That is, I can experience anger while *at the same time* explicitly denying that any unfairness, injustice, or wrongdoing attaches to its object. But the very fact that, in cases like this, I regard my anger as unfitting shows that *my anger* in some sense affirms what *I* deny.

This is akin to cases where my eyes deceive me. Consider the familiar Müller-Lyer illusion in which lines of equal length appear to be of different lengths because one is framed by inward-pointing fins and the other by outward-pointing fins. I know the lines are equally long: I have encountered the illusion before, measured the lines, even covered the fins up to erase their distorting influence. And yet, when I encounter the illusion anew, the lines look to be of different lengths. I reject what my senses tell me *even as they tell it to me*.

Similarly, I can reject what my anger tells me even as it tells it to me. This is why Zagzebski denies "that an emotion includes a judgment or belief." Instead, emotions are a matter of appearances:

> Something can appear fearsome to the agent when she does not judge it to be fearsome. In fact, she may judge that it is not fearsome. But if something appears fearsome to her when it is not, there is a misstep of some kind—a lack of fit between

---

5. See Aristotle, *Nicomachean Ethics*, 1106a–7a.
6. Zagzebski, *Exemplarist Moral Theory*, 33.

> her faculties and her environment. The faculty or disposition through which something appears to her in her emotional state is misrepresenting the object.[7]

In other words, like sense impressions, emotions represent the world to us in a particular way. On Zagzebski's account, they present to us their objects as possessing what she calls "thick affective properties":

> In a state of emotion, the object appears to fall under what I call a thick affective concept. *Pitiful, fearful, admirable,* and so on are thick affective concepts in the sense I mean. They are concepts that combine a descriptive part and an affective part in a way that cannot be pulled apart.[8]

Once again there is a resemblance here between emotion and sense experience. Consider my visual experience of the can of lemon seltzer in front of me. The way the can's surface reflects and absorbs wavelengths of light results in "yellow" wavelengths hitting my eyes in higher proportion than others. My brain processes this input to produce the subjective experience I call yellow. But people were experiencing yellow things long before anyone knew about wavelengths of light. And when I call the can yellow, it's not on account of scientific studies about how different wavelengths of light reflect off its surface. Instead, I have an immediate experience, this wholly subjective sense of "yellowness" distinct from my subjective sense of "greenness"—what philosophers call the "qualia" of sense experiences. The qualia of colors inform our color concepts: when I say the can is yellow, I have this subjective experience at the front of my attention. But despite the ineradicably subjective nature of my experience of an object's yellowness, we treat my color attributions as saying something *about the world*. We say this because my color experiences *track* reality, even if the way colors "look" to us is "just in our heads." Hence, when I say the can is yellow, what I say fits reality, making the statement true.

Still, sometimes sense experiences go wrong. Suppose I'm in a room suffused with yellow light. Or, more seriously, suppose I acquire an ocular disorder that makes everything take on a yellowish cast, such that I can no longer distinguish white cans from yellow ones: they all produce in me the same "quale" of yellowness. If I know that something like this

---

7. Zagzebski, *Exemplarist Moral Theory*, 33. For a similar point, see Baillie, "Learning the Emotions," 224.

8. Zagzebski, *Exemplarist Moral Theory*, 34.

is happening, I can resist calling the can yellow even as it retains that appearance. Still, there is a judgment *correlated* with my sense experience in the following sense: I *would* reach a given judgment based on appearances *were* I to trust appearances.

Returning to emotions, we might say our emotions represent the world in a certain way, making something appear fearsome, funny, or tragic. These appearances correlate with the judgments we *would* reach if we trusted appearances. To say emotions can be fitting or unfitting is to say these appearances can track or fail to track reality. The judgments correlated with them can be either true or false. In other words, there are things that *really are* fearsome and funny, and there are things that really aren't, even if our emotions represent them that way.

Suppose I am terrified of bunny rabbits because of an early childhood exposure to the killer bunny scene from *Monty Python's Holy Grail*. I experience bunnies as fearsome even though they are not *in fact* fearsome. And if I am raised by White supremacists, I might experience the humiliating abuse of a Black teen as funny even though it is not. In each case, I experience an emotion: fear or amusement. In each case, the emotion is *about* something: bunny rabbits or the teen's humiliating abuse. In each case, my emotions present something to me in a certain way—the bunny as fearful, the humiliation of the teen as funny. And in each case, my emotional state presents its object to me *wrongly*, rendering the emotion unfitting.

But the ways my emotions can go wrong differ importantly from how my senses can go wrong. Sense experiences track the descriptive properties of our world, but emotional experiences track descriptive properties *in relation to the domain of values*. Some thinkers take emotions to *be* affectively-laden value judgments. Robert Solomon, for example, calls emotions "self-involved and relatively intense evaluative judgments" that "are especially important to us, meaningful to us, concerning matters in which we have invested our Selves."[9] R. T. Mullins suggests something similar when he characterizes emotions as "evaluations of what one takes to be worthy of attention."[10]

But as we've seen, Zagzebski denies that emotions *are* judgments, since our explicit judgments can conflict with our emotions. Instead, she think emotions *present* their objects to us *as possessing* a particular

---

9. Solomon, *Passions*, 127.
10. Mullins, *God and Emotions*, 14.

sort of positive or negative value, such that we *would* adopt certain value judgments if we accepted what they present. When Magda Arnold, the groundbreaking psychologist of emotions, defines emotions in terms of attractions towards and aversions from "anything intuitively appraised as good" and "anything intuitively appraised as bad," we can suppose that she intends the "intuitive" qualifier to distance emotions from *explicit cognitive judgments* in something like the way Zagzebski does by treating emotions as appearances.[11]

For present purposes we need not decide between the view that emotions are value judgments and the view that they are representations that would issue in value judgments were we to trust appearances. Although I favor the latter, the emotional dispositions of the blessed would be perfected and hence would not misrepresent reality. As such, there would never be a case in which, say, their emotions represent a state of affairs as tragic (they feel grief about it) but they explicitly judge it otherwise because they see their emotions as unfitting.

Another important insight of Zagzebski's thought is that emotions represent their objects not as *generically* good or bad but as possessing distinct *kinds* of goodness or badness. This is what distinguishes emotions from one another, even when they have the same evaluative *valence* (positive or negative). Admiration presents its object to us as admirable, which is a different kind of positive value from being funny. Grief presents its object to us as tragic, which is a different kind of negative value from being offensive. Values are more fine-grained than "good" and "bad," just as colors are more fine-grained than "light" and "dark"—and our emotions, when functioning well, track these nuances. While Zagzebski makes this point using the idea of thick affective properties, others make similar points in different terms.[12] For our purposes, however, the crucial point is that emotions represent the world to us in *evaluatively laden terms*, as possessing different sorts of goodness and badness, rightness and wrongness, and hence can go wrong in *both* descriptive *and* normative ways.

In the case of experiencing bunny rabbits as fearsome, there is a descriptive error: rabbits do not in fact have the capacity to rend the throats of armored knights via leaps of such blazing speed and precision that

---

11. Arnold, *Emotion and Personality*, 182.

12. For example, according to Ronald de Sousa, there are distinct kinds of values—like danger and loss—that function as the "formal objects" of emotions, allowing us to distinguish them from one another. See De Sousa, *Rationality of Emotion*, 122.

self-defense is impossible. Nor are rabbits disposed to behave in these ways. But in the case of experiencing the humiliating abuse of a Black teen as funny, part of what makes the racist's amusement so egregious is that they are getting the situation *descriptively* right in terms of what is being done to the victim. The error lies with the value judgment associated with their amusement. Humiliating abuse of a person based on their race *is not funny*. Both the rabbit-phobe and the racist have unfitting emotions, but for different reasons, based on whether the error is descriptive or normative.

OBJECTIVE AND SUBJECTIVE VALUES

This interpretation of emotions presupposes that there are objective values, and that our subjective values can conform or fail to conform to them. As R. T. Mullins puts it, "one can argue that it makes no sense to talk of emotions being subject to standards of correctness and justification if there are no objective values in the world. Part of what it means for an emotion to be appropriate or reasonable is for the emotion to justifiably represent its object as having certain values."[13]

While the reality of objective values is controversial in many contexts, it is not generally controversial in the Christian context. Granted this context, if emotions present the world in value-laden terms, they can go wrong with respect to values. They can get the descriptive facts wrong, as with one who finds rabbits fearsome, *and* they can get the *normative* facts wrong.

To make sense of this, we need to clearly distinguish between objective and subjective values and how they connect with emotions. Again, Mullins puts the distinction well: "Objective values are the evaluative properties that things have regardless of whether or not someone recognizes them. . . . Subjective values are the patterns of commitments and judgments that a person has. A person's subjective values may or may not line up with the objective values that exist in the world."[14]

When we have strongly held subjective values, our emotions typically reflect them, representing the world in a way that matches the values we already embrace. The racist feels amusement at the humiliation of the Black teen because of the racist values that represent what is happening

13. Mullins, *God and Emotion*, 12.
14. Mullins, *God and Emotion*, 12.

as possessing the positive value property of being *funny*. But what is happening is *not* funny. The racist's subjective values, reflected in their amusement, clash with what is objectively valuable. Put another way, while strongly held subjective values powerfully shape which emotions we experience, the fittingness of those emotions is a function of objective values.

In the case of the person with the rabbit phobia, the *value judgments* at issue are uncontroversial. Fear is tied to a perceived threat to something of value. A flop-eared beast both capable of and prone towards sudden leaps of fang-rending fury poses a threat to human lives. There is no error in valuing those lives, and so no disconnect between subjective and objective values. The error lies in taking rabbits to pose such a threat.

In sum, emotions can be unfitting because they can represent their objects in ways that mischaracterize the truth either factually or normatively (or both). The normative error arises because the values subjectively posited in the emotional state clash with objective values.

But this does not mean all subjective values either conform to or conflict with objective values. Some values are *purely* subjective: there are no objective values that either undergird them and make them correct or clash with them and make them incorrect. In other words, human beings can subjectively value things in ways that go beyond what objective values call for without thereby coming into *conflict* with objective values. I doubt violin music is more or less valuable than guitar music *objectively*. But I love the former more than the latter. So long as I do not act as if this subjective preference reflects an objective truth—so long as I simply hold that violin music has greater value *for me*—there is no conflict with objective values.

Such purely subjective values still play a role in my emotions. If a great violinist is coming to town, I will anticipate the performance in a way others will not. And if the performance is cancelled, I will feel greater disappointment. These emotions, while not unfitting, are no more fitting than the emotions of others with different subjective values. Emotions that reflect purely subjective values will be fitting or unfitting only in relation to the descriptive facts: if I'm sad about the cancelled violin performance, this might prove to be unfitting if the performance hasn't been cancelled. Later in the chapter we will consider a special case of such subjective values: what Eleonore Stump calls "desires of the heart." For now the point is this: our subjective values can *shape* our emotions in ways that go beyond their fittingness.

EMOTIONS AND MORAL CHARACTER: INCONTINENCE, CONTINENCE, AND VIRTUE

As we've seen, if my emotions misrepresent objective reality, I might notice this and so make cognitive judgments at odds with my emotions. And if I don't accept the way my emotions present the world to me, there is another issue that arises, having to do with the motivating capacity of emotions. Emotions are correlated not just with cognitive judgments but with characteristic behaviors. Even if I reject the judgments correlated with my emotions, I might act on those emotions anyway—because I lack impulse control.

These relationships between emotions, judgments, and behavior reveal just how deeply implicated emotions are in our moral lives. To explore these implications more fully, consider another example. Suppose a restaurant server spills water on me, and I surge to my feet in outrage. My anger might be unfitting because I am mistaken about what happened. Perhaps I think she did it on purpose. But suppose I have the facts right: I correctly think she *accidentally* spilled water after inadvertently tripping while in a state of exhaustion at the end of a double shift. Suppose I am outraged about *that*.

Even though I have the facts right, my outrage is unfitting because my level of anger represents an accidental stumble at the end of a long shift, resulting in spilled water, as *outrageous*—that is, as blatantly wrong and blameworthy. But for the server's behavior to count as blatantly wrong and blameworthy, the following moral judgments would have to be true. First, she would have to have *a moral duty* in her role as server to display levels of attentiveness and precise body control so high that an accident of this sort would not occur. Second, this duty to maintain such levels of attentiveness and control would have to be so pressing under the circumstances that exhaustion after a long day of work is no excuse.

But such moral judgments attribute to her duties that apply to surgeons performing life-and-death surgery, not to servers carrying water to a table. My emotional state in the aftermath of the accident represents its object wrongly, by mischaracterizing the normative state of things.

This error at the emotional level has the potential to affect me both cognitively and behaviorally. How it does so will have further implications for assessing my moral character. In fact, Aristotle famously identified distinct categories of moral character associated with distinct ways that unfitting emotions can impact someone at the cognitive and behavioral levels. Chief among these are vice, incontinence, continence, and virtue.[15]

First, I might *accept* the judgments correlated with my emotions. My emotions represent the server's accident *as if* it were comparable in severity to a surgeon fumbling the knife and risking a patient's life during a routine procedure—and I *accept* that representation of things and act accordingly, berating her as if her clumsiness has jeopardized human lives. In so doing, I have proved myself to have, with respect to anger, what Aristotle calls a *vice*—in this case the vice of short-temperedness.

Second, I might reject the appropriateness of my emotional response. I might recognize that the way my emotional state normatively represents its object is erroneous. But emotions are motivating: they push us towards certain ways of acting. And they can be motivating even when we don't trust them. Suppose I lack the self-control to resist that motivating impulse. I lash out at the server, realizing even as I do so that my response is unfitting. I feel bad afterwards. Maybe I apologize and leave a big tip. Or, if I'm a worse person, I slink out quietly . . . and look away quickly when the kitchen door swings open to reveal the server's tear-stained face. This kind of thing is what Aristotle calls *akrasia*, or "incontinence." I have an intellectual understanding of what is moral, but my emotions fail to reflect this understanding, and I lack the capacity to overrule their motivating force. My emotional impulses prevail over my better judgment.

Third, I might reject the fittingness of my emotional response *and* display the self-control to rein in the correlated behavior. Perhaps the server sees the flare of rage in my eyes and flinches back from it, but I contain it before it bursts free. I take a few deep breaths, assure her it is fine, and leave her a good tip. This is what Aristotle calls *enkrasia*, or "continence." I understand what is moral, and I am able to act on that understanding in the face of contrary emotions. My head is at odds with my emotions, but my head wins.

What I lack, even in this third case, is what Aristotle calls *moral virtue*. Moral virtue is that state in which my emotions don't go wrong because I have, through a process of habituation, developed my emotional dispositions to fit with my sound moral judgment. When I am virtuous, the normative judgments correlated with my emotions are correct. I might still make factual errors that lead me to have emotions that don't fit

---

15. What follows is my own synthesis of Aristotle's views, drawn especially from *Nicomachean Ethics* Bk II chs 5–9, Bk III chs 1–5, and Bk VII chs 1–10.

the *actual circumstances* (perhaps an unavoidable consequence of human finitude), but if I am morally virtuous I will no longer have emotions that don't fit normatively with the *perceived circumstances*. My emotions represent the perceived circumstances in a way that is normatively correct.

This last point shows that even though emotions can fail to fit their circumstances in two ways—descriptively and normatively—it is the latter that speaks most directly to moral character. A lack of fit between emotions and circumstances based on a *descriptive* error is, at least in many cases, morally innocent. I say "in many cases," because my descriptive error could be rooted in a culpable negligence. And then there are cases like the rabbit-phobia, where my rational judgment about the facts is at odds with how my emotions present the object: I may know that bunny rabbits are harmless, and yet my emotions continue to present them to me as dire threats. In such cases, I presumably have a duty to *work on* my emotional dispositions, even if their error is in terms of description rather than evaluation, and even if blame for the phobia's origins lies with my uncle who introduced me to Monty Python at a too-impressionable age. At least sometimes, a failure to try to overcome a phobia could be less than morally innocent.

One reason why this is so is because, if I am morally virtuous, I want my emotions to fit the *actual* circumstances. While I might excuse an emotion that doesn't fit the facts, I wouldn't justify it and might make amends were anyone hurt by the actions the emotions inspired.

TRUTH-DISCERNING EMOTIONS?

Although this Aristotelian portrait is helpful for thinking about how emotions, and the value judgments correlated with them, are tied to moral character, there remain interesting and important questions. Some pertain to the nature of the relationship between emotions and the subjective values to which they correlate. Do we have the emotions we have purely *because* of the subjective values we have adopted, or do we arrive at our subjective values in part through our emotional encounters with the world? And if the latter, are emotions producing values in a way disconnected from what is objectively good, or are they capable (however imperfectly) of *providing us with normative information* in something like the way our senses provide descriptive information about the world? While we might think emotional representations are just *projections* of pre-existing subjective values onto the field of experience, we might also think they can *produce* subjective values in us. And if the latter, we might think they produce values in a way disconnected from what is objectively good, or we might think instead that they are fallible faculties for *discerning* objective values. Which is right?

Clearly, it is sometimes true that our emotions reflect the subjective values we have. Because we subjectively value something, we hope for it, fear losing it, and are sad when it is gone. In such cases the subjective value judgment comes first: the emotion *expresses* subjective values. But is this the whole story? If it is, our knowledge of objective values would come from another source—our intellects, perhaps—and then we would train our emotions to reflect those objective values. The process of character development would be a "top-down" project wherein the faculties for discerning normative truths reside in the intellect and our task is to regulate our emotions until they are attuned to them.

But this way of thinking about matters does not do justice to the full range of human experience with emotions. Sometimes our emotional responses surprise us and shape our subjective values. Imagine the racist, laughing about the humiliating abuse of the Black teen, who inadvertently meets the teen's eye and feels a jolt of horror. Their laughter withers, replaced by a flush of shame. They come away shaken, their racist values unsettled.

Experiences like this are not fiction. When I facilitated weekend prison workshops, participants routinely shared stories of just such transformative experiences—as if a moral truth they'd shut out had been suddenly pushed into their awareness *by their emotions*.

Based on these experiences, we might think emotions can play a role in *discerning* normative truths.[16] Presumably, our intellects would guide such emotional discernment in something like the way intellectual standards of consistency and plausibility regulate our sense experience. On this view, character development would have a dialectical structure: our emotional capacity to discern and represent normative truths would shape our subjective values in dialogue with our intellects. The normative judgments we ultimately endorsed would be the outcome of a back-and-forth in which emotions provide normative data that the intellect tests and refines, and the intellect provides critical assessments and guidance to improve the accuracy of emotional discernment.

---

16. See Roberts, *Emotions in the Moral Life*, 115.

I lean towards this understanding, most significantly because my own experience with powerful emotions is that they can be *transformative*, helping our character evolve through a deepened understanding of the domain of value. But in this book, our focus is on the emotions of the blessed, who by hypothesis are *morally sanctified*. Being sanctified, their emotions will *perfectly reflect* objective values whether that is because the emotions have been trained to consistently embody the insights of a perfected intellectual faculty or because the emotions' capacity for value discernment in cooperation with the intellect has been perfected.

Thus, while I think emotions contribute (imperfectly) to our understanding of objective values, most of the arguments in this book will not depend on this assumption. This is especially the case because, whether or not emotions are part of our apparatus for *discovering* normative truths, I think a Christian worldview clearly favors the view that they are part of how we *connect* to such truths: we are more fully aligned with normative truths when our emotions, not just our intellects, affirm them. There is a difference between acknowledging intellectually that a child's death is bad and being grieved by it. In either case, we disapprove of it; but in the latter case, we *feel* its badness. Our whole selves are attuned to it: we know it in our hearts *and* in our heads.

This is why the person heartbroken by suffering has a positive moral quality lacking in those who merely acknowledges its badness. Our emotions *connect us experientially* to morally laden realities in a way our intellects do not, and such connection is part of a more fully developed moral character. Aquinas thus notes that "sorrow is a good inasmuch as it denotes perception and rejection of evil."[17] Stated more fully:

> Supposing the presence of something saddening or painful, it is a sign of goodness if a man is in sorrow or pain on account of this present evil. For if he were not to be in sorrow or pain, this could only be either because he feels it not, or because he does not reckon it as something unbecoming, both of which are manifest evils. Consequently it is a condition of goodness, that, supposing an evil to be present, sorrow or pain should ensue.[18]

By implication, of course, the blessed would feel sorrow in response to tragic truths.

---

17. Aquinas, *Summa Theologica* I–II, Q. 39, Art. 2.
18. Aquinas, *Summa Theologica* I–II, Q. 39, Art 1.

LOVE AND GRIEF

In the last chapter, I developed the Christian understanding of moral sanctification that includes being perfected in agapic love. Such love is not contingent on someone's moral worth, utility, or on the prospect of reciprocity. Instead, it responds to the inherent worth possessed by every person and values three objective goods: a person's existence, their welfare (understood to include their self-actualization and moral development), and fellowship with them (understood as a *healthy* reciprocal relationship in which selves mutually share themselves).

While such agapic love might not be strongly emotional itself, this is because, as finite creatures, we cannot be personally acquainted with all persons on the deep level that generates a strong experiential understanding of the inherent value of their existence, welfare, and fellowship. But the morally sanctified will experience a more personal and emotional love where and to the extent that finite human nature provides the needed experiential understanding. Where it doesn't, the morally sanctified will *apply* the lessons of such experience to all persons.

Insofar as the blessed fully actualize such love, they recognize the inherent value of each person and so recognize the value of their existence, welfare, and fellowship. The emotional dispositions of the blessed will be perfectly attuned to these values, even if this does not mean the blessed will be *fond of* or *feel affection* for all persons. They will, for example, be happy when they learn that the flourishing of another human being is advanced—even if it's a stranger. When someone is the target of unjust harm, this will anger them—even if the target is not one of their loved ones and so not among those whose inherent worth they have directly experienced. When they are aware that a person's existence or welfare is in jeopardy, they will fear for them. And were a person destroyed, or their welfare permanently compromised, or fellowship with them no longer even possible, those perfected in agapic love who were aware of this loss would grieve.

This is so because of what the emotion of grief *is*. Grief is the emotional experience of loss—the loss of what we value. The object of grief is, generally, a person or relationship lost through separation or destruction. The judgment correlated with grief is that the person or relationship had significant positive value. *This good is gone.* In keeping with this perspective, philosopher of grief Michael Cholbi argues that the fittingness of grief is a backward-looking affair that takes losses as their object. Grief is fitting to the extent that it reflects the magnitude of the loss.[19] Cholbi, however, holds that the proper objects of grief are "agent-relative losses" that depend on "the relations between the bereaved and the objects of their grief" and so do not require that there are "objects with properties that render them intrinsically grief-worthy."[20] But the Christian perspective—which takes all persons to be inherently valuable, personally loved by God, and the proper objects of a love we are called to cultivate—offers a basis for thinking the loss of any person *is* intrinsically grief-worthy.

Or perhaps it is better to put the point this way: even if no one in *this* life relates to every person in terms of love's values, the blessed in heaven do. Being morally sanctified, they value the existence, welfare, and fellowship of every person, every child of God. Relative to *such* agents, the eternal damnation or annihilation of anyone would constitute a loss to be fittingly grieved. They would not just acknowledge the loss intellectually. To the extent that human finitude allows, they would attribute their emotional experience of the value of concrete loved ones to every human being and so feel heartbreak for all the lost.

More, they would know that for God, whom they love with all their heart and soul and mind, each of these losses is deeply personal—the loss of the Heavenly Father's beloved child. And there is something transitive about deeply personal losses: when my beloved has her heart broken by the death of a loved one, my heart breaks with her. As such, even were the proper objects of grief always relative to specific personal relations, the blessed relationship to God makes grief for all the lost a fitting emotional response.

CLASSIFYING LOSSES: SELF-REGARDING AND OTHER-REGARDING, FUNGIBLE AND NON-FUNGIBLE

Grief is a complex emotion because our values are complex, and when we lose persons to death or separation, we lose many things. We can classify these losses in several ways. First, some losses are fundamentally self-regarding: they are about the diminution of our own welfare. We need a range of things in order to promote our welfare—what we might call our welfare-needs. Some of these are survival needs, required for bodily health. Others are necessary for our flourishing, such as moral virtue,

---

19. Cholbi, "Grief's Rationality," 267.
20. Cholbi, "Grief's Rationality," 267.

meaningful activities and projects, and intimate relationships. Most crucially, according to the Christian tradition, we need a relationship with God, our creator. Our hearts do not rest until they rest in God.

Different people in our lives play distinct roles in helping to meet these welfare needs, such that their loss can diminish our welfare. But if we love someone *for their own sake*, valuing their good as we do our own, we will also grieve apart from how their loss affects our welfare. Most obviously, we will grieve for lost objective goods: their *being*, the *relationships* they helped to constitute, and their *flourishing*. Grief over such objective losses is the grief Wolterstorff describes when he speaks of his awareness that a "person, an irreplaceable person, is gone"[21]—gone in all the concrete ways that, as the father of the one lost, he knows intimately. This grief stands in contrast to the self-focused grief C. S. Lewis derides in himself when he describes the "bath of self-pity, the wallow, the loathsome sticky-sweet pleasure of indulging it."[22]

Of course, self-regarding losses are real, and insofar as we should love ourselves, we should grieve losses to our welfare that spring from losing someone. But self-regarding losses might be *replaceable* in ways a person and the relationships they help constitute are not. For example, the *companionship* they provided might be replaced with companionship of a similar kind and quality. In other words, the distinction between self-regarding and non-self-regarding goods tracks another distinction: that between fungible and non-fungible goods.

With respect to many self-regarding losses, if not all, the objects of grief might at some point cease to present themselves as *losses* because the lost goods have been replaced. We might fittingly stop grieving them, not because we can or should stop valuing our welfare and the way these goods contribute to it, but because we can achieve these goods in a different way. Even if a particular person has historically been instrumental in meeting my welfare-needs, over time I may learn to meet them in new ways. These losses can, in short, be *overcome*—and when they are, it would no longer be fitting to grieve them.

But while a lost loved one's role in meeting my welfare-needs can be replaced, the person—and the unique relationship I had with them—cannot. The person and our relationship are inherently valuable. If my subjective values extend beyond my welfare to encompass all objective

---

21. Wolterstorff, *Lament for a Son*, 33.
22. Lewis, *Grief Observed*, 8.

goods (as they would were I morally sanctified), then I would continue to feel the loss of others *as loss* even when I have found other ways to meet my welfare needs.

DESIRES OF THE HEART

Eleonore Stump argues that in addition to those goods that are objectively necessary for our welfare, human beings are constituted such that some things—especially particular persons—can *become* necessary for our welfare because we have performed the subjective act of *setting our hearts on them*. These "desires of the heart" tie our flourishing to individual persons (or sometimes life projects) in such a way that what would not be essential for our flourishing *absent* the subjective act of setting our hearts on them *becomes* essential. Their role in promoting our welfare thereby becomes *non*-fungible. For example, the role my wife plays in promoting my welfare is not limited to the company she provides, the help with the tasks of daily life, the engaging conversations, and all the other things that someone else could provide were my wife gone. Because I have set my heart on *her*, something of great importance to my happiness would be lost were she to die, even if all the other welfare needs she helps to satisfy were to be instantly satisfied in some other way.

Part of what it means to live a fully human life is to make choices about what to care about in the deepest way. Such choices express our nature as creatures who are free and creative beings. As such, we would be less fully actualized were we *not* to put out hearts into specific persons and relationships and projects. As Stump puts it, it is "essential to a person's flourishing that he set his heart on things not essential to his flourishing."[23] And setting our hearts on *specific* people reflects our finitude: "Human beings are not like God in being capable of sharing intimately with endless numbers of people. Human beings are built for shared union in love with particular people—in fact, those few people on whom they have set their hearts."[24]

There is a reason Stump identifies *persons* as the primary objects of our heart's desires. Even if our heart's desires are subjective, they are most fitting when they track objective value:

---

23. Stump, *Wandering in Darkness*, 438.
24. Stump, *Wandering in Darkness*, 438.

> Since shared union in love with particular people is the greatest good for a human person, it is of universal objective value that the deepest things a person sets his heart on are persons. That is, for every human person, there is something right, something conducing to human flourishing, about having particular persons as the deepest desires of the heart.[25]

The key insight here is that while the full actualization of human welfare depends on healthy relationships with persons, *which* persons (other than God) isn't specified by a general understanding of human flourishing. Had my life taken a different course, I might have had a different wife and children than I have. But in the real world I have set my heart on *these* individual human beings.

And when people become the objects of our heart's desires, their loss will be a special source of grief. Not only is an objectively valuable human being gone (something to be grieved from the standpoint of agapic love), and not only have we been deprived of someone who met a range of our welfare-needs, but *that* human being, an object of our heart's desire, is gone. And *that* human being cannot be replaced within the scheme of our personal welfare. Thus, there is a grief that does not obtain when confronting the loss of someone who is not an object of our heart's desires—even if in both cases we have lost someone who played a role in meeting our needs, and even if in both cases a person of sacred worth has been taken from the world.

ESSENTIAL AND ACCIDENTAL LOSSES

We will explore Stump's thinking about the loss of our heart's desires in more depth in chapter 7, as we consider how she tries to solve the problem of heavenly grief. For now, let us turn to a distinction that arises when we consider C. S. Lewis's grief over the loss of the precise form his relationship with his wife took. Lewis protests that "the thing I want is exactly the thing I can never get. The old life, the jokes, the drinks, the arguments, the lovemaking, the tiny, heartbreaking commonplace."[26] Lewis knows that, even if Christianity's Easter promise is true, *this* will not be restored: "Reality never repeats. The exact same thing is never taken away

---

25. Stump, *Wandering in Darkness*, 439.
26. Lewis, *Grief Observed*, 11.

and given back."[27] His yearning is not just for his wife's existence and a relationship with her, but for these goods in the form with which he is fondly familiar. This yearning impedes his capacity to be consoled by the promise of her ongoing existence and the prospect of restored relationship—even if, following the Christian portrait of heaven, the promised future relationship would be of *greater objective value* than the relationship he had with her in this life.

In other words, part of his grief is about the loss of *the accidental properties* that used to attach to their relationship, as opposed to being about the relationship as such. This is akin to someone in an ongoing relationship, one at least as good as it was years ago, reflecting on what the relationship used to be like and grieving the loss of properties the relationship used to have. We might say the grief here is really about *change* rather than *loss* in any metaphysically substantive sense: the relationship still exists, but with a new set of accidental properties.

I say Lewis's grief is *akin* to this, not identical. Even with the Christian promise of a future restoration of relationship in a fully actualized form, the death of a loved one causes an essential change to the relationship, not merely an accidental one. When a loved one dies, there is no longer the relationship between two living, interacting persons. Instead, one has a relationship with memories (something about which Lewis was deeply suspicious) and, perhaps, glimpses of the lost loved one's enduring nature (something Lewis sensed later in his grief journey). The relationship between two embodied persons is gone. What the Christian faith promises is that it will come back in a perfected form—in other words, that the essential loss is only temporary, even if the accidental losses might be permanent.

I do not mean to suggest that accidental losses are *not* something to be grieved, only that such grief has a different relationship to Christian love than does grief over essential losses. To be perfected in agapic love involves, as we saw, valuing the existence and welfare of persons as well as genuine fellowship with them. But genuine fellowship comes in different forms, and a single relationship can change over time even if it consistently achieves true fellowship. What Christian love recognizes as inherently valuable is such fellowship. We may attach subjective value to the specific ways the relationship expresses itself at a given time: the shared morning coffee on the patio, the playfully trash-talking games of

27. Lewis, *Grief Observed*, 23.

Scrabble. But if those expressions give way to other ones while genuine fellowship remains, the object of agapic love has not been lost.

THE GRIEVING PROCESS AND MOVING ON FROM GRIEF

In sum, losing someone through death or separation leads to a range of different kinds of losses and hence a range of objects of grief. Not all of these losses call for *enduring* grief. At least some of what we grieve when we lose someone can eventually cease to fittingly pain us because we undergo a *process* that *resolves* the grief—what is typically called the *grieving process*. Related to the *emotion* of grief, then, is this goal-oriented process aimed at coming to terms with loss and learning how to go on in the face of it.

A significant part of this process has to do with fungible self-regarding losses. We need to find new ways to meet welfare-needs that, previously, were met by the lost loved one. We have to be *willing* to look elsewhere for what they gave us, and the process of *becoming* willing may involve building a new self-understanding, a sense of who we are now that this person is no longer part of our lives. This is a case in which objective goods—dimensions of our own welfare—have been lost but can be restored. If a process can help reclaim these lost goods, we should not resist it, since agapic love extends to ourselves and includes valuing our own welfare. If this process enables us to find new sources for fungible self-regarding goods, grief over their loss would fittingly end.

Or consider the loss of a particular accidental form a relationship once took. While there is nothing about being perfected in Christian love that precludes experiencing grief over this, the purely subjective character of the value we attach to such a loss means we can change our values—find other things to value in that subjective way—without any corruption of our moral character.[28] I value playing the violin in a subjective way, and so would grieve the loss of my capacity to do so if a finger injury meant I could never play again. But if, after the injury, I cultivated new creative hobbies to fill the gap, and through a change of habits reached a point

---

28. While our heart's desires are arguably an exception to this general rule about subjective values, Stump notes that heart's desires can be unfitting—and it seems unfitting to make the accidental form a relationship takes at a particular time into the object of a heart's desire, such that even changes which increase its objective value are seen as irreparable loss. In any event, most subjective values are not heart's desires.

where violin-playing no longer held the place in my subjective values that it used to, continued grief might no longer be fitting. And there is nothing morally wrong with undergoing such a process of changing my subjective values.

But not all losses can be repaired in these ways. First, there is the loss from the world of an objectively valuable person—and in the case of a loved one, a person whose objective value we have experienced directly and so keenly feel. Second, there is the loss of a heart's desire: a person to whom we have attached our flourishing in a way that makes them irreplaceable to us. In the case of the former, changing our subjective values so we stop caring about what has been lost is morally untenable: it would mean our subjective values become at odds with the objective order of values and hence defective. In the case of the latter, changing our subjective values so that we *stop* making the lost person crucial to our welfare seems to run directly contrary to what a heart's desire *is*. If I could do that, it seems I never set my heart on them in the first place.

Even so, a grieving process may *reduce* the pain it is fitting to feel, especially in a Christian context. If Christian promises are true, even the loss of objectively valuable persons may prove only temporary. Stump appeals to the promise of having the heart's desire restored—as a gift of God—to address the pain of the loss of our heart's desires.[29] But in the immediate aftermath of a loved one's death, the wound can be so raw it is hard to hold onto promises that seem ephemeral in comparison. What we see in Lewis's memoir is an agonizing process in which the restoration of religious hope comes in fits and starts alongside the release of purely subjective values and the discovery of new ways to meet welfare needs.

In sum, the grieving process is a goal-oriented one in which fungible losses are replaced, subjective values adjusted, and, for some, religious hopes reclaimed. A new normal is eventually reached—but the lost loved one remains gone. Objective goods remain lost. And the heartbreak that accompanies the loss of a heart's desire is at best softened to something more like heartache. While the mourner can move forward, a wound remains.

This *partial* attenuation of grief is the end-point of the grieving process for many who face significant losses. But it is not complete attenuation. Grief endures. And given the reality of losses that cannot be replaced, grief that never leaves entirely in this lifetime seems fitting.

---

29. This aspect of her treatment of heart's desires will be considered in more depth in chapter 7.

THE CASE FOR ENDURING GRIEF

But there are people who, after a period of grief, move on with what appears to be as much joy as they did before the loss. Given that the emotional pain of grief is so great, there may be self-regarding reasons to develop psychological and practical mechanisms to eliminate grief's pain—for example, the pretense I discuss in chapter 2, facilitated by physical and temporal distance. Those mechanisms might be so effective that they eventually remove *all* the pain, even the pain linked to objective, non-fungible losses.

Such complete attenuation appears to be a reality for many: their emotional "resilience" is so robust they eventually move forward without evidence of enduring pain.[30] But is that *fitting*? Or are they adopting unfitting emotions as a practical concession to getting the most out of life?

If universalism is true, then the complete attenuation of grief *is* fitting, at least eventually. All loss is temporary, ending with restoration of every objective good and every heart's desire. But most scholars who reflect on grief do so on secular assumptions, and so do not suppose the losses tied to death are restored. These scholars wrestle with the fittingness of grief's complete attenuation when the loss remains. How they wrestle with this question has direct bearing on the issues central to this book, since on non-universalist assumptions the blessed in heaven face losses every bit as permanent as the losses non-religious scholars presume death to inflict. And so I will have to consider arguments about the fittingness of grief's complete attenuation absent any hope of restoration—but I put off doing so until chapter 7, when I consider purported solutions to the problem.

For now, I want to summarize a positive case for thinking that the eternal loss of anyone would, for the blessed, be a source of enduring grief. Many of the losses we grieve when someone dies are fungible losses relative to our welfare needs and so needn't occasion permanent grief. And much of what we grieve is tied to purely subjective values we can let go of without a vitiation of our moral character. But for those perfected in Christian love, these fungible and subjective losses are incidental. The most important losses relate to the being and welfare of the lost, and fellowship with them. Since such being, welfare, and fellowship are

---

30. For a summary of empirical research on resilience after grief—including how much *forgetfulness* features into that resilience—see Bonnano, *Other Side of Sadness*, 65–98 (chapter 4).

objective goods, a change of subjective values cannot erase the conditions for fitting grief. And even if, when someone who contributed to my welfare is lost to me, I can find some other way to meet my welfare needs, such functional replacement only restores the *instrumental* value they served in terms of advancing my welfare, not the inherent value of their existence, their welfare, and fellowship with them. Furthermore, my tendency to make some persons into objects of my heart's desires—and thereby wed my welfare to them by a subjective choice—is a fitting way for a finite being like myself to reflect the objective value that every person possesses.

Thus, if any person is eternally lost, the blessed would experience this loss as permanent and irreplaceable. Failure to do so would require a misalignment of subjective and objective values, an imperfection to which the blessed would not be subject. Furthermore, given that setting our hearts on specific people is part of a fully actualized human life, the blessed will have set their hearts on at least some people. Were those objects of their heart's desires eternally lost, it seems unfitting for the blessed to sever that special connection for the sake of avoiding grief. As such, not only would the blessed value all the lost on account of their objective value, but they would value some of the lost in a much more intimate way.

If the blessed never stop valuing the lost, and if the lost are never restored, then the emotional experience of such loss—grief—appears eternally fitting. While the blessed might, through a grieving process, purge their grief of those elements tied to merely subjective values or fungible losses, a core object of grief would remain. Thus, if non-universalism is true, an element of grief would remain as an enduring feature of the heavenly state.

UNIVERSAL AND PERSONAL FORMS OF THE ARGUMENT FROM HEAVENLY GRIEF

In chapter 3, we saw that the argument from heavenly sympathy has both universal and personal versions. The universal version takes it that the blessed are perfected in agapic love, and as such would feel sympathy for the eternal misery of anyone, assuming they were aware of it. The personal version does not assume the blessed would love all the damned but, rather, that they would continue to love those among the damned they loved personally in this life—and would thus sympathize with *their* suffering, assuming they were aware of it.

As with the argument from heavenly sympathy, the argument from heavenly grief has both a universal and personal version. On the universal version, the blessed would love all the lost and so grieve for them all, at least to the extent that they are aware of them. The reasons discussed in chapter 3 for thinking the blessed would be aware of the fate of the *damned* apply without substantive modification to the fate of the *lost*. First, the blessed would presumably be epistemically perfected and hence be aware of any fact—such as whether all are saved—that they *could* know and would *care* about. Second, the blessed's joy would be not just subjectively supreme but supremely *worthwhile*, meaning it would not depend on error for its persistence.

On the personal version of the argument from heavenly grief, the blessed would continue to love those they loved in a personal way in this life, and so would grieve for any of their eternally lost loved ones, assuming they were aware of their loss. In addition to considerations of epistemic perfection and supremely worthwhile joy noted above, the personal version offers a further reason to suppose the blessed would be aware of the eternal loss of any of their loved ones: absent a memory wipe, they would be *on the lookout* for them and so *note* their absence.

The considerations of the last two chapters offer reasons to support the universal version of the argument, given that moral sanctification entails perfection in agapic love, a love that values the existence, welfare, and fellowship of all inherently valuable persons. But the universal version does not *exclude* the personal one, and there are good reasons to affirm it as well—especially if we take seriously the idea that some of the damned will be the objects of a blessed person's heart's desire.

In fact, I think the strongest version of the argument pays attention *both* to the agapic love that encompasses all persons and to the more personal love the blessed would have for specific loved ones they knew in this life. Assuming limited salvation, all the blessed will love *all* the lost in the agapic sense, and most will presumably love *some* of the lost in a more personal way. Since both kinds of love create a problem for the *perfect* blessedness of the saved, it makes sense to formulate the problem of heavenly grief in terms of both.

Furthermore, as already noted, for finite creatures like us, these two kinds of love are intimately connected. My personal love for friends and family is not just the result of some purely subjective decision to hold them in my heart, as if I could as readily make reams of blank paper the objects of my deepest heart's desires. My personal love for friends and family involves the direct emotional experience, in my life, of their inherent value. This experience is undoubtedly tied to how they contribute to meeting my subjective values and my welfare: I directly experience how my life is better with them in it. But my emotional love for those closest to me cannot be reduced to such subjective and fungible valuations.

Shortly after each of my children were born, there came a moment when I held them in my hands: a tiny, precious *person*. I was in awe. I knew nothing about their character. It was their existence itself that moved me—underscored by the fact that so recently they hadn't existed at all. I felt in those moments—and still feel today—the value of their very being. My children are, in Stump's language, among the deepest desires of my heart. But if this is so, it is in large measure because I have deep emotional knowledge of the value that attaches to their being, to their flourishing, and to my loving relationship with them, a knowledge tied to my sustained attention to them as individual persons. I suspect the desires of my heart are shaped by what I pay the deepest attention to—and those desires are most fitting when my attention becomes fixed on what has the greatest inherent worth. And because persons have an inherent worth other things lack, the heart's desires that fix on persons are the most fitting, expressing a direct experience of profound worth. Presumably, this is what God experiences with respect to *all persons*, rendering every living person an object of the desires of God's heart.

For finite creature like us, it is by immediately experiencing the value of particular persons that we come to understand the value of persons in general and can, at least somewhat, *feel* the stranger's value rather than just acknowledge it intellectually. The sanctification of the blessed entails they will have perfected this capacity. As such, if any are eternally lost, the grief the blessed would feel over the loss of friends or family would function as a model for how they should relate to those among the lost who are strangers to them. Hence, they would grieve not just for those whose worth they have personally felt but for all the lost on account of this understanding of their worth. The lost are not just subjectively valuable. They are not just fungible sources of welfare goods for the blessed. They are *persons*. And according to non-universalism, their loss is not temporary. And so the occasion for grief never ends.

Finally, our human experience of grief testifies to the following fact: grief disrupts joy. In fact, there are few emotions that do more to disrupt it than grief, as personal testimonies like those explored in chapter 2 so vividly demonstrate. Perhaps this is why Scripture, in Revelation 21:4, singles out the end of *grief* in one of its most powerful and comforting promises.

All these considerations give us reason to conclude that, if the doctrine of limited salvation is true, the doctrine of perfect blessedness is false. But is there an uncostly way for non-universalists to avoid this conclusion and so hold onto the doctrine of perfect blessedness? In the next two chapters, we will consider such purported solutions to the problem.

6

Purported Solutions

Limited Love

THE PROBLEM RESTATED

THOSE WHO WANT TO affirm both the doctrine of limited salvation and the doctrine of perfect blessedness face a problem: the two doctrines appear to be in conflict. So far, I have been making the case that this apparent conflict is real by developing the *argument* from heavenly grief. A solution to the problem would show why Christians can reject one or more of the argument's premises—either without cost, or with costs less serious than those associated with escaping the problem by relinquishing one of the doctrines.

I noted in chapter 1 that we can formulate the argument in terms of four key premises. In light of material covered in the intervening chapters, we are now in a position to flesh out these premises more fully:

The Love Premise: The blessed will be perfected in love, meaning they will fully actualize (a) an agapic love that values the being, welfare, and fellowship of all persons (hereafter "love's values") and (b) a personal love for some persons based on direct experiential awareness of the inherent value of their being, welfare, and fellowship.

The Fitting Grief Premise: Those perfected in love will fittingly experience enduring grief if any persons succumb to the permanent vitiation of any of love's values; that is, they will grieve in an enduring way if any person permanently ceases to exist or exists in a permanently vitiated state, or if any person's welfare is permanently compromised, or if any person is permanently cut off from fellowship with others (especially from those perfected in love)—whenever they are aware of such loss, and especially when those they personally love are lost.

The Awareness Premise: If any human beings are eternally lost, the blessed will be aware of this, especially with respect to anyone they personally love.

The Incompatibility Premise: Experiencing enduring grief is incompatible with enjoying perfect happiness.

To see why these premises put the doctrine of limited salvation at odds with the doctrine of perfect blessedness, assume that the former doctrine is true. If so, some persons succumb to the permanent vitiation of at least some of love's values. From the standpoint of these values, creation endures a permanent loss. Based on the love premise, the blessed are perfected in love; and based on the fitting grief premise, they therefore experience enduring grief over this permanent loss if they are aware of it. And based on the awareness premise, they are aware of it. Hence, the blessed experience enduring grief. Given the incompatibility premise, it follows that they do not enjoy perfect happiness. Hence, the doctrine of perfect blessedness is false.

In the preceding chapters, I have offered reasons to accept each of these premises, with a special focus on the love premise and the fitting grief premise, explicated and supported in chapters 4 and 5 respectively. In the course of reviewing arguments from heavenly sympathy in chapter 3, we encountered reasons to accept the awareness premise. The case for the incompatibility premise rests largely on our experience of grief, as presented in chapter 2, which intuitively puts the burden of proof on those who would reject it.

Solutions to the problem will have to show that, despite the reasons to accept these premises, rejecting them is more defensible. This is done by showing either that rejecting at least one of these premises does not have the costs it initially seems to have, or by showing that, though costly, rejecting it is *less* costly to the Christian faith than escaping the problem by, say, embracing universalism. My project in the next two chapters focuses on solutions of the former kind: attempts to show that rejecting a premise does not have the costs it initially seems to have.

In this chapter, I look at purported solutions that target either the love premise or the awareness premise. Such purported solutions have something in common: they seek to solve the problem by denying that the blessed *actively* love the lost in the way the love premise posits. Solutions that reject the love premise deny this directly. But those that reject the awareness premise also deny it. Agapic love may ground a *disposition* to respond to everyone in ways that express love's values; but that disposition will never be active towards the lost if the blessed are never aware of them. The blessed love them in theory, we might say, but not in practice.

LOVE WEBS

I begin by considering a purported solution to the problem of heavenly grief put forward by James Spiegel in his book-length defense of annihilationism. As an annihilationist, Spiegel sees grief over the *loss* of the unsaved as a problem that persists even if sympathy for the damned is off the table. His proposed solution thus addresses precisely the issue at the heart of this book.

According to Spiegel, there is "a crucial premise of the problem of heavenly grief that deserves to be challenged, namely that among the residents of hell will be loved ones of the redeemed." He asks us, instead, to imagine the following possibility:

> All of those people who were loved by the redeemed eventually find their way to salvation and eternal life in heaven, even if for some the route to redemption runs through hell. This is not to suggest that universalism is true. Rather, this is only to suggest that none of those who are ultimately damned were ever loved ones of the redeemed. On this view, all of the redeemed constitute a closed community or "web" of love, such that everyone who loves or is loved by the redeemed person will ultimately find salvation.[1]

In response to those who find this possibility "highly unlikely" from "a statistical standpoint," Spiegel invokes the power and resourcefulness of God: "God is a miracle worker, able to achieve outcomes that surprise

---

1. Spiegel, *Hell and Divine Goodness*, 119.

and defy all odds."[2] God could achieve these closed communities of love either "by ensuring the salvation in this life of all of those in the web" or by ensuring that anyone in the love web of someone who is saved would eventually be saved as well, perhaps after enduring a finite hell. This view, he thinks "would ensure that no one in heaven would grieve the permanent loss of a loved one and would thereby solve the problem of heavenly grief without selling the eschatological farm to the universalist."[3]

In short, the infinitely resourceful God will deploy those resources to guarantee that for each of the blessed, *everyone* in their network of personal love relationships (their "love web") is saved. Furthermore, since love admits of degrees, Spiegel concedes "that even the slightest trace of Christian love would be sufficient to ensure the salvation of the spiritually beloved."[4]

But even with this concession, he thinks his solution avoids "selling the eschatological farm" to universalists because, presumably, there will be some inherently valuable persons, bearers of God's image, for whom *none* of the blessed show *even the slightest trace of Christian love*. In short, Spiegel rejects the love premise as formulated above—specifically, clause (a) which affirms that the blessed have agapic love for all.[5] But as we shall see, Spiegel accepts clause (b), about personal love, and does not believe that any of the blessed will lose the love they have for anyone they've loved in this earthly life. Good parents will love their children, even when those children descend into wickedness—and would grieve their eternal loss. His love webs are designed to address the concerns that arise from this kind of personal love.

In short, Spiegel's approach to solving the problem of heavenly grief is two-pronged: to solve the universal version of the problem, he denies that the blessed have agapic love for all; and to solve the personal version, he posits closed love webs among the blessed. I want to begin my assessment with the second prong. What assumptions would we need to make in order to affirm *both* that God can guarantee such closed love webs *and* that God does not save all?

---

2. Spiegel, *Hell and Divine Goodness*, 119.
3. Spiegel, *Hell and Divine Goodness*, 120.
4. Spiegel, *Hell and Divine Goodness*, 120.
5. Were it not for his explicit challenge to the view that the blessed love everyone, we might take Spiegel instead to be denying the fitting grief premise: perhaps the blessed do love everyone in some sense, but the kind of love that is universal doesn't inspire grief when a loved one is lost. This is a view we will look at in the next chapter.

RESISTIBLE AND IRRESISTIBLE GRACE

On Spiegel's proposal, if you are loved by one of the saved even a little, God will take action to ensure that you are saved too. What would such divine action look like? The most obvious answer is that God would bestow what is called "efficacious grace" on all who are both loved by one or more of the saved and who, absent such grace, would be lost. By "efficacious grace," I mean grace that is *sufficient by itself* to bring about salvation.

But some clarification is needed here. Christians generally hold that some human choices are a necessary condition for salvation. The most obvious is repentance: a reorientation of our wills *away* from sin and *towards* God. A key point of contention among Christians is whether God can permissibly *produce* such repentance. Calvinists claim God can and does: all the saved are saved because God has directly caused the reformation of their wills. On Calvin's view, God "does not move the will in such a manner as has been taught and believed for many ages—that it is afterward in our choice either to obey or resist the motion—but by disposing it efficaciously."[6]

Opposition to this Calvinist view comes from the conviction that respect for freedom matters—to God and to us—and that freedom is *incompatible* with being determined in one's choices. This leads to the view that God would not save us through efficacious grace but would rely only on grace that is resistible. Thus, for example, Jerry Walls favors the view that, in pursuing human salvation, God relies on "optimal grace," a grace "that represents the optimal amount of influence toward good which God can exercise on that person's will without destroying his freedom."[7] The capacity to resist God's grace, to say *no* to it, is essential for freedom. God's respect for freedom limits how far God will go to secure our salvation.

This theological debate is tied to a philosophical one. Philosophers of freedom distinguish between the "compatibilist" view that a choice can be free even if determined (which appears to be Calvin's view), and the "incompatibilist" view that it cannot. Incompatibilists will either affirm determinism and hence deny that we have free will (a view sometimes called "hard determinism" or "hard incompatibilism"), or reject

---

6. Calvin, *Institutes*, 303 (2.3.10).
7. Walls, *Hell*, 88.

determinism and affirm the existence of a kind of freedom distinct from the compatibilist kind, generally called "libertarian" freedom.[8]

On at least some Christian theologies, God either cannot or morally may not save any who have not freely repented in the *libertarian* sense—a kind of free choice incompatible with being irresistibly caused by God to repent. Such theologies are, following the terminology introduced in chapter 1, broadly Arminian: theologies in which God could not or would not save anyone using efficacious grace. Instead, all receive a grace that is *resistible* in the sense that the libertarian freedom to reject it is retained. In addition to the bestowal of such resistible grace, a libertarian free choice to accept (or at least not rebuff) that grace is needed—and is the only thing standing in the way of salvation.[9]

While the clearest alternative to this broadly Arminian view is classical Calvinism, according to which all the elect are saved through efficacious grace and all others are damned, these are not mutually exhaustive. Spiegel could, for example, couch his love webs solution in a more "broadly" Calvinist theology (as defined in chapter 1) by holding that some among the blessed are saved by responding favorably to God's resistible grace, while others are saved because, being loved by one or more of the blessed, God chooses to bestow efficacious grace apart from any libertarian free choice they make.

Still, it is worth asking whether Spiegel's love web view is compatible with the broadly Arminian idea that God bestows only resistible grace. Would Spiegel's love web solution to the problem of heavenly grief be available if divine use of efficacious grace is not an option?

It is *here* that the objection based on statistical probability applies with greatest force. In a world where salvation depends on libertarian free choices, could God manage to arrange things such that those who are saved have in their network of loved ones *only* persons who are *also* saved? Keep in mind that the saved are presumably those most likely in this life to live up to Jesus' injunction to pursue the great commission, spreading the gospel to the unrepentant. They would thus be those most

---

8. For a good overview of recent philosophical discussions about freedom in these senses, see Levy and McKenna, "Recent Work on Free Will." For a deeper exegesis of the various positions, see Kane, *Contemporary Introduction to Free Will*, especially chapters 1–3.

9. In the tradition, such resistible grace has been dubbed "sufficient grace"—a problematic label, since unlike efficacious grace, where the bestowal of grace is sufficient to produce everything necessary for salvation, sufficient grace is not sufficient. Thus, I prefer—and will use here—the term "resistible grace."

likely to go where unregenerate sin is rampant, befriending those hostile to God, sharing God's love with them, etc., rather than isolating themselves from those most likely to be lost. The saintliest among us wouldn't shy away from reaching out to a recalcitrant sinner just because they think the probability of inspiring repentance is low. In fact, the most saintly are those most likely to reach out and make caring human connections with the least saintly—thus maximizing their chances of coming to know and personally love, at least a little, those *most likely to be lost*.

Unless God has a way to ensure that those most likely to reject divine grace will nevertheless freely (in the libertarian sense) accept it eventually, it seems God cannot guarantee for the blessed, using resistible grace alone, "a closed community or 'web' of love" that includes none of the lost. And if God *does* have a way to guarantee that those *most likely to reject divine grace* will nevertheless freely (in the libertarian sense) accept it eventually, it seems God would then have a way to guarantee that those less likely to reject divine grace will freely receive it eventually and so be saved. In other words, if God has a way to guarantee that those most likely to reject grace will freely receive it in the libertarian sense of "free," then God has a way to guarantee that everyone will do so.[10] In short, to solve the personal problem of heavenly grief through the postulate of love webs, Spiegel must hold either that God can and morally may bestow efficacious grace that guarantees the salvation of any recipient, or that God can deploy resistible grace in a way that guarantees the salvation of any recipient.

Either way, God has at God's disposal a morally permissible means to save any person God chooses to save—but uses that means, not to save all, but to secure closed love webs for the blessed. The reasonable question to pose here is why, if such a means is available, God stops short of saving all.

LIMITED LOVE?

The Arminian view is that free rejection of grace is *the* crucial impediment to God achieving the desire to save all: if all are not saved, it is because God cannot guarantee the salvation of all using only resistible grace. God's love extends to all but is defined by both a desire for their salvation and a respect for their (libertarian) freedom, the latter constraining God's

---

10. In fact, I think God does have such a means, as I will argue in the last chapter.

means of pursuing the former. It thus seems clear that *if* Spiegel thinks his love webs solution can work within an Arminian account of grace, his only way to avoid "selling the eschatological farm to the universalist" is by rejecting the Arminian account of God's love.

More plausibly, Spiegel can follow a path that is more thoroughly Calvinist, holding both that God can and may use efficacious grace and that the reason God does not use this grace to save all is that God *does not love everyone*. Instead, God only loves some created persons—the elect—and, motivated by love for the elect, ensures that their eternal joy is unmarred by grief by creating closed love webs in which the elect love and are loved only by others of the elect.

In sum, Spiegel's love-web solution will work only if God has a means of guaranteeing the salvation of anyone God chooses to save; and his love-web solution will avoid "selling the eschatological farm to the universalist" only by positing limits on God's love. It isn't just the blessed in heaven—who, by virtue of their limits, *cannot* personally experience the inherent value found in the personhood of every human being—who fall short of loving all created persons. God—who is directly personally acquainted with the inherent worth of every person, who discerns and immediately experiences the image of God that exists in every human being God has made—*also* fails to love all.[11]

And note that, for reasons already discussed in chapter 1 but worth revisiting, if our aim is to solve the problem of heavenly grief, we cannot say that God *does* love all but that the expression of this love is constrained by other demands of divine goodness at odds with acting on that love towards all—demands such as the requirement to have vessels of eternal wrath to manifest God's justice. Because in that case, the problem of heavenly grief does not vanish but is written into the eternal and immutable nature of God: an eternal and tragic conflict within God's moral nature requiring that God lose those God loves, that their inherent goodness be permanently vitiated or destroyed, and that the goods God wishes to bestow upon them be eternally withheld.

---

11. But even if one puts limits on both blessed and divine love, the love-webs view may still push us towards universalism granted that "the slightest trace" of love is enough to secure someone's salvation. If I'm saved and I love Bob even a little, Bob is saved, and so are all those he loves even a little, and so on in an exponential propagation that even reaches back in time (since those I loved even a little as a child loved others when they were children, etc.).

When Abraham climbed the mountain to sacrifice his beloved son Isaac at God's command, surely his heart was tearing in two. Surely, if he loved his son, obedience to God was in this case a source of anguish. Even if we grant the premise that obedience to God was for Abraham more important than what his love for Isaac called him to do, we would surely insist that if Abraham didn't grieve for what he was about to do it would indicate a serious moral failing, a deficiency of love. Likewise, if God loves created persons like a father, and if that love extends to those the divine nature requires that God annihilate or damn, we have a cosmic tragedy—one that would be a source of heartbreak for God and any who love God with all their hearts and souls and minds, as the blessed in heaven do.

To avoid this cosmic tragedy, Spiegel must hold that God's love is as limited as he takes the love of the blessed to be, that God does not love the lost even though God is more fully aware of their worth than any finite creature could ever be—that, contrary to a long tradition of thought on the nature of goodness, *God's love does not track what is objectively valuable.*

ENDURING PERSONAL LOVE

But Spiegel's rejection of the love premise is only partial: the love web solution denies that the blessed would have agapic love for all but affirms that they would persist in having personal love for those they counted as loved ones during their earthly lives. His reasons for the latter are instructive, and warrant some attention before we critically assess his reasons for rejecting the universal dimension of the love premise.

So, why does Spiegel think the blessed would continue to love those they loved during this earthly life? First, Spiegel distinguishes two ways we might stop loving someone we loved in this life. The first is selective amnesia, whereby we forget that our loved one existed. The second is "love reorientation," where we "retain all of our memories of them, including the fact that we loved them, even very intensely. But our love towards them itself disappears."[12]

It is the latter I want to consider here, since selective amnesia relates to the awareness premise and so will be explored in the second half of

---

12. Spiegel, *Hell and Divine Goodness*, 114.

this chapter. In addressing love reorientation, Spiegel considers Randy Alcorn's claim that the blessed would stop loving the lost because they cease to be lovable. According to Alcorn,

> What we loved in those who died without Christ was God's beauty we once saw in them. When God forever withdraws from them, I think they'll no longer bear his image and no longer reflect his beauty. Although they will be the same people, without God they'll be stripped of all the qualities we loved. Therefore, paradoxically, in a sense they will not be the people we loved.[13]

Spiegel identifies two problems with this argument. First, "that someone could stop bearing the image of God yet remain the 'same' person is dubious, if not unintelligible."[14] I would add that if, as King and others maintain, the image of God is our very personhood, we would cease to bear God's image only if we ceased to be persons. But my personhood is essential to me: for me to stop being a *person* is for *me* to stop existing.

Of course, ceasing to exist is what annihilationists take to be the fate of the lost, and so Spiegel—an annihilationist—does not take this to be the chief problem with Alcorn's view. Instead, the problem is that "it does not address one basic dimension of heavenly grief: *the loss of our loved ones*."[15] He continues:

> Stripping a person of their beauty, goodness, and even *imago Dei* is horribly sad and tragic, as is the prospect of someone being imprisoned by their bad desires, even if this is deserved. The fact that there would be nothing left to love in one's close friend or family member would itself be cause for tremendous grief.[16]

In short, grief is about the *loss* of the person we loved. Spiegel's point is that the transformation of a loved one into something unlovable amounts to the loss of the loved one—and so, rather than accounting for why we *wouldn't* grieve for the lost, it serves as the explanation for why we *would*. Spiegel brings this point alive with a zombie metaphor: suppose you live in some zombie apocalypse, and your spouse has not just died but become a zombie. Wouldn't this magnify the grief? But we don't

---

13. Alcorn, "If Our Loved Ones Are in Hell," para. 11, quoted in Spiegel, *Hell and Divine Goodness*, 114.
14. Spiegel, *Hell and Divine Goodness*, 115.
15. Spiegel, *Hell and Divine Goodness*, 115.
16. Spiegel, *Hell and Divine Goodness*, 115.

need horror story metaphors to understand this idea. It should be clear to anyone who has looked on a loved one's corpse and discerned that the loved one isn't there anymore. Absent hope of persistence beyond death, the loved one has been replaced by something unlovable: a corpse. It's not because we love the unlovable corpse that we grieve. We grieve because the person we loved is gone, replaced by this valueless corpse. Grief is the experience of that *absence*, the lament that a sacred locus of inherent value is lost.

In short, Spiegel's point is simply that grief is a fitting emotional response to *loss*, and the loss is not diminished but, rather, *increased* if the loved one is reduced to something unlovable. But in a sense this response sidesteps the main issue. Even granted that *Alcorn's* response is wholly inadequate, why couldn't the blessed avoid grief over lost loved ones by simply changing their affections so they stop valuing the person who is gone?

The answer, of course, is that ceasing to love those we loved in this life means disconnecting ourselves from the objectively valuable goods that our love for them connects us to: their being, welfare, and fellowship. What makes it "horribly sad and tragic" if a person is stripped "of their beauty, goodness, and even *imago Dei*" is not merely my subjective appreciation of that beauty, goodness, and divine image. What makes it horribly sad and tragic is that these objective goods have been erased from God's creation. Because these goods are objective, my appreciation of them is fitting—and to simply decide to stop valuing them is to decide to make my subjective value system *less* in tune with the objective order of values, thereby *diminishing* my moral character. This is not a decision the blessed would make. And since grief is an appropriate emotional response to seeing the inherently valuable beauty, goodness, and *imago Dei* of loved ones erased from the world, the blessed would grieve.

Put another way, to cease loving those one has loved personally would mean ceasing to value someone whose objective value one has personally experienced. But ceasing to value inherently valuable persons, when we have directly experienced that worth, is *even less excusable* than ceasing to value them when we haven't directly experienced it. The blessed will have no shortcomings in *need* of excusing, which is why we would expect them to value *all* the lost, and grieve for them all, whether or not they have personally experienced the objective worth of what is now gone.

But Spiegel thinks otherwise, despite the assumptions about fitting emotional responsiveness to lost goods that underlie his telling response to Alcorn. Can Spiegel justify this perspective?

SPIEGEL'S CASE FOR LIMITED LOVE

Spiegel offers a three-pronged defense of his view that the blessed need not love everyone. The first invokes Calvinist theology:

> Eric Reitan declares, "anyone in a state of eternal blessedness possesses both perfect bliss and universal love for all persons." But why assume that the love of the redeemed in heaven must be universal? It is possible, after all, that God does not love every human being, and those whom he never loved will not be saved. Such is the classical Calvinist take on the matter, and for all we know, that might be correct, in which case the love displayed by the redeemed in heaven might match that of God in being so limited and thus sidestep the objection.[17]

The second prong of his response holds that "even if God does love all human beings, it doesn't follow that in heaven we must have the same depth of love that God has for every human being" since "as finite beings our loves must always be limited and somewhat selective." He elaborates that "our love for family members and good friends on earth would presumably be far more personal and intense" than any general love for all persons—which, arguably, might not be intense or personal enough to pose "a threat to heavenly bliss."[18]

The third prong challenges Schleiermacher's claim that "the perfecting of our nature" entails that "sympathy must be such as to embrace the whole human race."[19] In response, Spiegel holds that "our sympathies will advance considerably" in heaven even if it excludes the lost because "the extension of our deep affections from hundreds or thousands to, say, billions of fellow redeemed souls will constitute an enormous advance in our capacity to love."[20]

The second and third prongs of his answer can be set aside quickly, in that they only have merit if we accept the first prong that doubts God's

---

17. Spiegel, *Hell and Divine Goodness*, 121.
18. Spiegel, *Hell and Divine Goodness*, 121.
19. Schleiermacher, *Christian Faith*, 721.
20. Spiegel, *Hell and Divine Goodness*, 122.

love for all. Consider the second prong. Even if we concede that the blessed would experience varying *depths* of love insofar as they remain finite creatures, it hardly follows that they would not love everyone if God does. First of all, they could still love all in the agapic sense in which they attribute to all the inherent worth they have directly experienced only with some. Secondly, we should recall that, in developing his love-web view, Spiegel wisely insists that "even the slightest trace of Christian love would be sufficient to ensure the salvation of the spiritually beloved."[21] Agapic love values the inherent worth of persons one doesn't know, recognizing that the value one has directly experienced with the beloved applies to the stranger. Surely this counts as at least "the slightest trace of Christian love." When my wife hears a story of a child killed in a distant land, it bring tears to her eyes even though she does not know the child at all. Why? Because her experience with children (she is a school teacher and a mother) leads her to emotionally grasp the inherent value of children and to attribute this value to the child she has never met. Such attribution is not some purely intellectual exercise but a real recognition of the lovability of the child, even though a stranger. For me, her tears represent an attainment of agapic love greater than my own.

Insofar as agapic love can encompass all persons, the finitude of the blessed is no barrier to them loving all *at least a little*. And if God loves all, the blessed would surely seek to love all as far as they *could*. Furthermore, the blessed would surely love God personally—indeed, with all their heart and soul and mind. And if God loves all persons, including all the lost, then the loss of these persons becomes a matter of grief for the blessed in much the way I grieve for someone I love personally if they experience a tragic loss. Hence, even if we deny that the blessed love all, if God loves all, the blessed would have reason to grieve if any are lost.

What about the third prong? When Schleiermacher speaks of general sympathy for all humanity, he surely has in mind something more like agapic love than personal love. What Spiegel suggests is that, in effect, expanding the scope of personal love to encompass billions would amount to an increase of love even if it were accompanied by a failure to love any of the lost, even in an agapic sense. But consider Martin Luther King Jr. who sought (however imperfectly) to embody agapic love for everyone, even the racist bigots who fought to preserve segregation. Suppose that, upon entering heaven, King's capacity for personal love

---

21. Spiegel, *Hell and Divine Goodness*, 120.

expanded to encompass all the saved—but that this expansion of his personal love were accompanied by the complete *extinguishing* of his agapic love.

This is exactly what would happen if he loved none of the lost. Agapic love is a responsiveness to the inherent value of all persons. It begins with the recognition that love's values extend to *every* person of sacred worth, every bearer of God's image. Any love that selectively excludes some persons thus fails to meet a necessary condition for *being* agapic love. Hence, were King to love none of the lost once in heaven, what follows is that a kind of love he imperfectly embodied in this life—agapic love—is *extinguished altogether* in heaven.

Isn't this a moral diminishment, even if it is accompanied by a widened scope of personal love? After all (following Matthew 5:44-48), even tax collectors love their *friends*. *That* is not the kind of love Jesus singles out as what we are to strive for as part of the call to be children of our Father in heaven, perfect as God is perfect. In our effort to be children of God, it is the kind of love that encompasses *enemies*—and hence the unsaved—that Jesus lifts up.

By Jesus' standard here, a love that extends to friends but excludes enemies is defective. And this remains true even if one has *lots* of friends. Spiegel's point that the blessed would in effect have more friends than they ever had before cannot, then, vindicate them of the charge of a moral deficiency if that bevy of friends is restricted to the blessed, and no trace of love extends to anyone beyond heaven's borders.

If we accept what seems to be the clear meaning of Matthew 5:44–48—namely that God loves all and we should strive to do likewise—the second and third prongs of Spiegel's argument have little force. Spiegel's case against the love premise thus depends on the merits of his first prong, which says we cannot rule out the idea that God does *not* love all.

GOD'S LOVE FOR ALL

Let me be forthright here: I *do* rule out the idea that God does not love all. A God who loves all created persons is central to my reading of Scripture and my understanding of the Christian faith. Perhaps, then, I should simply set aside those theological frameworks that say otherwise and direct my arguments to those who share my conviction that God is love and that divine love is not limited or exclusionary. I might then move forward in the hope that most of my readers share this starting point and that those who don't will still find value in work that wrestles with the implications of such a theology.

But I think there is merit in offering a sketch of why putting limits on God's love strikes me as, for Christians, a *problematic* way to try to solve the problem of heavenly grief. There are *costs* to solving the problem this way, costs that need to be weighed against the costs of alternative solutions and escapes.

Consider the following well-known scriptural verse: "For God so loved the world that he gave his only Son, so that everyone who believes in him may not perish but may have eternal life" (John 3:16). This verse extends God's love to "the world" and identifies this love for the world as the driving motive for what Christians take to be God's most important act in human history. As such, God's love for the world is not peripheral to the Christian faith.

Were this passage taken in isolation, one might perhaps read God's love for "the world" in a way that excludes some people from its scope. Perhaps God's love for the *whole* does not entail love for every *part*, and some persons are among the unloved parts. Such a reading clashes with the theological tradition that takes persons to have an objective worth that a morally perfect God would value. But the broader scriptural witness also counts against it.

Consider the tension between such a reading and the Genesis 1 narrative, in which God creates the world in stages and, at each stage, *sees* that what God made is good. Does God not love what is good? And doesn't the Genesis story entail that everything God made is, as a creation of God, good? And aren't all human beings created by God? Consider, furthermore, the scriptural assertion (Gen 1:26) that human beings were created in God's image. Would God not love that which bears God's own image? The doctrine of original sin does not entail that persons created by God have ceased to bear God's image or ceased to have inherent value. On the contrary, it is because of the great value of what has been corrupted by sin that the corruption is so dire, and God's desire to save us from it so important.

Furthermore, such a limited view of divine love is hard to reconcile with the scriptural claim that God "desires everyone to be saved" (1 Tim 2:4). If God's saving work through Christ is attributed to God's love for the world, and if those God wants to save includes *everyone*, how then can we coherently take it that God's love the world should be construed such that "the world" does *not* include everyone? The resulting view would go something like this: what motivates God to take such astonishing steps to secure human salvation is God's love for the world, but there are some created persons who are *not* included in his love for the world even though they are part of the world, even though God wants to save them, and even though God's saving work is said to be motivated by love for the world. Surely such a reading of God's "love for the world" is, at best, problematic.

And then we have passages like Luke 15:7, which declares there is "more joy in heaven over one sinner who repents than over ninety-nine righteous people who need no repentance." This and similar passages not only reinforce the idea that God (and the whole kingdom of heaven) desires the salvation of each and every person who has fallen away, but that each and every instance of repentance is a source of joy. Such joy is what we would expect from those who care—that is, from those who love. And it is clearly a better fit with the meaning of the passage to suppose that the love precedes the repentance: those one loves, whose good has to this point been compromised by their bondage to sin, have now turned toward God and in so doing started on a course towards redemption and sanctification and the fulfillment of their potential. God and the hosts of heaven rejoice when those they loved *while yet they were sinners* repent.

One might, I suppose, argue that the passage is not intended to apply to all sinners in need of repentance but only to some: God loves some of those sinners in need of repentance, and so is filled with joy when *those* sinners repent (perhaps the ones God has predestined to be recipients of efficacious grace), while not loving other sinners (perhaps those God predestined to never receive the grace needed to repent). But this is obviously not a distinction that is made in the passage, nor is it a natural reading of the passage. The most natural and straightforward reading of the passage is that God—who Scripture says *is* love, who Scripture says desires the salvation of *all*, who Scripture says loves the *world*—in fact loves each and every sinner in need of repentance and so is filled with joy when they repent. Other readings are at best strained. That a purported solution to the problem of heavenly grief requires such a strained reading is surely a cost of that purported solution, even if we are sometimes required to pay such a cost because there is no alternative.

More significantly, however, there are all the passages that speak to God's endorsement of a love that extends to all: the call to love not just friends but enemies in order to be perfect like God (Matt 5:44–48), Paul's claim that "love is the fulfillment of the law" (Rom 13:9–10), Jesus' claim that we should love our neighbors as ourselves (Matt 22:38), and Jesus' answer to the lawyer who asks, "Who is my neighbor?" (Luke 10:29–37). What emerges is a human ethic that calls for loving without discrimination or distinction. How can we make sense of the idea that God calls *us* to love without discrimination or distinction if God's love discriminates and distinguishes? Are we called to love in a way different from the way God loves, even though the message of 1 John 4 is that our love for others is supposed to be an extension of God's love for us? This hardly *seems* plausible—but if it *is* plausible, Spiegel is too quick in claiming that if God does not love all, then neither would the blessed. Put simply, the portrait of moral perfection Jesus commends to humanity is one in which love extends without distinction or discrimination. Presumably this means the blessed should love in this way *even if God does not*—since it is what God has commanded. Of course, the more coherent reading is that God loves in this way, too.

One might try to explain a distinction between divine love and the kind of love we are called to embody by holding that the command to love without distinction or discrimination is a *concession* to human finitude: since we don't know who is loved by God and who isn't, and we should love everyone God loves, the safe bet is to love everyone. But this concession would not apply to the blessed in heaven, since they would know who is loved by God and who isn't.

Such a reading is, however, difficult to reconcile with the fact that Jesus ends his call to love without distinction and discrimination in Matthew 5 with the closing injunction to "Be perfect, therefore, as your heavenly Father is perfect" (Matt 5:48). The straightforward reading here is that Jesus is calling us to love in this way because *this is how God loves*, and we are to strive to be like God.

Arguably, it is these sorts of scriptural challenges that lead many Calvinists, such as Piper, to hold that, even though God predestines some for glory and others for damnation, there remains a sense in which God loves all. Piper's view, as we saw in chapter 1, is that while God loves all, only some are beneficiaries of that love. For others, God's love does not culminate in the beneficence towards which divine love is oriented because such beneficence conflicts with the use to which God must put them as instruments for displaying divine glory. Such a display of God's glory requires an eternal manifestation of wrath against sin by the creation of vessels of wrath, that is, persons predestined to suffer eternally for their sins.

There are many who are suspicious of the coherence of this view, on the grounds that it is hard to see God's love for these vessels of wrath as sincere if the only difference between them and the ones God saves is that God gives the latter the grace needed to repent but not the former.[22] But in the context of this book, the deeper worry, as I have already argued, is that this view does not solve the problem of heavenly grief but seems to make it worse by transforming it from a problem tied to contingent circumstances resulting from human choices (ones that might have been different) into an essential problem at the heart of reality itself, a tragedy bound to the very essence of God.

Hence, a broadly Calvinist theology can *solve* the problem of heavenly grief only if it takes the form Spiegel attributes to it rather than the form Piper articulates—one in which God's love is narrowed in order to make room for unloved vessels of wrath. But in addition to this view being in deep tension with scriptural passages that posit divine love for all, there are difficulties with the positive scriptural case offered in its favor. The heart of that case rests on Romans 9:13–24, in which Paul speaks of God's right, as creator, to make some people into vessels of wrath and others into vessels of mercy. Paul ask us, what if God did this? Who would we be to complain?[23] But it is hardly a straightforward inference to draw from this passage the conclusion that God *will* make some into *permanent and eternal* vessels of wrath, especially given the overarching narrative, introduced in Romans 9 and culminating in Romans 11.

In that narrative, Paul argues that "a hardening has come upon part of Israel *until* the full number of the gentiles has come in. And in this way *all* Israel will be saved" (Rom 11:25–26). In other words, Israel's heart is hardened by God as part of a strategy for winning over the gentiles, and once that goal is accomplished, Israel will be saved, too. Paul's conclusion is that God's ultimate aim is to make *all* into vessels of mercy:

---

22. For developments of this view, see McCall, "We Believe in God's Sovereign Goodness"; Walls, *Does God Love Everyone?*, especially chapter 5.

23. It is worth noting here that any statement about what God has the right or authority to do tells us little about what God *will* do—how God will exercise that authority—especially if we think God's authority is unlimited. If we turn to Scripture to answer questions about what God will do, we must look to what it says about God's promises, plans, and character, not God's authority.

> Just as you [gentiles] were once disobedient to God but have now received mercy because of their [Israel's] disobedience, so also they have now been disobedient in order that, by the mercy shown to you, they also may now receive mercy. For God has imprisoned all in disobedience so that he may be merciful to all. (Rom 11:30–32)

Put in more classical Calvinist terms, Paul claims that God makes all persons vessels of wrath at one time or another as part of a strategy whose goal is to make all into vessels of mercy. Rather than being two distinct and final categories of humanity, *all* human beings are vessels of *both* wrath and mercy.[24] This conclusion fits Paul's earlier claim, in Romans 5:18, that "just as one man's trespass led to condemnation for all, so one man's act of righteousness leads to justification and life for all." While the point here is to contrast the effects of Adam's sin and Christ's atoning work, the common theme is that all people are objects of both divine condemnation and mercy—but *mercy* is the final word.[25]

Even if one rejects a universalist reading of Romans, it is hard to deny that Paul describes the process of hardening hearts as something God does to Israel as a *stage* in the process of making both Israel and the gentiles into vessels of mercy. One might argue that not every object of divine mercy is saved, perhaps because some rebuff or reject that mercy—but in that case, it is not because God has hardened hearts with the aim of making vessels of eternal wrath. Any hardening God does—at least on this reading of this Romans account—aims at the good of all.

In short, we can read Romans 9 as affirming God's *right* to fashion people as God likes, even if that means fashioning some into vessels of wrath and others into vessels of mercy, and that we have no right to complain no matter how God might exercise that right. And we can then read the narrative that follows, culminating in Romans 11, as an account of how God in fact *makes use of this right*—a use so glorious and generous in its aims that not only does no one have a *right* to complain, but no one has any *cause* to complain: God's generous mercy is the final word for all.

---

24. For a detailed explication of this reading of Romans 9–11, see MacDonald, *Evangelical Universalist*, 90–95.

25. All of this fits seamlessly into a stream of the theological traditional that sees God's wrath and judgment as God's angry love: condemnation and judgment are one side or expression of God's love, not a sign of its absence. For example, Barth asserts that God's holiness "is not side by side with, but in His grace, and His wrath is not separate from but in His love." See Barth, *Church Dogmatics* 2.1, §30, 363.

Given how natural and coherent this reading of Romans is, and given how well it coheres with scriptural themes of a divine love that extends to all, I find a theology that denies the universal scope of God's love harder to fit with Scripture as a whole—not to mention with dominant themes in Christian ethics—than a theology that affirms God's love for all. And if God loves all, then so would the blessed, if not in the personal way that requires direct experience of the inherent worth of all, then in the agapic sense that attributes to all what is directly experienced only with some.

If that is right, and if Spiegel is right that God can and will secure the salvation of all those loved by the saved in order to spare the saved grief, what follows is that God will save everyone. Spiegel's love webs reconcile non-universalism with the doctrine of perfect blessedness only if there are limits to God's love and the love of the blessed. But for the reasons mentioned here, positing such limits is a costly way to solve the problem of heavenly grief.

CHALLENGING THE AWARENESS PREMISE

In a pair of articles responding to Thomas Talbott,[26] William Lane Craig levels three connected challenges to the awareness premise. He formulates these challenges merely as "defenses," meaning he is not committed to the truth of his proposals, nor even their plausibility. For reasons mentioned in chapter 1, I do not think a mere defense in this sense can serve as an adequate *solution* to the problem of heavenly grief, since a solution by way of rejecting the awareness premise needs to show that the costs of rejecting it are lower than the costs of alternative solutions and escapes. A minimalist "defense" that establishes the logical compatibility of non-universalism with the perfect blessedness of the saved if only we grant a premise that, while utterly implausible, cannot be *proven* to be false *necessarily*, doesn't qualify as a solution in my sense. Hence, I will treat Craig as if he thinks his proposals are *plausible* in the light of the broader network of beliefs it is reasonable for Christians to accept. If they are not—if accepting his proposals has high costs in terms of requiring that we embrace highly implausible claims or reject highly plausible ones—then their adequacy as solutions to our problem is in doubt unless

---

26. Craig, "Talbott's Universalism"; Craig, "Talbott's Universalism Once More."

and until we can establish that *all other proposals and escapes are even more costly.*

He offers two *main* challenges to the awareness premise, which I will call *the challenge from overwhelming bliss* and *the challenge from blessed ignorance*. The former proposes that the overwhelming joy of the beatific vision drives all awareness of the damned from the minds of the blessed. The latter proposes that God shields the blessed from the knowledge that any are damned, if necessary by erasing their memories of lost loved ones, to prevent any distress such knowledge would produce.

But these challenges most directly challenge the claim—made by Schleiermacher—that the blessed would be aware of the fate of the lost. What Talbott claims is that, whatever the truth about the final fate of persons, it must be of a kind that would not undermine the supreme happiness of the blessed *were they* to become aware of it. Otherwise, their supreme happiness would not be supremely worthwhile. More precisely, Talbott articulates three conditions for blessedness:

> (a) that S is reconciled to God and in a state of supreme happiness; (b) that S is filled with love for others and therefore desires the good for all other created persons; and (c) that there is no fact F such that (i) S is ignorant of F, and (ii) were S not ignorant of F, then S would have been unable to experience supreme happiness.[27]

In short, Talbott thinks that for subjectively supreme happiness to be supremely *worthwhile*, it cannot depend on moral imperfection or wickedness, and it cannot rest on false beliefs. For Talbott, (b) expresses the first of these conditions and (c) the second. Given (c), there could be no facts whose disclosure would disrupt the joy of the blessed. If there are such fact, no one is perfectly blessed even if there are persons who meet conditions (a) and (b).

Exploring Craig's challenge to this view—what we can call *the challenge from the nature of supremely worthwhile happiness*—will serve as a useful starting point for thinking about Craig's more direct attacks on the awareness premise.

---

27. Talbott, "Providence, Freedom, and Human Destiny," 239.

THE NATURE OF SUPREMELY WORTHWHILE HAPPINESS

Craig challenges Talbott's condition (c)—the idea that, to be supremely worthwhile, the happiness of the blessed must be able to survive a full disclosure of the truth—as follows:

> It seems to me dubious and even false that supremely worthwhile happiness entails the ability to survive a full disclosure of the truth. For a happiness which would, *ceteris paribus*, be diminished by the disclosure of a tragic truth about a loved one seems more worthwhile than one which would survive undiminished.[28]

Craig's claim here is that a happiness that would be diminished by the disclosure of tragic truths is more worthwhile than a callous happiness that would persist even in the face of tragedy. From this he concludes that Talbott's view is mistaken and that the happiness of the blessed could be supremely worthwhile even if it is *vulnerable* to being dislodged by awareness of tragic truths (but isn't dislodged in fact, because they remain oblivious).

But this misses Talbott's point. Talbott agrees that a happiness that would be diminished by the disclosure of tragic truths is *more* worthwhile than a callous happiness. What he denies is that such happiness can be *supremely* worthwhile if there are tragic truths of which one is unaware. This is because Talbott makes a further claim: supreme happiness that depends for its persistence on blissful ignorance is worth less than supreme happiness that fittingly reflects a reality that *warrants* such happiness.

In response to this, Craig simply asserts that "the mere possession of more information seems irrelevant to the worth of one's happiness. What is relevant is how one's happiness would be affected by the disclosure of such painful knowledge."[29] Craig thus concludes that Talbott "needs to prove that it is logically impossible that the blessed should be unaware of the existence of the damned."[30] In short, Craig thinks Talbott's condition (c) is false, and so thinks that in order to conclude that anyone's eternal damnation would undermine the blessedness of the saved,

---

28. Craig, "Talbott's Universalism Once More," 508.
29. Craig, "Talbott's Universalism Once More," 509.
30. Craig, "Talbott's Universalism Once More," 509.

one needs Schleiermacher's premise that blessedness is incompatible with lack of awareness of the damned. This explains why Craig's main challenges, while occasioned by Talbott's thinking, more directly target Schleiermacher.

But Craig's rejection of Talbott's condition (c) amounts to invoking Craig's intuition that the existence of information that would undermine one's happiness were one aware of it is irrelevant for assessing the worth of that happiness. Talbott's contrary intuition is that such information is highly relevant. Is a clash of rival intuitions all we have here?

Consider again what Talbott maintains. For Talbott, perfect blessedness is not just about being supremely happy and perfectly loving. It is about existing in an environment so good it *warrants* supreme happiness among those who are perfectly loving. Talbott, in effect, sees happiness as an emotion in the sense explicated in chapter 5: in addition to how it feels, happiness is *about* something and involves a value judgment. Those who are happy *approve* of the state in which they find themselves and are more or less happy depending on how much they approve, or how unmixed their approval is with disapproval. "The state in which they find themselves" is ambiguous, and deliberately so. Different people have broader or narrower conceptions of what constitutes their "state," paralleling the extent to which they include or exclude others' welfare. But someone perfected in love would care about the condition of *all* persons and so would be *supremely* happy only if they approve unconditionally of the state of everyone—in other words, only if all are saved.

Talbott's view, in short, is that if the blessed believe that all are saved and this belief is false, their happiness is worth less than if it is true. It may not be worth less *morally* (what Craig apparently takes to be the only measure of the worth of happiness). But if the judgment associated with the supreme happiness of the blessed is false, the blessed are living an eternal *mistake*—eternally out of touch with reality. Can we really call that *perfect* blessedness?

Talbott's point is that supreme happiness may be unfitting because of a distorted value system *or* a mistaken conception of the facts. Even if living a lie is, as Craig seems to think, *better* than suffering on account of tragic truths, both appear to be defects to one's state. And if the state of the saved is marred by a defect, it fails to qualify as *perfect* blessedness.

Once we view happiness as an emotion, susceptible to the same standards of fittingness as other emotions, Craig's intuition becomes hard to sustain. Rejoicing over the rescue of everyone trapped in the Twin

Towers on 9/11, given that so many were not rescued (and, in fact, many of the rescuers were themselves killed), amounts to a kind of tragic farce. Craig asks us to imagine God presiding over an *eternal* farce in which the blessed joyously celebrate the homecoming of *every single* prodigal child—in the midst of a reality in which prodigal children writhe in eternal torment, never to come home.

But suppose for the sake of argument that Craig's implausible intuition is correct. Even if blissful ignorance over the fate of the lost is perfectly good *because* of the bliss and in *spite* of the ignorance, that won't matter if Schleiermacher is right to think the blessed in heaven would, precisely because of their blessedness, be aware of the lost.

OVERWHELMING BLISS

As noted above, Craig offers two reasons to think the blessed might be unaware of the lost. He expresses the first as follows:

> It is possible that the very experience itself of being in the immediate presence of Christ (cf. the beatific vision) will simply drive from the minds of His redeemed any awareness of the lost in hell. So overwhelming will be His presence and the love and joy which it inspires that the knowledge of the damned will be banished from the consciousness of God's people. In such a case, the redeemed will still have such knowledge, but they would never be conscious of it and so never pained by it.[31]

This challenge from overwhelming bliss holds that even if the supreme happiness of the blessed couldn't survive *awareness* of the fate of the lost, *knowledge* of their fate needn't produce such awareness. And Craig posits a reason to think blessed knowledge of the lost *wouldn't* entail awareness. Perhaps the beatific vision would drive such awareness from their minds, such that even though the blessed *know* that some of God's beloved children are eternally lost, they know it in something like the way one might know, during a cocaine high, that children are starving in Palestine.

On this view, failure to be aware of the fate of the lost is not only *consistent* with perfect blessedness but *entailed* by it—specifically, by the experience of the beatific vision, which keeps unpleasant facts, even when known, from entering the conscious awareness of the blessed.

---

31. Craig, "Talbott's Universalism," 307.

If this thinking is correct, the awareness premise is false even if the blessed suffer no defects of *knowledge*. As such, in order to be spared grief over the tragic final state of God's creation, the blessed need not suffer from any epistemic defects of ignorance. Even though not *ignorant* of the tragic fate of some of God's beloved children, the overwhelming nature of the beatific vision would make them *unaware* of it.

Craig concedes that "Talbott could amend clause (c) ... by substituting for 'ignorant' something like 'unaware' or 'unconscious.'"[32] But Craig dismisses such a move because "we are surely justified in doubting that clause (c) is a necessary condition of salvation,"[33] since there is nothing that "seems to justify this condition either philosophically or biblically."[34]

But is this right? If your happiness depended on lacking *awareness* of facts that, were you *aware* of them, would lead you to judge your happiness unfitting, wouldn't your happiness fall short of being supremely worthwhile just as surely as if you lacked knowledge?

But this point aside, there is reason to suppose that if the blessed knew of the fate of the damned, they would be aware of it—by virtue of their moral sanctification. Even if we don't go so far as to *identify* love with attention, as Simone Weil does,[35] attention to someone's condition is surely an element of love for them. The first thing the good Samaritan did on that Jericho road was *pay attention* to the injured robbery victim. To fail to do likewise—to ignore those who suffer when you *know* of their suffering, as the priest and the Levite did—looks to be a failure of love. If the priest's excuse is that he was too high on cocaine to maintain awareness of the robbery victim he knew to be suffering, the implication seems to be that the drug has made him unable to love his neighbor as he should. Is the Levite's excuse any better if he claims to have been so caught up in rapturous prayer he couldn't pay any attention to the poor man on the road?

This point is strengthened if we accept Luther's idea that to love one's neighbor is to "'put on' his neighbor, and so conduct himself toward him as if he himself were in the other's place. ... A Christian man lives not in himself but in Christ and his neighbor. Otherwise, he is not a Christian."[36] If we take this to mean Christians should care nothing

---

32. Craig, "Talbott's Universalism," 307.
33. Craig, "Talbott's Universalism," 307.
34. Craig, "Talbott's Universalism," 307.
35. Weil, "Forms of the Implicit Love of God," 149.
36. Luther, "Freedom of the Christian," 79–80.

about their own welfare and needs, there are reasons to be skeptical of Luther's claim. But it is hard to affirm that we should love our neighbors *as* ourselves if we deny that our attention and care should encompass them. After all, our self-love includes such attention and care. If Craig's account of the effects of the beatific vision is correct, then the beatific vision *diminishes* our capacity to love by disabling our ability to attend to our neighbor's plight. In other words, his view seems to imply that the direct experience of God's goodness has an *anti-sanctifying* effect. Instead of union with the God of love perfecting our love, it so distracts us from our neighbors that we *can't* love them as we do ourselves. As Talbott puts it, the beatific vision could "drive all knowledge of the lost from the consciousness of the redeemed (without obliterating it altogether) only if it is possible that the beatific vision will make the redeemed less loving and thus more calloused."[37]

Craig replies that someone would be less loving and more callous "only if he fails to love all those persons of whom he is aware; but it would be fatuous to so describe someone for failing to love a person of whose existence he is completely unaware."[38] But this response misses the key point, which is this: when we love others, their suffering *demands our attention*. Loving others requires caring about their condition. Knowing that their condition is miserable and yet *eternally* failing to pay any attention to it exhibits a failure to love. If, like a drug, the beatific vision compromises the capacity of the blessed to pay attention, what follows is that their *capacity to love* is compromised.

But this way of putting things assumes the lost are *suffering*. That is Craig's assumption, since he is defending the doctrine of hell. But even if his argument from overwhelming bliss fails in its intended context, might it work as an annihilationist response to the argument from heavenly grief? If the lost are annihilated instead of tormented, there will be no suffering for us to care about—and, arguably, their eternal absence is not something that demands out attention.

But the deeper point here is that moral sanctification entrenches the blessed more fully in their allegiance to the good and concern for the good, and the experience of the beatific vision is not divorced from moral sanctification but vitally tied to it. To experience the beatific vision is to be united with the supreme good, namely God, in such a direct way that

---

37. Talbott, "Craig on the Possibility of Eternal Damnation," 510.
38. Craig, "Talbott's Universalism Once More," 510.

our wills are wholly and fully aligned with God's will. This experience is *both* a source of joy *and* a driver of moral sanctification. The joy found in the beatific vision is more like the joy tied to living a morally good life than it is like the overwhelming bliss of a cocaine high. The latter takes you *out* of the world: you are so full of euphoric feelings you lose touch with reality. But the former involves a deeper entrenchment in reality through attunement of the self to the ultimate reality and the ultimate good. If we are permanently distracted from the fact that objectively good persons have been annihilated, that means we are less attuned to reality and the good than we were before. But surely that is the *opposite* of what the morally sanctifying experience of the beatific vision bestows.

To experience the beatific vision is to be united with God, bringing our will into alignment with God's will. If God is love, that means we will value the being of persons, their welfare, and the prospect of fellowship with them. It means our emotional dispositions will be perfectly attuned to such values. Thus, it is untenable to suppose that, were non-universalism true, the beatific vision would keep the blessed blissfully oblivious of this truth. Such inattention to the things love cares about simply cannot be coherently construed as an effect of loving union with the God of love.

But Craig has a final argument: reasons to think the blessed might not even know about the lost. Does his challenge from blessed ignorance fare any better than his other arguments?

BLESSED IGNORANCE

Schleiermacher's view is that ignorance of something as significant as the suffering of the damned is *incompatible* with blessedness. We have already explored a range of reasons for thinking this is true. First, given that our intellectual faculties are central to our human nature, it seems blessedness would involve these faculties achieving their fullest potential. At the very least, as we argued in chapter 3, we would expect our epistemic powers to be sufficiently actualized that we would avoid outright errors in our beliefs, especially errors that feature into moral choices—errors such as, for example, the error of thinking all are saved when they are not, and thus adopting an attitude of perfect joy that is unfitting to the actual circumstances. To this we can add the point that the blessed would surely be on the lookout for a loved one, desiring a heavenly reunion.

As such, it seems that, barring divine deception, they would notice their absence from the community of heaven.

Craig's argument from blessed ignorance needs to be assessed in light of these considerations. The crux of his thinking is the proposal that God will actively "shield" the blessed from the "painful knowledge" that some are damned—and do so in a way that does *not* amount to immoral deception.[39] He offers a pair of points in defense of this proposal. First, he notes that "we can all think of cases in which we shield persons from knowledge which would be painful for them and which they do not need to have," a shielding we regard as virtuous.[40] But while withholding painful information may be fitting in *this* life—where we must choose between the imperfections of ignorance and pain—blessedness is supposed to be a *perfected* state, not one in which God must choose which imperfection to subject us to.[41]

Craig's second point is no more compelling. He imagines God keeping the "terrible secret" about the damned buried forever in the divine breast "in order that He might bring free creatures into the supreme and unalloyed joy of fellowship with Himself." Craig takes this to be "a beautiful extension of Christ's suffering on the Cross."[42] But would God really facilitate "the supreme and unalloyed joy of *fellowship* with Himself" if God eternally *withholds* God's grief over the fate of the damned? Loved ones who keep their grief to themselves are walling off a part of themselves, a part that *matters*, and thereby placing a significant limit on the degree of fellowship or loving union they allow with others. If God, to preserve the joy of the blessed, erects such a partial wall, God is imposing just such a restriction on loving communion. But surely it is contrary to Christian assumptions to say the blessed are rendered more blessed by God erecting such walls. Instead of the blessed enjoying union with God and the damned enduring separation, there are only degrees of separation. But adopting such a theology is surely a high cost for solving the problem of heavenly grief.

And then we have Craig's final point: this divine "shielding" of the saved does not amount to *deception*. Craig argues that while it "*would* be deceptive of God to make the blessed believe that the lost were saved when in fact they are not," it is not similarly deceptive if God simply wipes

---

39. Craig, "Talbott's Universalism," 306.
40. Craig, "Talbott's Universalism," 306.
41. See Talbott, "Craig on the Possibility of Eternal Damnation," 508–9.
42. Craig, "Talbott's Universalism," 306–7.

all knowledge of the lost from their minds, since this does not result in any false beliefs.[43] This is, presumably, how God gets around the fact that the blessed would be on the lookout for loved ones. The lack of a heavenly reunion would not drive home the fact of their absence if the blessed have completely forgotten that their lost loved ones ever existed.

There are two problems here. First, to ensure their supreme happiness, the blessed can't be merely *agnostic* about whether any are lost. The *supreme* happiness of those perfected in love involves the judgment that all is well, in other words, that *all* are saved. Thus, God's blessed memory wipe must lead the blessed to think all are saved. So, even if God is not *explicitly* lying to the saved, God is tinkering with their minds with the aim of producing a false belief.

If there is a distinction between this and lying, it is a distinction without a moral difference. On Craig's picture, the blessed are supremely happy based on the judgment that such happiness is fitting given the circumstances. But they are wrong about this. Their attitude is one they would never adopt if they knew the truth. At a minimum, God could have disavowed them of their false judgment but chose not to. But if God is in the business of erasing memories, God's responsibility is more active: God is *acting* to ensure that the blessed respond emotionally to the state of the world as if the world were in a different state than it is actually in. God is actively producing error.

Finally, the kind of memory erasure Craig posits is hardly harmless. Talbott doubts "that Craig has any conception of how much a person's mind that would destroy."[44] James Spiegel makes the same point in greater detail:

> At least when it comes to loved ones who are close family members, such as a parent, child, or sibling, memory erasure would demand such a deep and radical restructuring of one's memories that it would constitute revising one's personal identity. Consider for a moment how many of your memories involve or are built around your parents and their influence on you. Thorough removal of memories of one of them would not only be significant in itself but would necessitate alteration or removal of countless other memories of people you know who had close relationships to them.[45]

43. Craig, "Talbott's Universalism Once More," 510.
44. Talbott, "Craig on the Possibility of Eternal Damnation," 508.
45. Spiegel, *Hell and Divine Goodness*, 111.

Spiegel notes that severe, permanent amnesia can render someone "a completely different person," and suggests that the partial amnesia Craig envisions would differ only in degree, not in kind, in terms of its identity-erasing impact.[46] The result would be "an extreme loss" of a sort "utterly inconsistent with any plausible account of heavenly bliss."[47]

In reflecting on Craig's proposal here, I cannot help but reflect on my mother's dementia. For me, the most agonizing thing has been to watch her forget the very existence of her grandchildren: people she loved dearly, lost to a fog of forgetting. With each person forgotten, the dementia tugs another thread from the weave of my mother's life story. Although this forgetting spares her grief over the death of my father and her brother and so many others, that freedom from grief is achieved by *diminishing* her.

If that is the only way to spare the blessed grief over the lost, then it is a cost too high. But more to the point, it is a *cost*. A diminishment. Blessedness involves the perfection of our natures. To be afflicted with forgetting is a vitiation.

CONCLUSIONS SO FAR

Based on these considerations, I do not see much promise in denying either the love premise or the awareness premise of the argument from heavenly grief: the costs of both are high. Those who want to *solve* the problem should, I think, look instead to the fitting grief premise or the incompatibility premise—arguing either that persistent grief is *not* a fitting response to the eternal loss of persons, or that persistent grief over the fate of the lost is in some way compatible with perfect blessedness. I take up these responses in the next chapter.

---

46. Spiegel, *Hell and Divine Goodness*, 112.
47. Spiegel, *Hell and Divine Goodness*, 112.

7

Purported Solutions

Unfitting Grief

IN THE LAST CHAPTER we examined purported solutions to the problem of heavenly grief that deny that the blessed *actively* love the lost—either because their love does not extend to the lost or because they remain blissfully unaware of them and their tragic fate. In this chapter we consider proposed solutions that challenge the fitting grief premise (questioning whether enduring grief for the lost is an emotionally fitting response to awareness of their fate) and the incompatibility premise (questioning whether enduring grief really precludes perfect joy).

IMPASSIBILITY

In responding to John Kronen's and my formulation of the argument from heavenly sympathy, Eric Yang challenges the fitting grief premise by invoking the doctrine of divine impassibility. Yang lays out his challenge as follows:

> Currently there is much suffering in the world, but God is fully aware of the suffering of creatures and yet remains perfectly in bliss. God is also aware of those who are damned and even loves those consigned to hell, yet his happiness is not diminished in any way. Moreover, it is reasonable to suppose that the blessed will have become more like God in some (but not all) respects. Perhaps, then, something akin to impassibility might

be attributed to them.... Thus, the residents of heaven can be completely aware of the fate of the damned and yet not be harmed by such knowledge.[1]

In other words, based on the doctrine that God is impassible, it follows that *God* can know perfect joy despite knowing that those God loves are in torment. If this is possible for God, why not for the saved?[2]

If any readers find this "impassibility" account of God's attitude towards the damned to be a bit cold—turning God's love into a distant and alien response quite unlike what we normally associate with love, let alone the love of a parent—they are hardly alone. Many theologians reject divine impassibility in favor *passibilism*. R. T. Mullins defines the passibilist as one who "claims that God's happiness is disturbed by what transpires in the universe because a morally perfect God cannot be unmoved by the evils of the world."[3] The biblical image of God as Father favors this view. An emotionless response to the *eternal anguish* or *annihilation* of my beloved child, one that leaves my happiness unfazed, seems deeply inconsistent with love that is anything like a father's love.

But let us bracket the question of whether divine impassibility is a doctrine we should accept. Even if we grant the impassibilist conception of how God responds to the eternal misery or destruction of God's beloved creatures, it doesn't follow that we can simply impute a parallel response to the blessed. If God lacks emotional responses—or, at least, negative ones—then God's nature in this respect is so unlike ours that it seems we could not share God's perspective and remain human. Human beings are by nature emotional beings. Eternal blessedness on Yang's view thus sounds like the *swapping out* of our human nature for something else rather than the *perfection* of our human nature. It ceases to be *human* blessedness. That having a body is part of what it is to be human has led the tradition to hold that the blessed will have perfected bodies rather than sharing in God the Father's disembodied state. Likewise, since having emotions is part of what it is to be human, shouldn't we hold that

---

1. Yang, "Heaven and the Problem of Eternal Separation," 161.

2. Yang cites Athanasius as a historical precedent for the view that the blessed will share in God's impassibility. See Athanasius, *Against the Arians*, Discourse III, 34, cited in Yang, "Problem of Eternal Separation," 162.

3. Mullins, *God and Emotions*, 28. For some examples of passibilist defenses, see chapter 7 of Hill, *Divinity and Maximal Greatness*; O'Connor, "Tears of God"; Oord, "Strong Passibility"; Wessling, *Love Divine*, chapter 4; Wolterstorff, *Inquiring about God*, chapter 10.

the blessed would have perfected emotions rather than sharing in divine impassibility?

But Yang refines his response in a way that might address this concern, through an appeal to recent work by Anastasia Scrutton. Scrutton argues that divine impassibility should be construed, not as the absence of all emotions in God, but as the absence of all *passive* emotions, or "passions." The presence of active emotions, or "affections," should be affirmed. For Scrutton, the distinction lies in the source of the affective state: "what makes an affection an affection rather than a passion lies in the fact that it is a movement of the will, which is part of the higher, inner, intellective self, while the passion is an act of the appetite, an aspect of the lower, outer, sensual self."[4] The distinction here is between emotions that express reason, ones we actively adopt as rational agents because they are fitting (affections), and emotions that are purely reactive and irrational, that happen *to* us as unreflective responses to environmental stimuli tied to our sensual appetites (passions). Yang argues that the perfection of our human natures would entail the elimination of all such passions, even as we retain our affections.

But this account would solve the problem of heavenly grief only if grief were a passion rather than an affection—something one might reasonably suppose if all grief were "the bath of self-pity, the wallow, the loathsome sticky-sweet pleasure of indulging it" that Lewis describes as the first reaction to his wife's death.[5] But we saw in chapter 2 that grief is not reducible to such self-indulgent wallowing.

Consider the following perspective on divine grief and sadness described R. T. Mullins:

> When [God's covenant people] are unfaithful to the covenant, God is grieved by their unfaithfulness because He correctly perceives the disvalue of their immoral actions. God's grief is a rational and moral response to their behavior. Yet, when God's unfaithful people suffer, God feels sorrow for them because He cares for them and wants them to flourish according to His covenantal promise.[6]

Were grief nothing but a reactive and irrational response to stimuli tied to bodily appetites, this account of divine grief would be incoherent.

---

4. Scrutton, *Thinking Through Feelings*, 38.
5. Lewis, *Grief Observed*, 8.
6. Mullins, *God and Emotions*, 28–29.

But the account is *not* incoherent precisely because there is a form of grief that has an intentional object and features a value judgment about lost goods that can fit the objective order of values. Grief can be something grounded in a *discernment* of real goods lost. It can involve a fitting experience of that loss. While neither God nor the blessed will be mired in the wallowing grief Lewis found so loathsome, this does not mean they will not grieve. The kind of grief attributed to God in the passage above is affectional, not passional. Human moral sanctification would entail the perfection of our disposition towards grief in this affectional sense, such that if the world God made contains *eternal tragedies*, the blessed would experience enduring grief.

Finally—and most tellingly from a Christian standpoint—Jesus experienced emotions, including grief. Consider his emotional response to the death of Lazarus and to the grief of those who loved him (John 11:33–36) and his weeping over the impending fate of Jerusalem (Luke 19:41). To suppose the blessed do not grieve tragic truths is to suppose that the perfection of their natures makes them *unlike* Jesus, even though Jesus, in his humanity, is the Christian model of a perfected human nature.

REJOICING INSTEAD OF GRIEVING

As part of a series of articles for *Church Life Journal* attacking universalism,[7] Fr. James Dominic Rooney addresses the problem of heavenly grief by arguing that the blessed should rejoice over what God has done for the damned rather than grieve. Rooney's approach relies on a distinctive version of traditionalism according to which the damned suffer eternally because they reject God, but they are not objectively cut off from God's love. Instead, God embraces the damned in the midst of their anguish. Hell, which results from persistent, hard-hearted rejection of God's grace, does not involve any objective separation between the blessed and the damned. The damned are *subjectively* cut off by their willful attitude, but objectively remain in the presence of God and the blessed.

To clarify this vision, Rooney invites readers to imagine reaching the border of paradise to witness an unfolding tragedy: your loved one stands at a cliff's edge, their back to heaven. In despair, they prepare to fling themselves into the abyss. You try to talk them out of it, assuring

---

7. Rooney, "Incoherencies of Hard Universalism"; Rooney, "Hell and the Coherence of Christian Hope"; Rooney, "Hard Universalism, Grace, and Creaturely Freedom."

them they are loved, that God waits with open arms, but they refuse to believe it.

Trapped by delusions and despair, they leap. You spring forward, seizing their hand before they fall. Now they dangle over the void, begging you to let go, insisting that your portrait of the joy that awaits is a lie. They can't or won't believe your contrary assurances.

How long do you hold on? According to Rooney, if you love them as profoundly as God does, you'd never willingly let go. Of course, as a finite creature you may not be able to hold on forever. But God is not so limited. God could and would hold on forever.

And this is Rooney's portrait of damnation: God holding onto the damned despite their rejection, "bringing them into union with Christ" despite the hopelessness or bitterness or hostility that twists their view of reality:

> And that union, the presence of God's love to them, is good for the damned—indeed, Gods presence to us is among the greatest goods—even if they do not perceive it as such. Their pain is not good in itself, certainly, but the damned (by definition) see the world wrongly—the damned perceive the Good Himself as hateful and painful. But God is doing something good; we should not trust the damned in their perception of whether their state is good for them.[8]

God does for the damned the best God can do given their persistent, delusional rejection of divine grace. And God never *stops* doing for them the best God can do. It is in the context of this understanding of the fate of the unsaved that Rooney offers his solution to the problem of heavenly grief. Rooney argues that the damned "are better off in the resurrection precisely because of being in union with Christ, since the damned are closer to now [sic] him than to themselves, an eternal scar within the Heart of Jesus. On the true scale of value, the divinization and glorification that the damned undergo is enough to defeat any evil that persists."[9] On this basis he concludes, "From the perspective of the blessed, the presence of the damned need not be a cause for sadness, but for rejoicing."[10]

---

8. Rooney, "Hard Universalism, Grace, and Creaturely Freedom," 11.
9. Rooney, "Hard Universalism, Grace, and Creaturely Freedom," 11.
10. Rooney, "Hard Universalism, Grace, and Creaturely Freedom," 12.

Rooney personalizes this perspective using, again, the example of someone gripped by suicidal despair who attempts to fling themselves into the abyss only to be seized by God and those among the blessed who love them:

> It is true that the desire your beloved has to throw themselves away is still there. Their pain sits inside and . . . their suffering might never fully go away. Yet . . . I know that they can feel me with them. Far from serving as an obstacle to keep us apart, that pain and brokenness is part of what keeps us together. You will never leave or let go as long as your beloved needs you—and you will need each other forever. From my perspective, being forever with someone I love and cannot now lose is cause not for disappointment by rejoicing. You sit, side-by-side, holding onto each other as the Sun rises.[11]

Note that for hell to be eternal on his view, the impulse towards self-destruction, the refusal to see God's grace for what it is, must persist forever. While the image of a sunrise suggests an end to the darkness, the question at hand is whether grief is fitting on the assumption that the lost soul's darkness never ends. Rooney's answer is that it is not, because God's love embraces them despite their eternal rejection and resulting misery, and because their torment bonds the blessed to them through their unending need for the comfort the blessed eternally give and the lost eternally refuse to receive. And these are reasons to rejoice.

The problem here is that "rejoicing" can be construed in two ways: as a total state of one's being, or as a specific response to a specific good. In the former sense, being in a state of rejoicing rules out grief and suffering. But in the latter sense it does not.

Suppose I learn my child was in a car wreck. I rush to the hospital, fearing the worst. Upon arrival I learn they are alive and their injuries are not life-threatening, but their spine is damaged. They'll never walk again. While I might rejoice over their survival, I would at the same time grieve over what they have lost.

Rejoicing over a specific blessing is not the same as being in an overall state of rejoicing and does not entail perfect joy. On the contrary, it can be paired with grief over specific losses that *preclude* perfect joy. Rooney's thinking turns on this ambiguity. Suppose my child is eternally damned despite being rescued from the abyss by God's power. Suppose

---

11. Rooney, "Hard Universalism, Grace, and Creaturely Freedom," 12.

they remain perpetually tormented by a despair that feeds their misperception, which in turn intensifies their despair in an endless feedback loop. They are here with me, in what for me is heaven. I provide what comfort I can. They weep and beg for it to end while I continue to hold them, tears streaming down my face.

Do I rejoice that they are with me and alive rather than swallowed up by oblivion? Perhaps so. But does that rejoicing exist alongside bone-jarring grief and anguish for their misery? If I love them, of course it does. That God is doing the best God can for them short of transforming their will in ways that allow them to see the truth means there is something to celebrate *and* something to grieve. There remains the pain of the eternal "what might have been"—even if they're with me and I can hold them through their misery.

DEFEAT OF EVIL

But perhaps this analysis leaves something out. At one point Rooney says that "the divinization and glorification that the damned undergo" by virtue of being drawn into Christ against their will "is enough to defeat any evil that persists." Does his idea that God's divinizing grace *defeats* hell's evils offer a basis for concluding that grief is unfitting?

To answer this, we must consider what evil it is that persists as well as what it means for evil to be defeated. With regard to the former, there appear to be two persistent evils associated with Rooney's conception of damnation: the eternal rejection of God's grace and the eternal subjective misery that follows. In terms of what it means for an evil to be defeated, I will assume Rooney has the standard sense of "defeat" in mind: something we would ordinarily consider evil taken in isolation, call it E, is defeated when it is an integral part of a whole that is better than it would be were E missing from it.

But it is important here to distinguish between two species of defeat in this sense: relative and absolute. A relative defeat of E obtains when, given some *other* evil, F, a whole that contains *both* F and E is better than a whole that contains F alone. But the *absence* of the whole containing both F and E would be better still. Only *granted* that we have to deal with F do we think having E is better than not having E. Criminal punishment offers a good example. Suppose Jack murders Jess and is caught, convicted, and sentenced to prison. Jack suffers from his lack of freedom.

Suffering is ordinarily considered evil. But in this case, *given* that Jack murdered Jess and the suffering is the product of a just punishment, the evil of the suffering is defeated.

What is *not* defeated is the evil of Jess's murder. *Given* the crime, we would rather have Jack be punished despite his suffering than forego his suffering and let him go unpunished. But it would be even better had Jack never murdered Jess at all. Just punishment defeats—in a relative sense—the evil of the perpetrator's suffering, but it does not defeat the evil of the crime. The whole that includes the crime and the perpetrator's punitive suffering is better than the whole that includes only the crime, but a world in which neither occurs is better still.

By contrast, an evil, E, is defeated *absolutely* when it becomes an integral part of a whole of such great value that it is better that the whole exist, even if that means the existence of E, than for E to cease to exist and with it this valuable whole. In this absolute sense of defeat, a world containing the whole of which E is a part is better than a world without it, on account of the value of this whole. The *felix culpa* doctrine exemplifies defeat in this absolute sense: a world in which humanity fell into sin and God redeemed us through the radical sacrificial love of becoming human and dying on a cross is construed, on this doctrine, as *better* than one in which humanity never fell at all. Similarly, Marilyn McCord Adams represents her account of God's defeat of horror as *absolute*: God builds up around horrors a whole of such value that we would rather have the whole (once we fully perceive its value), despite the horrors integral to it, than forego the whole and the horrors.

So what kind of defeat does Rooney have in mind with respect to the eternal suffering of the damned? His view seems to be this: *given* that some eternally reject God, it is better that God continue to love and sustain them and pour grace on them, despite the suffering that their delusional experience of these gifts produces, than that God stop bestowing these gifts.

For this picture to constitute a case of *absolute* defeat of evil, it would have to be the case that a world in which some eternally reject God's grace and suffer eternally for it is better than a world in which all receive the offered grace and none suffer . . . and it is made better *by* the fact that they suffer eternally. It would have to be the case that, while a whole free of both eternal rejection of God and eternal suffering is fine, even better is a world in which some forever reject grace and are forever in torment because of it—and the inclusions of their torment is what makes it better.

As implausible as I find it to be, I can imagine some Calvinists adopting such a view—on the grounds that a world eternally embodying God's retributive justice (by virtue of containing persons writhing forever in unmitigated anguish as a punishment for their never-ending defiance of God) is better than a world in which all created persons align their wills to God, love as God loves, and bring about a final state of unending joy for all. But Rooney (to his credit, as I see things) gives no indication of being this kind of Calvinist. For Rooney, God desires that all freely receive divine grace, and it is a tragedy that they don't.

As such, what we have is at best a case of *relative* defeat: the evil of their rejection of God's grace is not defeated any more than the evil of Jack's murder of Jess is defeated. Just as it would be better had Jack never committed murder, so it would be better had the damned not rejected God's grace. Undefeated evil remains. Hence, so does cause for grief. Creation is permanently vitiated by the damned's eternal rejection of grace and by the eternal thwarting of God's desire that all be saved.

But it is even worse than this. In the case of Jack, his suffering is an integral part of the whole that relatively defeats his suffering: the tragic state of things, given Jack's crime, is made better *by* his punitive suffering. But the tragic state of things, given human rejection of divine grace, is not made better by the suffering of the damned. Rooney does not endorse a punitive understanding of their suffering. For him, their suffering is a natural outcome of their tragic rejection of God. Given this tragedy, it is better that God keep loving them and sustaining what goods God can— their being if not their subjective happiness, Christ's union to them if not their reciprocal response. But the fact that God can't bestow all of the goods God wishes to bestow on the damned—the fact that they remain eternally miserable and isolated despite God's efforts—doesn't make their rejection of God's grace *better* than it would otherwise be.

Rather than the tragic state of things, given the damned's rejection of grace, being made better by their suffering, the tragic state of things is made better by God's continued bestowal of every good God *can* give. We have a bad situation made better by the divine infusion of goods, not a situation made better by something that would ordinarily be bad (suffering) having its badness defeated by the role it plays in making the whole better than it would be without it.

So, this isn't even a case of *relative* defeat. The tragic rejection of divine grace by the damned remains an evil to be grieved, *as does their eternal suffering*. What God's persistent love and grace accomplish in this case is not the defeat of these evils. What they do is ensure that there is no *more* tragedy than necessary.

And so we are left with my original analysis of Rooney's picture of damnation: there are things to grieve and things to be thankful for, given that God has done as much good as God can for the damned consistent with respecting their freedom. But both their misused freedom and the eternal suffering it produces remain tragedies that the blessed, perfected in love, would grieve.

SETTING HEALTHY BOUNDARIES

In *The Great Divorce*, C. S. Lewis envisions an encounter between a damned husband and his blessed wife. The husband wants his wife to suffer on account of him. He tries to evoke her pity, but she refuses to be held hostage to his misery. Though she strives to convince him to release the petty attachments that keep him from knowing joy, when he ultimately refuses to do so she spares him no grief.[12]

In a subsequent conversation between the narrator and his guide (a fictionalized George MacDonald), the narrator struggles with the wife's apparent indifference to her husband's misery: "Is it really tolerable that she should be untouched by his misery, even his self-made misery?"[13] MacDonald replies that the alternative would be to let the damned subject the saved to emotional blackmail:

> That sounds very merciful: but see what lurks behind it. . . . The demand of the loveless and the self-imprisoned that they should be allowed to blackmail the universe: that till they consent to be happy (on their own terms) no one else shall taste joy: that theirs should be the final power; that Hell should be able to *veto* Heaven. . . . I know it has a grand sound to say ye'll accept no salvation which leaves even one creature in the dark outside. But watch that sophistry or ye'll make a Dog in a Manger the tyrant of the universe.[14]

This story seems to offer a response to the problem of heavenly grief, to the effect that ongoing grief for the damned is unfitting because it conflicts with something a fully actualized human would do: namely, set up

---

12. Lewis, *Great Divorce*, 120–33.
13. Lewis, *Great Divorce*, 135.
14. Lewis, *Great Divorce*, 135–36.

healthy boundaries that include a refusal to be manipulated or have one's emotional buttons pushed by wicked and self-serving people.

But such a view conflates two things: on the one hand, the wife putting herself in the power of her corrupted husband, allowing him to manipulate her emotions in the service of his distorted agendas; on the other hand, the wife recognizing as genuine losses her husband's fall into depravity and misery and the consequent impossibility of genuine fellowship with him—in other words, recognizing these as real losses to be fittingly grieved.

Lewis is surely right that the woman should not pander to her husband's egoistic efforts to evoke pity or pretend that genuine fellowship is possible and enter a sham relationship that makes her vulnerable to exploitation and abuse. But if she wisely separates herself from him and, from that place of separation, considers the loss of what could-have-been absent his corruption—and if she grieves that tragedy, not as a reaction to his emotional button-pushing but as a recognition of what has been lost because of his folly, she would be expressing a disposition towards grief worthy of the blessed. Perhaps she shouldn't *share* her grief with him or give him the satisfaction of letting him see her tears. But that doesn't mean she shouldn't shed them.

Or consider a related response. A clever villain who understands the character of saintly people will be able to elicit predictable emotional responses from them precisely because there is a consistency to virtue. To have a virtue is to have a disposition to respond in predictable ways. Should I, in order to foil a villain's attempt to elicit negative emotional responses out of me, compromise my own virtue? Or should I, rather, grieve for murdered children because that is the morally fitting response even if that means a particularly nasty villain could "push my emotional buttons" by murdering children? Surely the saintly should not compromise their saintliness for the sake of foiling villains. And does it change things if those villains are in a position where the only people they can harm are themselves? When precious children of God are so in bondage to sin that they mire themselves in endless misery, that is a tragic evil. Those with morally perfected emotions will experience the negative emotions that fittingly track such evil, not strategically shut fitting emotional responses down for the sake of denying these tragically broken people power over them. On the contrary, if I compromise my virtue in an effort to avoid the negative emotions a villain's actions produce in virtuous people, it is *then* that I am truly giving the villain power over me, by letting questions about how to thwart the villain dictate my character rather than forming my character in relation to moral standards of fittingness.

But in a recent essay, Eleonore Stump invokes this fictional George MacDonald's speech in her own account of why God's joy would not be diminished by grief over the eternally damned. Insofar as her account invokes a human mother's response to her son's damnation, it applies both to God and the blessed. Does her account add something to or reveal something I have missed about Lewis's perspective that can explain why enduring grief over the damned is unfitting?

Her account features two responses to the claim that God would fittingly grieve for the damned. Both are framed within a non-universalist theology that sees the unsaved as preserved forever in existence by God for the sake of the value of their being, and sees their suffering and isolation not as something God imposes but as the result of their choice to rebuff God's grace, thereby eternally miring themselves in willed loneliness. Because God respects freedom, God honors these choices even though they bring ruin to the damned. Within this framework, Stump raises the question at the heart of the argument from heavenly grief:

> Would God not wish for the Jerome who could have flourished in his true self if he had surrendered to God's love? And if God did long for the Jerome who might have been, then would God not mourn over what Jerome actually is?[15]

Her first answer is to say that, if God longed "for the Jerome who might have been," the object of God's love would be "a non-existent person." God would "yearn for a merely possible person and feel disappointed to have gotten Jerome instead." This would conflict with God's love:

> To love is to desire the good for the beloved and union with the beloved. To wish that Jerome was replaced by the person he might have been is not to desire the good for the actual Jerome; and it is a rejection of the actual Jerome in favor of desire for the non-actual possible person.[16]

But is this right? If God or the blessed grieve for Jerome, they are not grieving for the non-existent Jerome-who-might-have-been. Rather, they grieve for the Jerome who is before them, the actual tragedy-ridden Jerome, *on account of* all the goods that Jerome might have enjoyed—the goods that might have been—had Jerome been less of a sin-addicted fool.

15. Stump, "God of Love," 5.
16. Stump, "God of Love," 6.

Had the potential for something far better not been possible, there would be nothing to grieve. We are grieving because Jerome's reality is vitiated, deprived of the goods for which Jerome was made. It is this *lost good*—which we grasp by discerning the vast gap between Jerome as he is and the Jerome-who-might-have-been—that is the occasion for our grief. Because we value Jerome's existence, his welfare, and fellowship with him, we grieve that he is vitiated by sin, miserable rather than rejoicing in union with God, and that real fellowship with him is unattainable. To wish for the Jerome-who-might-have-been is to wish, not that the real Jerome be swapped out, but that the real Jerome have the goods for which he was made. And if Jerome is eternally lost, the grief is for all the goods of which the real Jerome is forever deprived.

Stump's second response recognizes this, insofar as it addresses the worry that God would be "sad over the condition of Jerome as he is."[17] Here is where Stump turns to how Jerome's human mother, Paula, might respond to him, were he to reject Paula and make choices that mire him in darkness, making it impossible for Paula to have a relationship with him.

Suppose it is the Nazi era, and Jerome has joined the Gestapo. Stump readily acknowledges that Paula will grieve *during the time when there is still hope of redeeming him*: "She will hope against hope that he can be redeemed" and "will weep during this time, as Jesus also wept over Jerusalem, with the sorrow that comes while hope is still live but unavailing." But once hope of Jerome's redemption is lost, the time for grief ends: "Paula will come to understand that Jerome is what his choices have made him. . . . At that point, Paula will no longer want Jerome's company."[18] She will still love him, but her love will take the form of "compassion for Jerome at a distance." More significantly,

> These changes in Paula's desire of love for Jerome will not leave Paula in a state of heartbrokenness if Paula has woven her desire for Jerome into a deepest heart's desire for God. Interwoven in that way, Paula's love for Jerome will be situated within Paula's participation in union with God, shared with other persons who are also united to God in love. The loneliness Jerome has willed for himself cannot take away the joy of that shared union for Paula.[19]

17. Stump, "God of Love," 6.
18. Stump, "God of Love," 6.
19. Stump, "God of Love," 7.

There are some puzzling features of this response. The first has to do with the dynamic of grief. As Stump describes it, grief persists while hope persists, and ends when there is no more hope of preserving or recovering the goods that Jerome's choices have stripped away. But in our ordinary experience of grief, hope *mitigates* grief. It is when all hope is lost that grief hits hardest. Lewis did not experience the most crushing grief while he could still cling to the hope that his wife might beat the cancer. That came after she died of it. And his grief journey *out* of devastation was mediated by the gradual restoration of hope—hope not for the return of the life they had, but hope tied to the sense that she was not after all gone but persisted in a new form.

Hope offers consolation in the face of grief, and grief is worse when that consolation is gone. But Stump tells the narrative of Paula's grief as if grief were tied to hope's persistence, with the death of hope bringing the fitting end of grief. This is at odds not only with our experience of grief but with what grief *is*: the emotional experience of loss. Hope mitigates grief because it offers the prospect of loss being limited or overcome. Loss without that hope would presumably warrant *greater* grief because the loss is more complete.

But what about her deeper and more central point, that if Paula finds her deepest heart's desire in God—weaving her love for Jerome in with her loving union with God and with all those others united in love to God—then the "loneliness Jerome has willed for himself cannot take away the joy of that shared union"?

Stump is not proposing here anything like Craig's notion that the beatific vision will drive out all awareness of the damned. Paula, through union with God, does not cease to be aware of Jerome. On the contrary, she continues to love Jerome in and through her place of loving union with God. Stump's view is that, by orienting her deepest heart's desires towards God, Jerome's loss ceases to hurt even though she continues to love him.

But why is that? If God loves Jerome, Jerome's loss matters to *God*. Wouldn't Paula, by weaving her love for Jerome into her love for God, have in relation to Jerome a love that reflects the eternal thwarting of God's antecedent desire that Jerome be saved? Stump is right that Jerome's rejection of God "cannot take away from God and the others united with God the great good of love that is reciprocated." But the point is not that these goods stop being goods worthy of attending to with joy. The point is that the joy is tempered with real loss.

Consider again the speech by Lewis's fictional MacDonald, who repudiates the emotional blackmail whereby those who have locked themselves in a hell of their own making insist that "till they consent to be happy . . . no one else shall taste joy." Lewis lays out a choice between two extremes: a world where no one tastes joy, and a world where grief over eternally lost loved ones is done away with. But there is a third option: joy, real joy, that is nevertheless not perfect *because perfect joy would be unfitting given the reality of total and permanent losses of objective goods that matter to all who love as God has called us to love.*

Those who damn themselves—or, on annihilationism, commit metaphysical suicide—cannot take away the goods that remain: all those who have not damned themselves, who have found union with God and one another, who have actualized their potential through intimate union with God. But they take *themselves* away, and that is a real loss. They have vitiated God's creation by removing *themselves* from the blessed community (or from existence). The result is not abject misery for those who remain. That would be unfitting given all the great goods that remain. The result, instead, is an emotional response that fits the mixed state of things: inherently valuable persons eternally lost, combined with a community of persons who have found life's meaning and formed a community of love in and through God.

The argument is not that if the blessed let themselves grieve for the lost they will mire themselves in eternal misery and so allow the lost to hold all their joy hostage. The argument is, rather, that given non-universalism the joy of the blessed would be *disturbed* by a fitting grief for the lost. And so they would not be *perfectly* happy.

The fear of the lost holding the happiness of the saved hostage is ruled out by the very thing that ensures the blessed will grieve for the lost: the community in which the blessed are united with God and one another. Love is the greatest good, and union with God, who *is* love, is the only thing that can provide *eternal* satisfaction for creatures made by God and made for love. And so those who have that good cannot be held hostage through the kind of emotional blackmail Lewis asks us to imagine. But such a community of love in and under God *perfects* the blessed in love. Hence, their love extends to the lost and experiences their loss as tragic. The result is not that "no one else shall taste joy," or that the Jeromes of the world will "take away from God and the others united with God the great good of love that is reciprocated." The result, rather, is that the joy found in that great good will be laced with grief.

As we saw in chapter 2, Mark Doty characterizes his grief as the cathedral in which the whole array of human experience is housed, including joy. Stump's insight is that when God becomes our center, the object of our deepest heart's desire, the joy of union with our creator becomes that cathedral. But that doesn't mean no grief for the lost is to be found within its rooms.

DESIRES OF THE HEART REVISITED

Perhaps, however, there is something essential to Stump's argument we are missing. The language she uses to develop her case explicitly evokes the terminology employed in her masterful work, *Wandering in Darkness*. It thus makes sense to take a closer look at her effort there to apply her Thomistic theodicy to the loss of our heart's desires.

As we saw, the desires of the heart are, for Stump, things we set our hearts on other than what is objectively needed for human flourishing—specific goods we care so much about that our happiness becomes tied to them. Stump thinks having such heart's desires is part of what it is to be human. Even if "no particular thing valued as a desire of the heart is essential to a person's flourishing, human flourishing is not possible in the absence of the desires of the heart."[20] While *some* heart's desires are unfitting because of the inherent disvalue or triviality of what is desired, she sets these cases aside—and for our purposes we can as well, since our focus is on the heart's desires for specific people. And not only are people objectively valuable, but Stump holds that "only persons *ought* to be the deepest desire of a person's heart."[21]

Stump defines love for someone in terms of the desire for their welfare and for union with them (things that presuppose their continued existence).[22] As such, her account of love aligns with the one laid out and defended here. So how is love for a person related to making them the object of a heart's desire? It is possible to love someone without making them, their welfare, and union with them the object of our heart's desire. But *when* a beloved person becomes the object of our heart's desire, our flourishing is then tied to their existence, welfare, and the prospect of fellowship with them.

---

20. Stump, *Wandering in Darkness*, 431–32.
21. Stump, *Wandering in Darkness*, 439.
22. For a fuller account of her view of love, see Stump, *Wandering in Darkness*, 91–97.

PURPORTED SOLUTIONS: UNFITTING GRIEF

It is in such cases that grief over the loss of someone is most intense. Not only is an objectively valuable person gone, but we have subjectively tied our flourishing to their existence and welfare and the prospect of union with them. And so we experience a substantial blow to our welfare.

In the face of this vulnerability to suffering brought about by heart's desires, Stump does not endorse the "stern-minded attitude" that counsels eliminating all other heart's desires so that we *only* care about God and union with God—a view she rejects for a range of compelling reasons I will not recount here, except to note their convergence with a key point made in these pages: God loves all persons, (antecedently) desiring their welfare and union with them, and hence so should we. But given our finitude, we cannot love all in a deeply personal way. Hence, we should pair a general love for all with a deeper love for those we set our hearts on.

If those we set our hearts on are miserable, or we are denied union with them, we will experience that as the loss of our heart's desires. And we will grieve.

For Stump, such loss and grief pose a distinct version of the problem of evil. Since she will not dismiss this suffering as the effect of humans culpably refusing to adopt stern-mindedness, her theodicy has to account for the pain of lost heart's desires in some other way.

Stump finds the clue to such an account in the story of Mary of Bethany's loss of her beloved Lazarus. Had Jesus come in time to heal him, Mary would have been spared the grief of losing him. Instead, Jesus comes later and restores Lazarus to life. And this means her heart's desire is fulfilled in a new and more profound way:

> Lazarus is the heart's desire of Mary of Bethany. But when Lazarus is restored to her through resurrection, she has Lazarus as given to her by Jesus in love for her. After the resurrection of Lazarus, Mary loves Jesus in loving Lazarus, and she loves Lazarus in loving Jesus. What is new is not her love for Lazarus or for Jesus, but somehow the interconnection for her of these two loves. . . . When Lazarus is restored to her through the miracle Jesus does, Mary's love for Jesus becomes part of her love for Lazarus. Her heart is still set on Lazarus, but it is set on Lazarus as gift, as something given to her by a person on whom her heart is set in an even deeper way.[23]

When the person who is my deepest heart's desire gives or restores to me another of my heart's desires as a gift of love, the latter heart's desire

---

23. Stump, *Wandering in Darkness*, 443.

is "refolded" into the former. And when I make God the object of my *deepest* heart's desire, I align my subjective values with objective ones. To make God one's deepest heart's desire is an act of surrender in which "one gives oneself, together with all the other desires of one's heart, to the person from whom the other heart's desires are hoped for as gifts." But "such surrender is not submission" since "the loving nature of the person to whom one surrenders" makes it "right to trust that in surrendering one is not giving up the desire's of one's heart."[24] As such, the one who surrenders in this way

> will also trust that the God who loves him will give him the other desires of his heart, as God can, compatibly with his flourishing. The suffering stemming from the loss of what he desires as gift in relation of love with God is still suffering, but it does not destroy either the center of the web of desire for him or his hope to have the other desires of his heart.[25]

Two elements from this pregnant passage deserve note. First, we are to trust that God will gift us with the desires of our hearts *as God can, compatibly with our flourishing*. When the heart's desire is for the welfare of and union with a *person*, the "compatibly with our flourishing" qualifier is no impediment to God extending such a gift, since the welfare of the beloved and loving union with them are clearly compatible with our own flourishing.[26] Hence, we should trust that God will bestow this gift unless God *cannot*. On Stump's view, the lost are precisely those God cannot save. Their salvation depends on loving union with God, which *requires* a free response. The damned are those who eternally withhold that response.

The second thing to note in the passage is that the suffering of loss *will persist as suffering*—albeit a kind that doesn't break us. Stump elaborates on this point as follows:

> If a person loses or fails to receive a heart's desire in the process of deepening her closeness to God, she will grieve, because she has lost something that she had set her heart on. But, even so, what is at the center of the web of desire for her is *not* lost. Things do not fall apart for her; the center holds. And, because what is at that center is a perfectly loving God, even in grief she

---

24. Stump, *Wandering in Darkness*, 445.
25. Stump, *Wandering in Darkness*, 446.
26. Even if some pretense of union with a broken, miserable person incapable of real union is not.

need not, should not, abandon her desire for the heart's desires she lost or failed to have. . . . [B]ecause the person who is her deepest heart's desire is also perfectly good and loving, she can trust him to give her the desires of her heart, in one form or another, but recognizable still in their particularity.[27]

Stump summarizes her solution to the problem of heart's desires as follows: "The suffering that stems from the loss of the heart's desire is defeated not just by flourishing but also by the gain of the heart's desires, even if in a refolded mode."[28]

But what is the heart's desire of Jerome's mother, Paula? If she loves her son, that means she desires his welfare and union with him. In making Jerome an object of her heart's desires, she is attaching the deepest longings of her heart to these things—which is not unfitting, since Jerome's welfare and fellowship with him are objective goods. On Stump's account, Paula grieves for the loss of these heart's desires *until* she loses all hope for their fulfillment, after which she adopts an attitude of distant, compassionate love for the broken creature who will never be happy or capable of fellowship. Stump thus concludes:

> What might have been an active desire on Paula's part to have Jerome as an intimate part of her life will become an encompassing compassion, content to offer as much care as possible to a person who has walled himself off from love. In this shape, Paula's heart's desire for Jerome *can* be satisfied.[29]

But is this right? Paula's heart's desire was for Jerome's welfare and for fellowship with him. What she has now is not this heart's desire satisfied in a new way—in some refolded mode in which they are offered to her as a gift of God—but, it seems, something else altogether: a one-sided compassion for a miserable person incapable of reciprocating or benefiting from it. The very desires that, for Stump, define love for another person—desire for their welfare and union with them—are the things Paula will now *never have*. This looks like the *loss* of the original heart's desire, not its satisfaction in some new form. It is true, of course, that Paula has the joy of union with God and the blessed, and that Jerome can't destroy that or take it away. But still, on the portrait Stump paints in *Wandering in Darkness*, the "suffering stemming from the loss . . . is still suffering"

27. Stump, *Wandering in Darkness*, 449–50.
28. Stump, *Wandering in Darkness*, 450.
29. Stump, "God of Love," 7.

even though it cannot break her,[30] and hence "she will still grieve, because she has lost something that she has set her heart on."[31]

In short, as opposed to calling into doubt the conclusion we drew before, a deeper look into Stump's arguments in *Wandering in Darkness* only reinforces them: although the blessed in heaven cannot be broken by the eternal loss of their loved ones, the damnation of those loved ones means God cannot restore Jerome to Paula, and so cannot give her the desires of her heart—the desires for Jerome's welfare and for union with him—as a gift of love. The hope for this is forever lost, despite God's love and trustworthiness. And this is a source of suffering, a reason to grieve. It doesn't follow that Paula or others like her in heaven will be miserable. What follows is that there will be what Schleiermacher calls a "disturbing element" in their bliss. They will not be *perfectly* happy, because, despite all of heaven's joys, they will have suffered an eternal loss.

THE FITTING ATTENUATION OF GRIEF

But perhaps there is an argument lurking in Stump's account that has yet to be fully developed. Part of her story of Paula's grief is its attenuation and eventual disappearance. Even if the end of grief coinciding with the loss of hope is at odds with our ordinary experience of grief, the gradual attenuation of grief fits our experience well. Even if we never reach a point where all grief ends, most of us experience a process in which the *intensity* diminishes with time. Given eternity, would it eventually go away entirely?

And could such complete attenuation be *fitting*? If so, then while heavenly grief for the lost is fitting for a time, it is not fitting *forever*. At some point, it's time to set the loss aside and look forward. Isn't this the emotionally healthy thing to do? To grieve, but not forever?

First off, even if the attenuation of grief is in a *sense* "emotionally healthy," this judgment is consistent with denying that such attenuation is fitting. Dan Moller powerfully argues for this view. His central point is that grief's attenuation over time is not ultimately about some change that renders continued grief unfitting. Instead, grief impedes the business of living, and we have reasons to get on with life weighty enough that it makes sense for us to be equipped with an "emotional immune system"

---

30. Stump, *Wandering in Darkness*, 446.
31. Stump, *Wandering in Darkness*, 449.

that helps us recover from losses and "continue functioning in the face of trauma."[32]

But even if this is so, such a grief-attenuation mechanism has another effect: it "renders us unable to take in and register fully the significance of our losses."[33] He offers a range of reasons to think that "the emotions are part of the means by which we perceive value," such that resilience in the face of loss becomes "a form of benign—or at least adaptive—blindness."[34] As we recover from grief and move on, then, we adopt a kind of blindness in order to escape the pain of remaining fully aware of the truth. "Failing to recognize how great a good we have irretrievably lost," Moller says, "means we are to some extent deluded about our own condition."[35] Our emotional "resilience" confronts us with an unsettling fact: "We may thus begin to think of ourselves as less substantial, more superficial beings," Moller says, on account of "our inability to hold onto our concern for great goods once we have lost them."[36]

Moller's thinking here is supported by the experiences of a friend I will call Maggie. Maggie's husband was in prison. The grief she felt over their separation cycled in intensity relative to the occasional weekend trailer visits the prison system allowed. Her grief increased after each such visit before fading back again in the weeks that followed. Put simply, the weekend visits brought to the forefront of Maggie's attention the good of which she and her husband were mostly deprived, rendering the magnitude of its loss more vivid, thereby triggering a renewed surge of grief. The further removed she was from such reminders, the easier it was to operate as if the losses weren't there. It became easier to stop *attending* to the loss.

Absent reminders of what we've lost, our grief may eventually fade to nothing—not because time's passage makes grief less fitting, but because it makes the loss less vivid and so easier for our emotional immune systems to hide from view. On this account, we might still justify the process of grief attenuation as a concession to the limitations and imperfections of the world. But while making such concessions seems unavoidable in

---

32. Moller, "Love and Death," 310.
33. Moller, "Love and Death," 310.
34. Moller, "Love and Death," 311.
35. Moller, "Love and Death," 312.
36. Moller, "Love and Death," 313. For another argument that elaborates on and defends Moller's perspective here, see Cholbi, "Regret, Resilience, and the Nature of Grief."

this life, do we really want to transfer them to the blessed? Do we want to say that, were their disposition towards grief morally perfected the blessed would grieve the lost forever, but an attenuation of grief is nevertheless justified *as a concession to the limitations and imperfections of the blessed state*?

This is not a solution to the problem of heavenly grief but an admission of the problem's insolubility. The blessed must choose between imperfections: unmitigated happiness at the cost of being blinded to and emotionally disconnected from loss; or enduring grief in the name of being more substantial, less superficial beings who fully affirm the value of what is gone.

To these points we can add several observations from chapter 2. First, as we become more temporally removed from the death of loved ones, their absence becomes less novel, and so—given our propensity to focus on the new at the expense of the familiar—their absence more consistently slips our attention. Second, over time we drift towards new activities and practices we didn't engage in *with* the loved one. And so the business of living brings fewer reminders of loss, making it easier to *pretend* the loss never happened. Third, the grieving process involves a kind of reshaping of subjective desires and a development of new ways to satisfy needs and interests that once depended on the lost loved one. Hence, a range of losses associated with the loved one's death are replaced, diminishing the sources of grief. But only if we are fixated purely on *self-focused* losses will this dimension of the grieving process produce *complete* attenuation. For those with love's values, the most crucial losses persist.

The blessed will attend where it is fitting, not where novelty attracts their eye. They will *not* be inclined towards pretense. And they will not be self-absorbed. Hence, the forces that attenuate our grief will either not affect the blessed or will produce only partial attenuation.

But there is one more argument for grief-attenuation's fittingness I want to consider. In a recent article, Oded Na'aman suggests that some backward-looking emotions, like grief, are "rationally self-consuming attitudes."[37] The idea is this: with emotions like grief, how long one has grieved is part of the story of fittingness, such that having grieved to some extent already has bearing on whether continued grief is fitting. In other words, there can be fitting or unfitting *durations* of grief. Unfortunately,

---

37. Na'aman, "Rationality of Emotional Change," 245.

Na'aman merely suggests that this might be the case with grief without explaining why this might be so. Perhaps the reason is that losses have different finite magnitudes, and how much grief fits this magnitude will be a function of not just intensity, but duration. Grieve at a certain intensity over a certain length of time, and the total will add up to an amount of grief that fits the loss. Thus, there will come a time when further grief is excessive.

This view is interesting, but there are reasons to be skeptical. Consider again the case of Maggie, whose grief was revived by each weekend reunion with her husband. The visits actually reduced the *magnitude* of her loss: a separation featuring periods of reconnection is *less* of a loss than never-ending separation. If we accept the above picture of grief, the fitting duration of Maggie's grief should be *shorter* if she is allowed to have recurring visits with her husband for the rest of their lives than if she is denied the chance to ever see him again. And yet it seems clear that the recurring visits function to *keep her grief alive*. Given our experience with those who've lost spouses to death, we expect that if she knew the separation from her spouse were permanent, her grief would be intense at first but would fade with time. But with the *lesser* loss, what we expect—and in fact observe—is a pattern of resurging grief in the wake of every visit followed by a diminution to a level consistent with living her life. And this pattern remains steady and shows no signs of diminishing over time.

If grief is rationally self-consuming such that one reaches a point where one has grieved enough, then reducing the severity of the loss by allowing occasional reunions *should* make it emotionally fitting to stop grieving the loss sooner than would be true were such reunions denied. But Maggie's case inverts this result. And there is nothing unusual about this. We expect that someone who loses their spouse once-and-for-all will grieve for a time and eventually move on, whereas people in Maggie's situation will have ongoing cycles of grief.

One could, of course, explain this fact, not by rejecting Na'aman's picture of grief's fitting attenuation, but by accepting it and, on its basis, concluding that people routinely display unfitting grief patterns. But this is a problematic move if the *point* of positing that grief is rationally self-consuming is to offer an account of grief that shows a common dimension of our experience of grief—its eventual disappearance—to align with what is fitting rather than clash with it. This feature of Na'aman's account ceases to be an advantage of it if actual grief patterns clash with what is fitting on *both* Moller's *and* Na'aman's accounts.

Furthermore, Moller's account of why grief abates has the advantage of explaining not only why grief attenuates over time, even though attenuation is unfitting, but why we observe the pattern we observe in Maggie's case. In fact, Moller's account *predicts* Maggie's experience in a way Na'aman's account does not. On Moller's view, the recurring experiential reminders of what she's lost help Maggie retain a grief more suited to reality than would likely have occurred absent those reminders. Even with those reminders, her emotional immune system kicks in after each too-short reunion. Absent recurring reminders of the value of what's lost, there would be nothing to counteract the emotional immune system's work, which explains why we would expect Maggie's grief to eventually fade away if she could never see her husband again. It would abate not for reasons of the fit between grief and loss, but because her emotional immune system deftly leverages familiarity and pretense in ways that help her get on with life at the cost of blinding her to the magnitude of her loss.

A second concern arises if we apply Na'aman's concept of rationally self-consuming grief to the losses the blessed face on non-universalist theologies. Since Na'aman's perspective involves an abatement of grief *over time*, to apply it to the blessed we must assume they have a temporal existence, with a sequence of moments in which they grieve. A defender of grief's complete abatement in heaven could then argue that the eternal loss of any one soul is of finite magnitude, warranting grief of finite duration—and if this is true for one lost soul, it is true for all. Eventually, the blessed will have grieved enough.

But in assessing this argument, we need to keep two senses of "finite loss" in mind. On the one hand, the totality of goods possible in God's creation at any moment would be reduced by only a finite amount for each lost soul—such that the grief of the blessed at any moment would be fittingly finite and as such only a "disturbing element" to their bliss rather than a source of devastation. On the other hand, non-universalism treats each of these finite losses as permanent, implying a finite reduction in the totality of goods possible in God's creation *at each moment in the infinitely enduring lives of the blessed*. Given that what we are considering is an infinitely enduring finite loss, it does not seem that the blessed would ever have grieved enough to fit the loss. Instead, what seems fitting is that at any moment their grief should be merely finite.

Another way to think of this is to contrast the state of the blessed confronting eternal loss with the state of the bereaved in this life if one assumes death is the end. In the latter case, when you lose a loved one your loss at any moment is finite—and since your remaining lifetime is also finite, the total loss to you is finite overall. Arguably, you have two fitting ways to grieve this loss. First, you might experience the grief steadily over the course of your remaining days in a way that fits the degree of loss. Second, you might immerse yourself in grief for a comparatively short time, but grieve so deeply that your total grief fits the loss over the total course of your remaining life. The latter might be the better choice if your days are numbered and there are goods worth having that would be rendered inaccessible by ongoing grief. Immersing yourself in grief for a time would enable you to escape Moller's dilemma, allowing you to fittingly grieve *and* get on with life.

But this possibility depends not only on the finitude of the loss to you at any moment, but also on the finitude of the timeframe over which that loss applies. For the blessed, the same escape from Moller's dilemma would be achieved were universalism true, since then every loss would end in heavenly reunion. But given non-universalism, the blessed will face a finite loss at every moment of an infinite existence. Immersion in grief for a time will not enable the blessed to reach a point where they have grieved enough to fittingly set grief aside.

PERFECT HAPPINESS DESPITE GRIEF?

Jerry Walls, in *Hell: The Logic of Damnation*, responds to Schleiermacher's formulation of the argument from heavenly sympathy in a way that might be construed as a challenge to the incompatibility premise. Like Yang, Walls supposes that the blessed might share God's attitude towards the damned. Unlike Yang, he concedes that God's attitude towards the lost would include an element of suffering, in the form of "an attitude of regret toward the loss of happiness by those who refuse his love."[38] But this attitude is "not a feeling which could come to dominate the divine consciousness."[39] He thus makes a point similar to the one I made in response to Lewis's worries about emotional blackmail: "The very fact that God's attitude of regret is a moral attitude is what makes it impossible that God should be vulnerable to emotional manipulation.... God views rejection with an attitude of regret because he *wants* human beings to be

---

38. Walls, *Hell*, 108–9.
39. Walls, *Hell*, 109.

happy for *their own* sake. But he does not need them to be happy for *his* sake."[40]

One *might* read Walls's point here as equivalent to Yang's: God is wholly impassible, such that God's happiness is undiminished by how God feels about the lost.[41] But Walls makes important claims at odds with such a reading. Specifically, he suggests that "perfect happiness," applied to God, might not mean "that he could not be happier." Instead, "God's perfect happiness may inevitably include an element of suffering, or at least regret."[42] He concludes that "the blessed may share God's perspective and consequently share God's perfect happiness, a happiness which could be compatible with some element of suffering."[43] The view, in short, is this: God and the blessed, by virtue of their moral perfection, are indeed disturbed by the eternal loss of persons to whom their love extends. But this disturbance is *compatible* with their perfect happiness.

This sounds like a denial of the incompatibility premise. But a closer look at his thinking suggests otherwise. Walls says that "perfect happiness may not conform to our *a priori* expectations" and may be a "more complex matter" than thinking of it as a state in which one "could not be happier."[44] As Walls puts it, "Since God's happiness is the greatest actual happiness, accounts of perfect happiness which exclude all suffering may be conceivable, but strictly speaking, unrealizable."[45] In other words, assuming the truth of Walls's non-universalist theology, *the happiness of God and the blessed could be greater than it is and would be were universalism true.*

As such, the happiness of God and the blessed is not perfect in the sense of realizing the best state possible—namely a happiness *fittingly* free from grief and sympathetic suffering. Instead, it is perfect in a *relative* sense: the best state realizable *given the tragically imperfect final state of creation.*

But this relative sense is not what most Christians envision when they think about the perfect joy of heaven. The happiest I can be *given my circumstances* will hardly be "perfect" if my circumstances are imperfect

---

40. Walls, *Hell*, 109.

41. In an earlier reading of Walls, this is precisely the interpretation I attributed to him. See Reitan, "Eternal Damnation and Blessed Ignorance," 432–34.

42. Walls, *Hell*, 109.

43. Walls, *Hell*, 109.

44. Walls, *Hell*, 109.

45. Walls, *Hell*, 109.

and my level of happiness reflects this. If God and the blessed, given non-universalism, can only achieve "perfect" happiness in this relative sense, where having it means falling short of the joy that is conceivable (and would exist were all saved), the conclusion to draw is not that the argument from heavenly grief fails because the incompatibility premise is false. Rather, the conclusion to draw is that the argument *succeeds*.

In other words, the most plausible reading of Walls here is not that he has *solved* the problem of heavenly grief by giving reasons to think the incompatibility premise is false but, rather, that he *avoids* the problem by rejecting the doctrine of perfect blessedness as it is typically conceived (that is, conceived in terms of the *non*-relative understanding of perfect happiness).

Adam Pelser, however, offers a different reason to think that some negative emotions—including sadness and somberness—are compatible with the perfect joy of the blessed. He invokes an Aristotelian understanding of joy as *eudaimonia*, and uses a pair of concrete examples to support the thesis that some negative emotions might be a *constitutive part* of perfect joy—in a non-relative sense. He then concludes that if this is true, sadness over the fate of the damned might be a constitutive part of the joy of the blessed.

One advantage of Pelser's argument, for our purposes, is that it starts with the same basic understanding of human emotions developed here, in which emotions involve a direct experiential encounter with value. As Pelser notes, "Insofar as there is legitimate badness in the world, affectively negative or painful emotions enable us to perceive, know, and appreciatively understand that badness in all its variety and particularity."[46] He also argues that emotions properly attuned to values both guide and motivate moral decision-making.[47] For these reasons, he finds it highly implausible to imagine that the blessed would be free from negative emotions, since that would entail an epistemic or moral limitation at odds with blessedness conceived as a *perfected* state. Pelser holds that "we should expect that emotional experience of God's divine perfections and of the heavenly perfections of resurrected humans will be partly constitutive of the state of eternal joy Christians have traditionally associated with Heaven." But by the same token, "insofar as any negative realities exist to be perceived, known, or understood . . . the residents of

---

46. Pelser, "Heavenly Sadness," 118.
47. Pelser, "Heavenly Sadness," 118–19.

heaven will experience, know, and understand them by way of affectively negative emotions."[48]

And so, invoking considerations similar to those developed here, Pelser rejects purported solutions to the problem of heavenly grief that deny that the blessed experience negative emotions. Instead, Pelser proposes that there may not be any conflict between perfect heavenly joy and the negative emotions the blessed experience.

At one point in his essay, however, Pelser concedes that *some* negative emotions are "incompatible with the experience of perfect heavenly joy," and he explicitly mentions "intense grief" as an example. He thinks intense grief has a kind of "totalizing impact on our experience of the world" such that "experiencing even part of the world" in terms of such grief rules out "full, complete, perfect joy."[49] What he seeks to reconcile with heavenly joy, then, are negative emotions with a lesser impact, specifically "a kind of sadness, short of overwhelming grief" as well as "an emotion of somberness."[50]

Pelser's response to the problem of heavenly grief, then, denies that the blessed would experience overwhelming grief while acknowledging that they might experience a milder grief or sadness—something more like the grief Lewis describes in the latter parts of *A Grief Observed* rather than the devastation that consumes him at the start. Given what I have already argued in response to Stump and Rooney, I am prepared to accept this point. What needs to be accounted for is not a grief so intense it drives out the capacity to appreciate heaven's goods. After all, such grief impedes the capacity to fittingly experience positive emotions in response to genuine goods, which is not something the blessed would experience. My argument, rather, is that their love for the lost, granted the permanence of the objective loss that non-universalism posits, entails the fittingness of experiencing that loss in a way that diminishes joy.

So, I accept Pelser's point that the fitting grief of the blessed would not be an overwhelming grief. But it remains to be seen whether the fitting grief of the blessed would be limited to a sadness compatible with perfect joy. Even if Pelser can show that *some* form of sadness can be reconciled with perfect joy, this will not solve the problem of heavenly grief unless the grief that would be a fitting response to the eternal loss of the unsaved is *that* form of sadness.

48. Pelser, "Heavenly Sadness," 119–20.
49. Pelser, "Heavenly Sadness," 126.
50. Pelser, "Heavenly Sadness," 127.

When Pelser defines sadness, he does so in terms that conform to the account of grief developed here, as a "perception of the loss of something or someone that (who) is valuable and important," where the loss is not "merely temporary or still recoverable" but "relatively permanent or irrevocable."[51] He stresses that sadness in this sense "is valuable as an accurate perception of the value of persons and the disvalue of the loss of persons and of those persons' loss of relationship with God."[52] Thus, he believes that such sadness will be part of the experience of the blessed, granted non-universalism. His aim, then, is to reconcile perfect joy with the experience of sadness, while construing "sadness" in a way that overlaps with what I mean by "grief."

His first step is to concede that he cannot achieve such a reconciliation "if heavenly joy is essentially characterized by unending and uninterrupted affectively positive emotional experiences."[53] But Pelser thinks there is a better way to understand heavenly joy, one "more closely akin to Aristotelian *eudaimonia* than to the kind of ignorant bliss or emotional aloofness that is sometimes thought to characterize life in heaven." And Aristotle, Pelser notes, "argued that it is possible to suffer some pain and need without such suffering detracting from one's overall flourishing and happiness."[54] The idea here is that heavenly joy is not an endless stream of pleasurable states but "a state of settled pleasure in the understanding, activities, and loving relationships proper to heaven's existence."[55]

But even Aristotle concedes that a life in which one develops oneself into a fully actualized or virtuous person and finds pleasure in virtuous activity could be affected by misfortune—and if the misfortune is serious enough, "he will not reach blessedness" even if by his virtue he avoids misery.[56] It is perhaps for this reason that Pelser emphasizes that in heaven "most of the negative emotions we have reason to experience in this life will have no place."[57] Guilt, shame, loneliness, self-hatred, anxiety, and despair will all be done away with in heaven. What will *remain*, given non-universalism, is sadness over the fate of the lost.

---

51. Pelser, "Heavenly Sadness," 127.
52. Pelser, "Heavenly Sadness," 128.
53. Pelser, "Heavenly Sadness," 129.
54. Pelser, "Heavenly Sadness," 129.
55. Pelser, "Heavenly Sadness," 129.
56. Aristotle, *Nicomachean Ethics*, 1101a.
57. Pelser, "Heavenly Sadness," 130.

Pelser seeks to show that such sadness can be reconciled with perfect joy by exploring, as a kind of case study, the way Christians on Good Friday remember somberly and with sadness "the sacrificial death of Jesus on a Roman cross."[58] Such sad remembrance has positive value. It has positive epistemic value in that it helps to sustain "a deep, appreciative understanding of the significance of the crucifixion and resurrection of Christ," and it has positive moral value in terms of how it reinforces dispositions to experience positive emotions such as "proper gratitude for salvation, a humble sense of the undeserved nature of God's gracious forgiveness of their sins, and reciprocal love for Jesus."[59] These negative emotions are "partly constitutive of the full wellbeing of human creatures," insofar as they contribute to virtuous traits like a disposition towards gratitude and mutual love for God, which are essential components of joy.

Pelser concedes that his case for the compatibility of perfect heavenly joy with sadness rests in an important way on this examination of Christian observance of Good Friday. What this example does is "help lend psychological plausibility to this compatibility claim" since "it does not seem that the affectively negative emotional experiences at the heart of these observances must detract from an ideally joyful life."[60] In fact, I agree with Pelser about the Good Friday case: it features negative emotions, but these emotions look to be contributing parts of a flourishing life (in something like Aristotle's sense) as opposed to being detracting elements. The question is whether the same can be said about the sadness or grief that fittingly accompanies awareness of the permanent loss of some of God's beloved creatures.

There are important differences between the sadness that fits such a permanent loss and the sadness that fittingly accompanies reflection on Christ's passion. First, there is *no* sense in which Christ's crucifixion is the tragic end to *anyone's* story. It is, on the contrary, part of a broader narrative that culminates in triumph, and it is understood to be an integral part of that triumph. While it is sad that Christ's anguish was necessary, this sadness is situated within a story of victory and redemption: the *ultimate* good news. Christ's crucifixion and death might have been tragic if they had been the end of the story. But they are not. Instead, they are the means through which God triumphs over sin and death. We can fully

---

58. Pelser, "Heavenly Sadness," 130.
59. Pelser, "Heavenly Sadness," 131.
60. Pelser, "Heavenly Sadness," 131.

appreciate that triumph and its significance only if we properly experience the reality of what Christ endured for our sakes—by experiencing the negative emotions that fit this reality. This reality's role in securing the greatest happy ending in human history is surely part of the reason the negative emotions tied to its proper appreciation do not diminish our joy.

Were the suffering of those in hell *redemptive*—were hell's miseries the pain of a refiner's fire that brings repentance and reconciliation—then the negative emotions associated with reflecting on the fate of the damned would play a similar role as reflection of Christ's suffering. In each case, the negative reality would be part of a greater whole whose final chapter is joyous, and within which the suffering is defeated by its role in advancing God's redemptive aims. But on non-universalism, the fate of the lost has a different trajectory: being lost is the end of their story, their final tragic fate. It is one thing to suppose that negative emotions tied to the negative aspects of events with a triumphant ending can be integral to a perfectly joyful existence. It is something else to suppose the same is true for negative emotions tied to never-ending tragedy. However plausible Pelser's view in relation to the former, it seems highly implausible with respect to the latter.

Pelser briefly mentions the Jewish observance of Yom Hasho'a—the Holocaust Remembrance—as a potential analogue to Christian observance of Good Friday and another possible example lending credibility to his claim that perfect joy is compatible with negative emotions. He does not, however, walk through the Yom Hasho'a observance in the way he does the Good Friday observance, revealing how the pain of reflecting on the negative reality contributes to a more joyful life. And there is reason to be skeptical. Of course, *given* the reality of the Holocaust, *given* the magnitude of its evils, it is fitting to remember it and feel it in affectively painful ways. And *given* that such a horrific evil slashes through human history, someone who remembers it with sorrow and somberness is a better person, more in tune with the good, than someone who ignores it. But it doesn't follow from this that the pain of such remembrance doesn't diminish joy. Instead, what follows is that the upper limit of joy has already been dragged downward by the monstrous evil that occurred. In the face of this evil, there is more meaning and hence more joy in facing the evil squarely than in ignoring it or finding ways to be emotionally cold to it. But in this case, the sadness is defeated in a merely relative sense: given the Holocaust, it is better to reflect on it sadly and somberly;

but a world in which the Holocaust never occurred, and no such sadness was necessary, would be better still.

At least, that is, absent some promise of redemption, some theological narrative according to which God works to repair *even this*, and will in the fullness of time produce a final state in which the concerted efforts of the Nazis to crush the good and lift up hate are turned into so much fluff and froth, impotent to diminish the good and the triumph of divine love. Faced with a divine redemptive project that has the defeat of even the most horrific evils as its final end, a sad and solemn reflection on the evil of the Holocaust might well be compatible with perfect joy. In that case, reflection on the evil reminds us of its total defeat, and so is situated within a larger story in which *even the Holocaust* failed to diminish in any way God's creation. Given an emotional appreciation of the evils God has overcome, the greatness of God's accomplishments shine more brightly.

But non-universalism is precisely the doctrine that some souls, mired in sin, are never redeemed. Some persons—created for union with God, loved by God, possessed of the sacred dignity of personhood and the incalculable objective value that goes with it—are finally and utterly lost. This is the Holocaust *without* redemption, not a tragedy redeemed. Its existence in God's creation *lowers the ceiling of joy* by making perfect joy unfitting.

Another way to think of the failure of Pelser's argument here is in relation to his definition of sadness. Although he explicitly defines sadness in terms of the experience of the irrevocable loss of something or someone of value, the sadness over Christ's suffering and death on the cross does not count as sadness *in this sense*. There is loss here, of course, but the gospel narrative is a story about *restoration*. The sadness we feel when we reflect on Jesus' suffering and death is not sadness in Pelser's stated sense, since the Christian narrative presents those losses not just as temporary but as the means whereby God restores all things. The empty tomb speaks to the defeat of death and the losses death brings, just as the atonement testifies to the defeat of sin and all the vitiation of the good it can bring. We feel sadness over the sin and death in the passion story precisely so we can more fully grasp what has been restored by God's work.

Nothing like that is in play when we consider the Holocaust absent any promises of divine redemption; and nothing like that is in play when we consider the final fate of creation on non-universalist theologies. When we consider Christ's suffering and death, what we are considering is a sadness subsumed and transformed by the divine promise that what has been lost will be restored. That such *transfigured* sadness should prove to be compatible with perfect joy does not entail that un-transfigured sadness—where one experiences the *irrevocable* loss of something or someone of value—is compatible with perfect joy.

Pelser's discussion of Aquinas may, however, offer a possible answer to this critique. It is true that, given non-universalism, the loss of persons to sin and death is not redeemed or defeated through the ultimate repentance and restoration of the lost. But perhaps it is defeated in another way: through the *retributive justice* that attaches to what the lost endure. Perhaps this justice can transfigure our sadness over the fate of the lost in something like the way Christ's resurrection transfigures our sadness over his death.

Pelser embraces Aquinas's view that the blessed will feel no compassion for the damned, because the suffering of the damned in *deserved*, and "compassion involves construing the suffering of the sufferer as undeserved."[61] Moreover, Pelser accepts Aquinas's view that the blessed "will be able to see the suffering of those in hell through positive emotions insofar as their suffering is a good manifestation of God's justice and a reminder of God's mercy and grace shown to those who have received his forgiveness and salvation."[62] But Pelser rejects the idea that the blessed will experience no negative emotions in relation to the damned, since it is only through the emotional experience of hell's badness that gratitude for what God has rescued them from can be fully experienced: "non-emotional (or wholly painless) knowledge of suffering cannot do much, if anything, to increase emotional appreciation of contrasting blessedness."[63]

Pelser's idea, in short, is that the sadness the blessed feel as they confront the misery of the damned will contribute to their heavenly joy because the negative emotion will be tempered by an appreciation of the justice of what the damned endure and will help constitute the positive emotion of gratitude, which the blessed cannot fully experience apart from emotional awareness of the misery they've been spared.

One serious problem with this line of argument is that it presupposes that the damned deserve eternal suffering. This is an assumption I will critically assess and reject in the next chapter, and so I will not explore it here. Here, I want to raise two concerns. First, the fittingness of

61. Pelser, "Heavenly Sadness," 123.
62. Pelser, "Heavenly Sadness," 123.
63. Pelser, "Heavenly Sadness," 123.

compassion for the damned aside, is there any good reason to think that *sadness* over their fate will be transformed by its justice into a negative emotion that does *not* diminish happiness? Second, is it true that sadness over the fate of the damned will contribute to a blessedness-enriching gratitude for the divine grace that has spared the blessed a similar fate?

With respect to the first question, it is important to notice something about the structure of deserved suffering. As noted earlier with respect to retributivist justice as a means of defeating the evil of suffering, it is better that those who deserve to suffer get the suffering they deserve than that they escape it. But it would have been *better still* had they not come to deserve suffering in the first place. In other words, that a person has acted so as to deserve suffering is a reality with negative value, and their receiving the suffering they deserve does not erase that negative value. It is the *suffering* that has its negative value defeated by the fact that it is deserved, not the wrongful behavior. And behavior that renders someone deserving of suffering *diminishes* them—moving them further from the actualization of their potential, further from the purpose for which God made them. While rehabilitative or restorative punishment—the sort of punishment in which universalists generally believe—might help restore these losses, purely retributive punishment does not. In other words, even if we grant the retributive view of justice, what follows from this is that the negative value of the *suffering* is defeated by its being deserved. But the fact that someone sinned and failed to repent remains an undefeated evil: a diminishment of them and God's creation.

And this means that even if we grant that the blessed should not be sad about the *suffering* of the damned, there remains something the blessed should be sad about, something retributive punishment does not fix. This is especially obvious from the framework of a love ethic, where the one who deserves to suffer is the object of our love. If my daughter descends into criminality and commits murder, I might see punishment as deserved. But the imposition of that punishment won't erase the fact that the beautiful child I invested myself in and whose well-being matters to me has, through her choices, *vitiated herself* and threatened the conditions for her own flourishing. These are tragic losses, whatever we might think of the fittingness of the punishment she endures. And because I love *her*, these losses hit especially hard because it is *her* moral worth that has been diminished, *her* character that has been corrupted, *her* potential to be what God made her for that has been compromised.

These losses are an object of fitting grief that punishment, no matter how fitting, cannot erase. But what about the idea that gratitude for God's grace depends on the negative emotion of sadness over the fate of the damned? The problem here is that such a gratitude-enriching emotional awareness does not require that anyone be *eternally* damned. Emotional awareness of the bad state of those who reject God's grace, even for a *finite* time, is sufficient for us to appreciate what God's grace spares us (and, eventually, them) from: absent God's grace, *that* bad state would be *permanent*. Dwelling emotionally on the badness of this state gives us immense gratitude for the grace that ensures that it is *not* permanent.

Anyone being lost *eternally* is thus, relative to our capacity to experience fitting gratitude, a superfluous evil. Worse: it decreases what there is to be grateful *for*. If some are eternally lost, *that* is a bad state that persists despite God's grace, meaning *here* is an area where gratitude for God's redeeming grace is unfitting, since *here* is a place where God's redeeming grace fails to redeem. Emotionally experiencing the eternal loss of some of God's beloved creatures amounts, then, to an emotional experience whose degree of negative affect is superfluous relative to what is required to be grateful for God's grace and which, furthermore, drives home the limits of what we have to be grateful for. If we are perfected in love, we *would* be grateful for the salvation of these lost souls. But they are unsaved. And so we are confronted with a gratitude-that-might-have-been. This drives home, on an emotional level, the fact that there is *less* to be grateful for than we can envision.

And so I can only conclude that when it comes to the suffering of hell, only if universalism is true can sadness about the fate of the (temporarily) lost be subsumed and transformed by the joyful story of which it is a part, and so be rendered compatible with the perfect joy presumed to prevail in heaven.

8

Escaping the Problem

OVERVIEW OF THE ARGUMENT

IN THE PRECEDING CHAPTERS we have examined a species of argument that was first unambiguously invoked to challenge non-universalism by Schleiermacher in the nineteenth century.[1] Recent as the argument is, it has considerable force: there is clear tension between the standard Christian view of the blessed state and the doctrine of limited salvation. Schleiermacher casts the tension in relation to the doctrine of hell, but a major aim of this book has been to show that the tension is no less present for annihilationism.

When it comes to the doctrine of hell, sympathy for those who suffer would seem to disrupt heavenly bliss. But so would grief—and grief would have this effect even given annihilationism. The blessed would grieve because every person has inherent value. Perfected in love, the blessed would recognize and fittingly respond to this value by desiring for each person their continued existence, their welfare, and their fellowship. And they would grieve because each of the lost represents the eternal frustration of God's antecedent desire for their salvation. They would grieve because, on account of sin, reality falls eternally short of containing the full measure of goods that might have been. And they would grieve to the extent that people they love more personally—perhaps even the objects of their heart's desires—are among the lost.

---

1. Aquinas anticipates and so gestures towards this argument, if only to quickly dismiss it, in *Summa Theologica*, Suppl., Q. 94, Art. 1–3.

Despite this apparent incompatibility between non-universalist theologies and the doctrine of perfect blessedness, Christians have persisted in embracing both, invoking a range of strategies to try to solve the problem. But none of these purported solutions comes without cost. Some—such as Spiegel's "love-web" solution—come at the cost of constricting God's love in defiance of key scriptural themes. Others come at the cost of attributing imperfections to the blessed state.

For example, Craig's proposal that God shields the blessed from knowledge of the damned not only posits an epistemic imperfection among the blessed but entails that the joy of the blessed is based on a false understanding of the truth and hence is a kind of farcical celebration. Furthermore, to maintain this blessed ignorance, God would have to withhold part of the divine self from the blessed, reducing the intimacy the saved could enjoy with their creator. And if the blessed must be stripped of their memories of loved ones to be spared the grief of losing them, the cost of Craig's solution rises to intolerable levels. God would be sparing the blessed grief by inflicting on them a kind of eternal dementia.

Other solutions come with other costs. Some force us to choose between costs, such as the solution that posits the eventual abatement of grief among the blessed despite the difficulty of justifying the fittingness of such abatement. It seems, in this case, that the blessed must choose between letting grief fully abate at the cost of falling out of tune with reality or remaining in tune with reality at the cost of having their happiness permanently disturbed.

Still other solutions seem based on confusion—such as solutions that fail to distinguish between allowing others to hold you emotionally hostage and responding fittingly to tragic truths. Or solutions that treat heavenly joy as an all-or-nothing thing, thus making the false inference that, since joy is possible for the blessed even if loved ones are eternally unsaved, it follows that their joy would be *undiminished* by eternal loss.

Absent solutions more compelling than these, Christians who embrace both the doctrine of perfect blessedness and the doctrine of limited salvation will have to pay a significant price.

GIVING UP ON PERFECT BLESSEDNESS

While all of this implies that the problem of heavenly grief is a serious one for which an uncostly solution remains elusive, it does not immediately follow that Christians should become universalists. There are two reasons why. First, one might seek to escape the problem by rejecting the doctrine of perfect blessedness instead of the doctrine of limited salvation. Secondly, even if there are costs to every non-universalist solution or escape, this would be a reason to embrace universalism only if the universalist escape is the least costly option.

I begin by considering the first point. Should Christians be willing to relinquish the doctrine of perfect blessedness? Presumably, were we to do so, we would still insist that the heavenly state is worth having and better than any alternative. We might say, with Walls, that the blessed are perfectly happy in a relative sense, that is, in the sense of being as happy as is consistent with grieving the tragedy that some of God's creatures are eternally lost. But we would give up the idea that it is a perfect state.

This escape has costs. If universalism is costly because it parts with the majority tradition, then rejecting perfect blessedness offers no advantage on this front. And while both escapes require setting aside mainstream traditional teachings, escape by embracing universalism amounts to conceding that God is even more successful in achieving God's loving aims than the majority tradition has held. Escape by rejecting perfect blessedness entails God is even less successful than the majority tradition has held. All else being equal, if one must choose between two escapes that require us to set aside traditional teachings, one of which takes God to be more successful and the other less successful than the tradition has held, the latter is clearly more costly.

Second, this solution does not merely give up on the doctrine of perfect blessedness but gives up on it by introducing *grief* into the heavenly state. But this appears to directly contradict a scriptural passage that has the form of a promise, a passage whose plain sense is as clear as it is comforting: in the end, God will wipe away every tear, and there will be no more grief. To abandon this promise is to let go of one of Christianity's greatest comforts in the face of this world's tragedies. Universalism, by contrast, puts no qualifiers on divine promises, no amendment of the form, "Scripture's promise here is not *really* as good as it sounds." Again, all else being equal, this renders universalism a less costly escape.

Even so, some may find themselves drawn to this escape in the light of the following fact: some of the most meaningful moments in our lives feature grief. When my father died, those who loved him best gathered around the dining room table in my childhood home. We drank wine from the little wine cellar he had stocked and curated, wines he would have served had he been alive. We told stories about him.

And it was like he was there.

In music theory, they speak of how the vibrations of two notes played together interact to produce a third: a sympathetic vibration we can hear even though it isn't played. The dinner table that night was like that. My father was there among us like a sympathetic note, and it was among the most beautiful moments of my life. Arguably, my grief imbued that moment with a resonant meaning it wouldn't otherwise have had. As my father's absence intensified our appreciation of what he was to us, all the moments of joy around that table—moments in which my father was present—came together like a knot in time.

If the eternal loss of some of God's creatures were like this, one might be tempted to think it a bearable cost, even a mixed blessing in the sense of having implications that are both positive and negative for our eternal lives. But *would* heavenly grief over the unsaved be like this? Arguably, that dinner would not have been what it was absent the numinous sense that my father *wasn't* forever ripped from the community of those who loved him. The joy we felt sprang, I suspect, out of *the synthesis of grief and hope*: the sense of a presence beyond death, of a meaning that transcends the blind forces of the physical world. Even those at the table with no spiritual beliefs felt it, this thinning of eternity's veil, this glimpse of the numinous made visible by our tears. For them it may have been a nameless beauty, but for me it was a crack through which the hope of redemption poured.

If the unsaved are lost eternally, no such transfiguring hope could turn grief over their loss into a source of unexpected wonder and joy. Anyone who looks to experiences like mine and sees in them a way to minimize the costs of relinquishing the doctrine of perfect blessedness may not be relinquishing that doctrine after all. Instead, they may be courting Pelser's idea that the right sort of grief can *contribute* to perfect blessedness. But if the kind of grief I experienced with respect to my father did that, it is because the grief opened something in me that allowed in hints of God's Great Day, offering intimations of a perfectly joyous ending to the story. Heavenly grief could do *that* only if universalism is true.

Furthermore, all who gathered to mourn my father came together to remember someone fundamentally oriented towards the good, a man who had actualized much of his potential and formed bonds of rich fellowship with each of them. I doubt the blessed will need to grieve losses of *this* kind, even if non-universalism is true. If they do—if, as some theologies would have it, God presides over a reality in which good people are lost eternally because they had the misfortune of living and dying as, say, devoted Sikhs who never explicitly accepted Jesus as savior—the problem of heavenly grief is magnified to such astonishing heights I can only imagine that heaven is a place of wailing and gnashing of teeth.

Let us set this view aside, and suppose that the ones eternally absent will be more like a beloved child who dies of an overdose after a years-long descent into self-absorption, criminality, and drug-induced escapes. Her potential squandered, her relationships broken—perhaps cut off as a final desperate act of tough love that failed to motivate reform—she is now dead. When her loved ones gather around the table, what will they feel? If they believe in a God of love and mercy, perhaps they might still hope that, where they failed to save her, God will find a way. But absent that hope? What then? Could their grief be anything but a disturbance to their happiness as opposed to a crack through which God's redeeming promises pour?

If we assume the unsaved are lost eternally, the grief of the blessed who love them will be untethered from redeeming hopes. It will be a grief in which the commiseration and condolences of other blessed souls will always be available, but also always *necessary*. If such a grief is part of heaven, then the plain meaning of the Revelation promise must be set aside.

COSTLY UNIVERSALISM?

Still, none of this favors universalism if, as many argue, universalism is as costly as any non-universalist pathway out of the problem.

Critics of universalism point to many purported problems. Some, rooted in confusion, can be set aside quickly. For example, there is the worry that universalism undercuts the Christian concept of salvation, since salvation conceptually requires that there be something we are saved *from*.[2] But universalists needn't deny that we are saved from something terrible. If a rescue team saves everyone on a sinking ship, the significance of what the rescuers have accomplished isn't *reduced* by the total success of their efforts. What makes the rescue significant is that, *absent rescue*, those aboard would have drowned. The complete success

---

2. Jerry Walls expresses a worry along these lines. See Walls, *Hell*, 6–7.

of the rescue amplifies its significance by sparing the saved such things as grief and survivor's guilt.

Or consider the idea that universalism undermines the Christian faith by implying that Christ's atoning work is pointless. This is a confused idea because *Christian* universalism holds that God saves all *through* Christ's atoning work. It disagrees with Christian non-universalism on *how many* are saved by Christ's work, *not* on whether that work has a point.

Others may worry that universalism undercuts any reason to evangelize, presumably because they see evangelism as aimed at saving people from damnation or annihilation. If all are guaranteed salvation, what's the point of that? But Christian universalists need not hold that unrepentant sinners face no painful post-mortem consequences. They need only hold that these consequences are not eternal. Even if all are *ultimately* saved, there is good reason to urge the unrepentantly wicked to change course if, absent doing so, they must endure a finite hell.

More important, however, is the fact that evangelism is better conceived, not as warning people of dire consequences should they fail to take action, but as sharing good news. On this view, evangelism is like letting people in bomb shelters know the war is won and no more bombs are falling. The reason to spread such news isn't that those who fail to hear it will get blown up by the bombs that aren't falling anymore. The reason is, first, that such news is something to celebrate *in itself*, as in when a couple joyfully announces the birth of a child, and second, that hearing such good news will spare people needless fear.

These purported problems with universalism, then, turn out to be pseudo-problems. But others are more substantive. In what follows, I will consider what strike me as the three most significant: the worry that universalism fails to reflect divine justice and holiness, the worry that it is unbiblical, and the worry that it fails to honor human freedom. I cannot *fully* explore these worries here. What I can do is offer reasons to think they are less serious than most non-universalists presume, and hence, that universalism is less costly than generally assumed. My aim, then, will be to motivate a more serious consideration of universalism as a potential pathway out of the problem of heavenly grief.[3]

---

3. For those interested in a more detailed and systematic defense of Christian universalism in the light of a range of challenges, see Kronen and Reitan, *God's Final Victory*.

DIVINE JUSTICE, HOLINESS, AND UNIVERSALISM

Divine justice would impede God's desire to save all only if we accept two things. First, we must accept that justice demands punishment proportional in severity to the gravity of an offense, and that this demand is not contingent on the *forward-looking* goods that such proportional punishment pursues (such as moral reform) but is intrinsically fitting even if nothing further is achieved. Second, we must take human sin to be infinitely grave and hence as demanding infinitely severe punishment.

If proportional punishment depends for its justification on a forward-looking aim like moral reform, eternal punishment that never achieves this aim would be pointless and hence unjustified. And if punishment of merely finite severity can meet the demands of justice with respect to human sin, then God could meet the demands of justice in a finite timeframe. If any remain unsaved, it would be for reasons other than because justice precludes their salvation.

So let us suppose that justice demands proportional punishment because it is intrinsically good; and let us also suppose, with Anselm, that human sin is infinitely grave.[4] Even granted these assumptions, Christians who seek to justify non-universalism by appeal to the demands of justice face problems. Anselm does not just hold that human sin is infinitely grave because it offends against God, a being of infinite majesty and worth. He also holds that by virtue of this infinite gravity, humans alone *cannot* meet the demands of justice. For Anselm, this is because justice demands that the offending party (humans) make recompense to God for the offense—and humans are simply incapable of doing this.[5] Even if we focus on punishment alone and not compensation, there is a deep problem: finite humans can only endure so much hardship at any moment. Even if punishment is meted out over infinitely many moments, one would never reach the end of this sequence and so never reach a point at which the punishment fits the offense. As Stephen Kershnar puts it, "the amount of suffering a person has undergone is a cumulative property had at a time and there is no time at which a person has had an infinite amount of it."[6]

Since Anselm believes humans cannot satisfy the demands of justice, he concludes that the infinite gravity of sin requires that justice—not

---

4. Anselm, *Why God Became Man*, 305–7.
5. Anselm, *Why God Became Man*, 307–9.
6. Kershnar, "Hell and Punishment," 116.

merely divine love and mercy—calls for a *vicarious* atonement. And so, Anselm argues, God becomes incarnate in Christ and pays the penalty for human sin on our behalf. Being fully human, Christ can stand in for human sin. Being fully God and so a being of infinite worth, Christ's suffering has the infinite significance required to satisfy an infinite demand.

If Christ's vicarious atonement doesn't meet the demands of justice for every sinner, what follows is that justice simply *cannot* be met. This is why the Lutheran Orthodox insisted on the doctrine of *objective justification*—that Christ objectively met the demands of justice on the cross, and all that remains is for us to subjectively appropriate the benefits of that justification. Put metaphorically, the king has granted clemency to every prisoner, unlocked every dungeon door, and declared the prisoners free to go. All that is left is for them to get up and leave. If this is right, the demands of justice no longer impose an impediment to salvation. They have been met on the cross—in fact, that is the only way they *could* be met. And so, if any are unsaved, it is for reasons other than what justice demands.[7]

Some will argue, however, that the vicarious atonement is *applied* only to those who appropriate it through faith in Christ. Those who don't are justly punished eternally. But if the vicarious atonement only succeeds in meeting justice's demands when it is subjectively appropriated by sinners through faith, it follows that with respect to those who don't so appropriate it, even if they are punished eternally, the demands of justice will never actually be met, and the work of Christ will eternally fall short of achieving its aims. Unless, of course, everyone eventually appropriates the merits of Christ's work. In short, on this view of things it is only if all persons eventually appropriate Christ's work through faith that the demands of justice are actually met—making universalism *less* problematic than non-universalism from the standpoint of justice. Non-universalism falls short *both* with respect to satisfying God's desire that all be saved *and* with respect to justice.

Some suggest that annihilationism avoids these concerns because, unlike eternal damnation, annihilation is imposed all at once. It is a completed punishment the moment it is inflicted—similar to the difference between imposing the death penalty and locking someone in prison for life. As such, annihilation can accomplish what eternal damnation

---

7. For a fuller development of these arguments and ideas, see Kronen and Reitan, *God's Final Victory*, 116–23.

cannot, namely meet the demands of justice.[8] But even if true, this succeeds only in showing that annihilation is a proportional punishment, not that humanity has paid the debt it owes to God—what Anselm takes to be a key a demand of justice. Furthermore, annihilation will be a proportional punishment only if either sin is less than infinitely grave or annihilation is infinitely severe. But if sin were less than infinitely grave, God could meet the demands of justice without annihilating the sinner. Hence, annihilationism can avoid these problems only if annihilation is an infinitely severe punishment that, unlike eternal suffering, can be inflicted all at once.

But annihilation seems, intuitively, less severe than eternal damnation. If eternal damnation cannot meet the demands of justice, how could a less severe punishment do so? And it's hardly clear that annihilationism avoids the need for a temporally infinite sequence of punitive moments. As a finite being, to be deprived of my being is only a finite loss unless that deprivation is extended over an infinite sequence of moments. If this is right, then to be infinitely severe my annihilation must extend over an infinite series of moments—at any one of which God could presumably restore my being, resulting in a punishment of finite severity.[9]

But let us set all of these problems aside and suppose that, through hell or annihilation, the infinite demands of justice can be met. Even so we face the following fact: if Christ has met the demands of justice vicariously on our behalf, either objectively in the way Lutherans hold or conditional on appropriation through faith, what distinguishes the saved from the unsaved will be how they respond to God's grace. It is no longer the demands of justice *as such* the preclude the salvation of all but rather the failure of some to make the subjective free choices that allow Christ's saving work to be applied to them. So the question becomes, not whether universalism is compatible with justice, but whether it is compatible with God's respect for human freedom.

But what about divine holiness? Here, the purported impediment to the salvation of all is the fact that God is so holy that God cannot endure sin's presence. But quick reflection should make it clear that divine holiness poses a more serious challenge to the traditional doctrine of hell than it does to universalism. On the traditional doctrine, the unsaved exist forever but are permanently cut off from God and from the grace

---

8. See Spiegel, *Hell and Divine Goodness*, 48–49.

9. For a fuller development of these arguments, see Reitan, "Is Annihilation More Severe Than Eternal Conscious Torment?"

necessary to overcome their own sinful habits and dispositions. They are thus eternally mired in their sinfulness, at least in terms of the orientation of their wills, even if they can never again act on their sinful inclinations.

If God is truly holy and pure, the eternal persistence of such sinful dispositions—of wills opposed to God and the good—is an affront to God's purity. And if everything that exists does so through God's sustaining power, God is never *wholly* absent from the damned. And so, if sin is an intolerable affront to God's holiness, traditionalism faces a serious problem: God must eternally endure the never-ending sinful wills of the damned.

This is a problem that both annihilationism and universalism *avoid*—annihilationism because sinners and their sinful wills are destroyed, universalism because all eventually receive moral sanctification. On neither universalism nor annihilationism must God endure sin's persistent existence. That problem only arises for the doctrine of hell.

UNIVERSALISM AND SCRIPTURE

Whether we think something is biblical will depend on our account of the nature and purpose of Scripture and our interpretive hermeneutic—what we might call our "theory of Scripture." An adequate exploration of alternative theories of Scripture, with the aim of determining which is right, would require far more space than I can offer here. Fortunately, something more modest is sufficient. My aim in this chapter is to show, not that universalism is *true*, but that the purported problems with universalism are less weighty than many take them to be. To accomplish that in relation to the charge that universalism is unbiblical, it is enough, I think, to show three things: (a) there are scriptural passages and themes that favor universalism; (b) passages and themes invoked to support non-universalism are not unequivocally non-universalist; and (c) it is possible to construct a coherent reading of Scripture that is universalist while offering a meaningful place for the purportedly non-universalist passages and themes.

If (a)–(c) are true, one can hardly say that universalism is *clearly* unbiblical, even if a final determination of which theology best fits Scripture depends on a deeper plunge into the theory of Scripture than can be pursued here. But are (a)–(c) true? Here again, I can offer only a sketch of ideas and arguments developed more fully elsewhere.

With respect to (a), it is worth laying out scriptural passages that favor universalism on their most straightforward reading. My point here is to identify passages that favor universalism, not claim that non-universalist readings are impossible. With that in mind, consider each of the following:

Lamentations 3:22, 31–33: "The steadfast love of the Lord never ceases, his mercies never come to an end. . . . For the Lord will not reject forever. Although he causes grief, he will have compassion according to the abundance of his steadfast love; for he does not willingly afflict or grieve anyone."

John 12:30–32: "Jesus answered, 'This voice has come for your sake, not for mine. Now is the judgment of this world; now the ruler of this world will be driven out. And I, when I am lifted up from the earth, will draw all people to myself.'"

Romans 5:18–19: "Therefore just as one man's [i.e., Adam's] trespass led to condemnation for all, so one man's [i.e., Christ's] act of righteousness leads to justification and life for all. For just as through the one man's disobedience the many were made sinners, so through the one man's obedience the many will be made righteous."

Romans 11:25–26: "I want you to understand this mystery, brothers and sisters, so that you may not claim to be wiser than you are: a hardening has come upon part of Israel until the full number of the gentiles has come in. And in this way all Israel will be saved."

Romans 11:32: "For God has imprisoned all in disobedience so that he may be merciful to all."

1 Corinthians 15:22: "For as all die in Adam, so all will be made alive in Christ."

1 Corinthians 15:28: "When all things are subjected to him, then the Son himself will also be subjected to the one who put all things in subjection under him, so that God may be all in all."

Colossians 1:19–20. "For in him all the fullness of God was pleased to dwell, and through him God was pleased to reconcile to himself all things, whether on earth or in heaven, by making peace through the blood of his cross."

The plain sense of these passages—that God *will* save all, that through Christ God *will* achieve the reconciliation of the world—is reinforced by some broader scriptural themes. Again, my point in identifying these themes is to call attention to elements of Scripture that favor universalism, not to claim that non-universalist readings are impossible.

Consider first the synthesis of the recurring themes in Scripture that God desires the redemption of all and that God achieves what God desires.[10] With respect to the former, consider not only 1 Timothy 2:3–4 but 2 Peter 3:9 (which states that the Lord does not want "any to perish but all to come to repentance") and Ezekiel 33:11 (which affirms God's desire "that the wicked turn from their ways and live"). With respect to the latter, consider Isaiah 46:10–11, where we find God "declaring the outcome from the beginning and from ancient times things not yet done, saying, 'My purpose shall stand, and I will fulfill my intention,'" and we hear the unequivocal pronouncement that "I have spoken, and I will bring it to pass; I have planned, and I will do it." This message is reinforced by such texts as Ephesians 1:11 and Job 42:2.

If we accept these two themes in tandem, what follows is that God saves all. Why? Because God wants to save all, and God gets what God wants.

Consider another pair of recurring scriptural themes that together support the same universalist conclusion: the theme that all those who declare Christ as Lord and Savior will be saved, and the theme that ultimately all will do exactly that. With respect to the former, the most obvious support comes from the luminous verse in the Gospel of John: John 3:16. With respect to the latter, we find God's declaration, in Isaiah 45:23, that "To me every knee shall bow, every tongue shall swear," a declaration Paul picks up on in Philippians 2:9–11, where he says that "at the name given to Jesus every knee should bend, in heaven and on earth and under the earth, and every tongue should confess that Jesus Christ is Lord, to

---

10. Thomas Talbott thus notes that there is a tension between three propositions, all of which appear to have biblical support on a straightforward reading of Scripture: the two "recurring themes" I mention here and non-universalism. See Talbott, *Inescapable Love of God*, 38.

the glory of God the Father." Paul here takes the divine pronouncement in Isaiah, that all will bow and confess before God, to be fulfilled when all bow at the name of Jesus and confess that he is Lord. Paul reinforces the universal scope of this message by stressing that it extends to all "in heaven and on earth and under the earth."[11] Looking at these texts, it certain *seems* as if Paul believes that *all* will ultimately bend their knee before Christ and confess him as Lord—a belief that arguably undergirds his confident declaration, elsewhere, that *all* will be made alive in Christ.

But how can this be? What about the verses that declare that God will distinguish between the righteous and the unrighteous, and that for those who have put themselves in defiance of God's goodness there will be wailing and gnashing of teeth as they are thrown out of the kingdom of God (Luke 13:28)? What about Jesus' assertion that all people will be gathered before the Son of Man, and that he will separate them into two groups, those who cared for people in need and those who didn't, and he will send the latter into "the eternal fire prepared for the devil and his angels" (Matt 25:41), which will be for them an "eternal punishment" (Matt 25:46)? What about the dire Revelation account of the fate of the Beast's worshippers—the "torment with fire and sulfur" (Rev 14:10), with the smoke of their torment rising "forever and ever" and the grim promise that they will have "no rest day or night" (Rev 14:11)? Or 2 Thessalonians 1:8–9, which takes the fate of those who don't know or obey God to be "eternal destruction" and separation from God?

The difficulty is that Scripture has passages and themes that lend themselves to both universalist and non-universalist theologies. Christians who seek to construct a theology consistent with Scripture must make sense of the tension. The most common approach, historically, has been to take the non-universalist texts and themes at face value and then interpret away universalist passages and themes to make them fit with non-universalism. For example, some thinkers argue that when Paul says that "For as all die in Adam, so all will be made alive in Christ," he means the first "all" in the conventional and natural sense that applies to everyone—but uses the second "all" to mean something different. F. F. Bruce,

---

11. There are readings of this text that resist its universalist implications by denying that the *kind* of bowing and confession is in every case the sort that brings salvation. For a discussion of these readings and reasons to favor the universalist one, see MacDonald, *Evangelical Universalist*, 97–100.

for example, claims the latter "all" means "all without distinction rather than all without exception."[12]

In his commentary on this, philosopher Keith DeRose notes that this "all without distinction" idea is generally unpacked in terms of the various groups or classes of humanity, with the idea being that when Paul says all are saved he means that members of all groups, without distinction, have representatives among the saved.

DeRose minces no words in dismissing this interpretation. He invites us to imagine a "slippery character" under legal investigation who is asked to hand over all files related to the case. When it's learned he handed over only half the files, he justifies his actions using Bruce's distinction:

> Well, I handed over several files from each of the 10 major categories into which they fell. And I didn't just pick the least damaging files to hand over. Rather, I picked in a random fashion the files I would hand over from each category, so that each file, regardless of its category, and regardless of how damaging it was to my case, had a chance to be handed over. So, you see, I really did hand over all the files—all without distinction, that is; not, of course, all without exception.

DeRose thinks this justification is utterly untenable:

> This won't fly, precisely because "all" just can't mean anything like what the "all without distinction" crowd says it sometimes means. My reaction, at least, is not that this fellow was being deceitful merely in using one sense of "all" while it has another good sense. He's worse than that: There's *no* good sense of "all" that would make true his miserable lie.[13]

By the same logic, when Revelation 21:4 tells us that every tear will be wiped away, maybe it means "every" tear without distinction, not every tear without exception: while there will be *loads* of tears in heaven, *some* tears from every *class* of tears (sentimental tears, tears over fictional stories, tears of grief) will be wiped away. And so, while it is true that the blessed in heaven will be weeping eternally in grief over the lost, it remains true that all tears are a thing of the past—all tears without distinction, of course, not all tears without exception.

To these concerns we might add that, even if there were this peculiar sense of "all," we ignore the obvious parallel between "all" who die in

---

12. Bruce, *Letter of Paul to the Romans*, 211.
13. DeRose, "Universalism and the Bible," sec. 3, para 3.

Adam and "all" who are made alive in Christ if we treat the latter "all" as meaning something *different* from the former.

But as strained as this reading of the Pauline universalist passages might be, the basic strategy—of looking for a coherent and plausible way to read the conflicting scriptural passages that makes the conflict disappear—makes good sense. In pursuing it, we may need to consider the original languages in which the Scriptures were written. Robin Parry, writing as Gregory MacDonald, does just this in his explication of 2 Thessalonians 1:8–9:

> The Greek simply says, "they will be punished with eternal destruction *from* (*apo*) the presence of the Lord." The word *apo* could be translated as "away from" . . . or "coming from," depending on context. Following Gene Green and Tom Talbott, I suggest that the context favours the translation "coming from"— the destruction comes from the presence of Jesus. . . .
> Second, the punishment is "eternal destruction" (*olethron aiōnion*). How are we to understand this expression? Well, we note first that the adjective *aiōnion* suggests that the destruction referred to is the "destruction of the age to come" (not *everlasting* destruction), and thus the phrase need not carry any connotations of eternal conscious suffering. Second, the word *olethron* can mean "ruin" or "destruction," depending on the context.[14]

Parry notes further that Paul uses the term *olethron* rarely, and when he uses it in 1 Corinthians 5:5, he clearly intends for it to name a punishment meant for the good of the one punished. All of this means that, given its original linguistic context, this 1 Thessalonians passage *could* be speaking of a punishment that *comes from* God, involves *less* than total destruction, and has a corrective in purpose.

Whether it has this or a different meaning cannot be answered by looking narrowly at this text. Elsewhere, Parry notes that Paul's focus in this passage is on "divine retributive punishment on the enemies of God's people" and the "relief from persecution" this will bring. Paul simply isn't addressing the question of whether those who are the objects of divine punishment and the ruin it brings may yet be saved, or whether the punishment might contribute to their redemption and salvation. But his failure to mention these issues in this rhetorical setting does not mean "that such a possibility is incompatible with his wider theology or with what

---

14. MacDonald, *Evangelical Universalist*, 152.

he says in this text." To determine that, we must look at Paul's theology more broadly.[15]

It is also worth noting that the term *aiōnion*, which is etymologically linked to the English term *eon*, is the term generally used in Scripture where, in English translations, we find the terms "eternal" or "everlasting." But this translation is problematic. Talbott notes that where it is used in reference to punishment in the New Testament, it can easily be taken to mean something more like "a form of punishment that has its causal source in the eternal God and thus manifests his presence in a special way."[16] Parry notes there is a solid case "for maintaining that it means 'pertaining to the age' and often refers not just to any age but to 'the age to come'" and that, as such, when the term is used to refer to punishment it does not clearly connote endless duration.[17] While there is a different Greek term—*aidios*—that unambiguously means "eternal," the New Testament uses that term only twice: in Romans 1:20 to describe God's power, and in Jude 1:6 to describe the chains holding disobedient angels for the day of judgment.[18]

The key insight is this: divine punishment of sinners is not incompatible with universal salvation. In fact, one might take corrective or reformatory punishment as one of God's tools for achieving the salvation of all. What is incompatible with universal salvation is punishment that has no end and so cannot be coherently conceived as rehabilitative or purgatorial. But it is less than clear that Scripture teaches *that*.

The question, then, is whether we can read the Christian Scriptures in a universalist way while still doing justice to themes that speak of God's justice and punishment for sin, texts that invoke fire and speak of destruction, all while taking seriously the evidence that some people, at

---

15. Parry, "Universalist View," 122.

16. Talbott, *Inescapable Love of God*, 85.

17. MacDonald, *Evangelical Universalist*, 147–48. Parry notes that this point holds both for punishment and life, both of which are called "aionian." His point is that the issue of the duration of the life and punishment is not addressed directly and that the argument that the same duration must be attached to both is weak. First, "texts like 1 Corinthians 15:42–44 clearly establish the indestructible nature of resurrection life," but there is no similar corroboration for the eternity of punishment (148). Second, he cites Chris Marshall's argument that the use of "aionian" to qualify fire, punishment, and life is meant to stress "that all three will serve to establish the rule of God," not that they are all three of endless duration. See Marshall, *Beyond Retribution*, 292.

18. For an in-depth discussion of the distinct meanings of *aionian* and *aidios* in Scripture and a defense of the view that only the latter unambiguously means "eternal," see Ramelli and Konstan, *Terms for Eternity*, esp. 47–80.

the end of their earthly lives, die in a state of rebellion against God, unfit for heaven's joys.

Here is an example of such a reading: *All justice-based impediments to the salvation of all have been swept away by Christ's holy work. The only remaining impediment is willful clinging to sinfulness. While all eventually repent, some must first go through hell, experiencing the truth about what they have chosen: a chasm between them and God and an existence stripped of all that gives meaning to life. They must endure the purging fire of God's angry love, in which their sinful character and false self are exposed and then burned away until the truth about who they are—Children of the Father and bearers of the divine image—becomes clear. While their sinfulness endures, there will be weeping and gnashing of teeth. But God's resourcefulness is greater than human willfulness, God's holiness too pure to endure sin's persistence, and God's love and Jesus' atoning work too complete to leave any sinner out forever. Eventually the sinful false self is utterly consumed. All see the light and are saved.*

Is this picture *unbiblical*? A definitive answer is impossible in the space available here. But absent non-universalist preconceptions, this reading strikes me as not just defensible but *more* defensible than those non-universalist readings that don't even *engage* with universalist passages and themes.

FREEDOM AND UNIVERSALISM

The strongest challenge to universalism, I believe, relates to human freedom. Roughly put, the challenge is this: God's only way to guarantee that all are saved is to miraculously transform the wills and characters of the stubbornly unregenerate. But this would be incompatible with humans accepting or rejecting God's grace *freely*. And since respect for freedom is essential to God's loving goodness, God would never intervene in human choices in the only way that could guarantee the salvation of all.[19]

Let's call this the freewill challenge to universalism. For a complete assessment of it, we must consider whether the understanding of human freedom the challenge presupposes is the most plausible one. Since philosophers and theologians (and even brain scientists) have devoted sustained attention to the nature of freedom, I once again cannot here

---

19. Versions of this freewill challenge are found in, for example, Walls, *Hell*; Kvanvig, *Problem of Hell*; Stump, "Dante's Hell."

offer a comprehensive examination of these issues. But hopefully I can shed enough light on them to show that the freewill challenge is far from definitive.

In chapter 6, we distinguished between two competing understandings of freedom: compatibilism and libertarianism. The former holds that an action can be free even if determined (by natural laws or by God). Even if my will is caused to be what it is, I am still free if nothing prevents me from acting on my willed intentions. Libertarians deny this. They assert that an act being free is incompatible with it being causally determined, but insist that freedom still exists—freedom of an undetermined kind, or "libertarian freedom."

On freedom in the *compatibilist* sense, there is no conflict between God causing my repentance (or my acceptance of grace, etc.) and that repentance being free: God can cause me to have the intention to repent and arrange circumstances such that nothing prevents me from acting on it. Hence, the freewill challenge to universalism must reject as inadequate the compatibilist account of freedom.

But what makes it inadequate? I think the most plausible answer is that *libertarian* freedom is essential for genuine *agency*. Agents act based on a consideration of *reasons*. While *causes* are forces that produce effects, *reasons* are abstract entities—judgments about facts and values that speak in favor of or against a course of action. The worry is that if my choices are causally determined, they cannot be based on reasons. *Deliberation*—reflection on the reasons for and against an action—cannot play the crucial role in my choices that real agency requires.[20] Since genuine agency is essential to personhood, our status as inherently valuable persons would thus be undercut were our freedom limited to the merely compatibilist variety.

Not everyone will find this reasoning compelling, but let us grant it. Let us suppose that human dignity is tied to the ability to deliberate and act based on reasons, that this requires libertarian freedom, and hence that God will not bypass or override our libertarian freedom to secure our salvation. Does it follow that God cannot guarantee the salvation of all?

---

20. This view of freedom converges with the view Thomas Talbott develops, in different terms, in his recent book on free will. As Talbott puts it, "The essence of freedom . . . is the ability to follow the dictates of one's own reasoning powers, provided that one has passed the relevant threshold of rationality." See Talbott, *Understanding the Free-Will Controversy*, 71.

Not according to the philosopher Thomas Talbott. To fully understand his thinking, we must make a few additional points. First, to have freedom in the libertarian sense does not mean we are wholly unaffected by causal forces. Often, we act without deliberation—such as when we are moved by biological impulses or habits. To be free is not to exist in a world without such forces but, instead, to be capable of interposing between these forces and our behavior a deliberative process that considers reasons, and to be able to resist the causal forces in favor of what our deliberations recommend.

But some causal forces may be so strong we can't resist them. Drug addiction may be an example, as may deeply entrenched habits. Christians who confess that we are in bondage to sin and cannot free ourselves appear to be adopting this view with respect to the impulse to sin. In those cases, we're in the grip of "controlling affective states" that impair our freedom. While we may not be able to resist such controlling affective states *directly*, we might still be able to make other free choices that help us break free. We choose, say, to check ourselves into rehab. Or we ask God to free us from bondage to sin.

But in addition to controlling affective states, our freedom might be impaired by *error*: *mistakes*, descriptive or normative or both, that distort our deliberations. For example, in deciding to lend someone money, we might have a mistaken belief about their character. Our reasons are objectively bad because we are ignorant or deceived, such that what we *actually* choose (to give money to a swindler who never intends to pay us back) is not what we *thought* we were choosing (to lend money to a friend who will pay us back when able). Because of the error, we choose one thing but get instead something we didn't choose.

To be genuinely free, then, we cannot be ignorant, deceived, or in the grip of controlling affective states. Talbott thinks this feature of freedom favors universalism, because anyone who is truly free—liberated from all ignorance, deception, and controlling affective states—will inevitably choose union with God over the alternative.[21]

Why? First, if there are no controlling affective states in play, then the person will actually be able to make their decision based on a consideration of reasons. And in the case of choosing to accept or reject divine grace, someone who isn't impaired by ignorance or deception would have *no* reasons to reject grace and *every* reason to accept it. After all, union

---

21. See, for example, Thomas Talbott, "Towards a Better Understanding of Universalism," 5.

with God is objectively better than the alternative in every conceivable way. And not just slightly better. *Infinitely* better. And there is no conflict here between different kinds of values: union with God is both morally better and better for our welfare.

So, consider the choice about whether to receive or rebuff the divine grace that will reform our wills and ultimately bring us into union with God. If we are truly free, that means we will understand just how choice-worthy union with God is, and hence how choice-worthy it is to be open to God's grace. We won't have any misconceptions that lead us to undervalue that choice or attach positive value to alienation from God. And we won't be in the grip of controlling affective states that prevent us from following the outcomes of our deliberations.

What will be the result? The choice between union with God and alienation is not like the choice between ordering the chocolate cake for $4.99 and ordering the caramel flan for $5.50, where I have reasons for (and against) both options. It's more like a choice between getting my favorite meal for free (prepared from healthy and humanely raised ingredients), and paying $10,000 for a plate of foul-tasting swill (made from unhealthy ingredients acquired through slave labor). The difference, of course, is that union with God is infinitely better than getting my favorite meal for free, and alienation from God infinitely worse than paying $10,000 for swill. If I am truly free, I will be neither ignorant nor deceived, meaning *all* of my reasons will reflect the truth that union with God is infinitely preferable to the alternative. This means *all* of my reasons will not only favor union with God and oppose alienation but will favor the former and oppose the latter as strongly and clearly as any human reasons possibly can. And there will be no controlling affective states that causally determine me to choose contrary to the weight of my reasons.

This means, on Talbott's thinking, that I will inevitably choose to receive the grace that leads to union with God—and it is inevitable *because* I am free. If God can guarantee the salvation of all simply by guaranteeing that each person is actually free—by removing all ignorance, deception, and controlling affective states—God's respect for human freedom poses no impediment to saving all.

As compelling as this thinking is, there are potential criticisms. Were we, under conditions of genuine freedom, to choose to reject God's grace, it could not be for any *reason*—since under conditions of genuine freedom there would be no reason for such a choice. But some choices appear to be made for no reason—that is, at random. Consider when you are stuck between menu options at a restaurant and others at your table are ready to order. Could the possibility of choosing at random be part of what it means to be free? And could this possibility explain why someone might eternally reject God's grace?

One problem here is that we usually choose at random because a review of reasons can't settle the matter, meaning we have a *meta-level reason* to choose at random: it is preferable to paralysis. But there is no such meta-level reason to choose at random when confronting the choice between union with and alienation from God. In fact, all meta-level reasons favor *not* choosing at random when something of such monumental significance is at stake and when we have utterly decisive reasons to favor union with God. If I am not ignorant or deceived at that meta-level, it seems we can make sense of this—of choosing to make the choice about union with God at random, or partly at random—as a free choice only if part of what it means to be free is that we might *untether our wills* from all reasons *for* no reason.

I tend not to think such conceptions of freedom are coherent. Even if coherent, freedom in this sense does not sound like something with a positive value—something the possession of which contributes to our dignity and which God would respect even at the cost of letting us be eternally lost.

But perhaps there is another way to make sense of a free choice to reject God. *Prior* to union with God, we might suppose there is an inescapable ignorance about what's best that impacts our deliberations, and perhaps also an inevitable degree of bondage to controlling affective states—freedom-impairments God can't do away with *except* by saving us. But if God saves us *so that* we can have unimpaired freedom to choose our own salvation, God would have saved us *without* the prior cooperation of our unsaved will . . . in order for us to be free to choose what God has already brought about absent our free choice. So, maybe God must choose between saving us without our prior free consent and letting our impaired freedom determine our fates. Perhaps God has good reasons to prefer the latter, and thus to prefer letting the *impaired* freedom of the unsaved determine their eternal fate, despite its inevitable impairments.

So let us grant this. Let us suppose that in the state we are in prior to salvation, when presented with the offer of salvation our choice *cannot* be perfectly free. Hence, it cannot be a choice in which we correctly see that every good reason favors accepting the offer and none counts against it. We see through a glass darkly until we get to the other side of the glass, and so cannot *know* that crossing to the other side is the choice that has every reason in its favor.

And this means our choice will be influenced by the element of arbitrariness that accompanies uncertainty. In a world where we can never be sure of what the best choice is, it might even make sense for a certain arbitrariness to always be at work in our choices. Some options *look* like the better choice even when they are not. If I *always* choose based on what looks like the best choice, I might never learn the truth when appearances are deceptive. And so it may make sense for persons who exist in such uncertainty to make choices that are inevitably influenced by an element of *whim*: the occasional propensity to choose without regard for the available reasons.

So let us suppose that, in the pre-saved state, such an arbitrary element is an inevitable feature of free choice . . . and that God honors this freedom and its outcomes, even the most tragic outcomes resulting from the most unfortunate cases of arbitrary whim. Let us call this the radical libertarian view of freedom. To be clear: my point here is that to salvage the freewill challenge to universalism, we need something like this. I am not convinced that this radical libertarian view is defensible. But if we grant it, what follows?

Even granting it, there remains a case for thinking God could guarantee the salvation of all while respecting freedom. If God desires our salvation, and if neither God's justice nor holiness conflicts with this desire, then God will never withdraw the offer of salvation. Instead, God will arrange the circumstances of the unsaved such that they will never lose the opportunity to accept divine grace and so be saved. The option to receive the fruits of Christ's work will have the form of a *standing offer*. If this is so, someone will be *eternally* damned only if they persist in rejecting God in the face of *infinite opportunity to change their mind*.

And if God desires the salvation of all, with the only impediment to that salvation being creaturely free choice, God will presumably do the best God can do for the unsaved, given their ongoing rejection of grace, at every moment that their rejection persists. This will presumably mean not only keeping the offer on the table but reminding them of the offer when and where such a reminder is most likely to do some good. It would likely also mean providing assurances of love, designed by divine ingenuity to have the best possible chance of breaking through delusional beliefs about God. It would presumably mean therapeutic interventions meant to jar people out of foolish choice-patterns, creative efforts to clearly show them the consequences of their current choice pattern, moral suasion when and where that will open their eyes, and reformatory punishment when and where that has the capacity to drive home the gravity of their wrongs. It will involve identifying and exposing where pride undermines their own good, perhaps immersing them in experiences that drive home the folly of their hubris.

In short, what we have to envision here is a person continuing to reject divine grace in a reality where God *never gives up on them*, where the fruits of their choice to reject God are experienced in all their intolerability, and new opportunities to rethink their choice keep coming up, new occasions for deliberating anew are presented . . . for as long as it takes.

To be eternally damned, one must reject God's grace *infinitely many times* while an *infinitely resourceful and loving God* is on the case, working to inspire a change of heart.

There are two ways to imagine such decisive rejection playing out. On the one hand, we can imagine that at each opportunity in an infinite sequence of opportunities, while truly free to change their mind, the damned soul persists in the horrific choice that perpetuates their misery. On the other hand, we can suppose that at some point they make a choice or pattern of choices that eliminates their future capacity to change their mind: they become *absolutely* hard-hearted.

With the latter option, their hard-heartedness must be truly *absolute*. It can't be like the hard-heartedness of Ebenezer Scrooge, susceptible to change through the right sorts of therapeutic interventions (the Ghost of Christmas Past), moral suasion (the Ghost of Christmas Present), and vivid presentation of the costs of one's choice (the Ghost of Christmas Yet to Come) . It must instead be a hard-heartedness that *eliminates freedom*. They stop being free because they have become causally determined to continue to choose as they do based on absolutely entrenched habits.

Let's start with the first option: a choice to reject grace that persists over infinitely many opportunities to accept grace, without the possibility of freely accepting it ever going away.

If I retain the freedom to accept God's grace over an infinite array of opportunities to do so, and if my freedom means it is truly possible for me to accept it, this means that at every opportunity there is a real possibility that I *will* accept it. But on the mathematics of infinity, if there is a real possibility of something happening and infinite opportunity for it to happen, the probability of it not having happened yet approaches zero as the opportunities proliferate. Put another way, if Scrooge's conversion is a real possibility, the probability that the actual world will be one in which Scrooge continues to reject divine grace becomes increasing unlikely as the timeline moves forward, approaching zero as the timeline approaches infinity.

Consider an analogy. If I'm rolling a (non-weighted) six-sided die, the chances that I will roll a six is low for any give toss. But since there is a real possibility of this roll, the chances that I *have* rolled a six at some point becomes increasingly likely as the number of rolls increases. If I've rolled it a hundred thousand times, the likelihood that the actual world is one in which I have not yet rolled a six is very low. In fact, the probability that I have rolled a six approaches 100 percent as the number of rolls approaches infinity.

This is true even if it's a thousand-sided die, or a hundred-thousand-sided die. The point is that so long as the probability is not infinitesimally small, we can have a *mathematical* guarantee that given indefinite opportunity, a six will eventually come up.

I am not saying here that choices are like chance events—even if, as may be the case, we sometimes choose at random. Choosing *at* random (rather than based on reasons) is still choosing, which is a different thing than an event *happening* at random. What I am saying is that for the choice to accept or reject grace to be free in the radically libertarian sense, it has to be *genuinely possible* for me to accept it. And if it is genuinely possible at any given choice opportunity, the way the roll of a six on a die is genuinely possible for any given roll of the die, then given infinite opportunity to repent it becomes staggeringly unlikely that anyone will remain unregenerate forever.

Once we add the doctrine of the preservation of the saints—the idea that once someone has been saved by grace they are confirmed in that choice—the outcome is this: so long as God ensures that the unregenerate remain free to change their minds indefinitely, the salvation of all is mathematically certain even if we grant the radical libertarian view of freedom. And the doctrine of the preservation of the saints makes sense based on what we have already said. Our hearts are restless until they rest in God. But once they rest in God, we have found what we've been looking for. On this side of salvation it is as if we are looking through a glass darkly, creating the uncertainty that makes it possible for us to (mistakenly) judge rejection of divine grace to be a good choice. But once we have opened ourselves to that grace and allowed it to transform us, we have passed to the other side of the glass. We see clearly the utter choice-worthiness of union with God and so become confirmed in that choice.

But all of this assumes that human beings who reject divine grace *remain free* to change their minds, and that if they become hard-hearted, it is Scrooge's kind of hard-heartedness: a character-defining rejection of the good that, nevertheless, is susceptible to transformation given the right experiences, persuasion, and therapeutic interventions.

What I have been sketching here is a formulation of the "Infinite Opportunity Argument" that John Kronen and I develop and defend in *God's Final Victory*.[22] But this argument *fails* if human beings can and do bring themselves to a state of *absolute* hard-heartedness: a state of God-rejection that *completely extinguishes their freedom to change.*[23]

But if God wants to save all, and if the only impediment to achieving that desire is God's respect for freedom, it is hard to fathom why God would design us so that, in a state of God-rejection, we could extinguish our own capacity for free choice *completely* and thereby put ourselves outside of God's saving reach. Why would a God who desires to save all and desires the repentance of all—and who respects human freedom—design us so we can extinguish our freedom to repent and thus permanently block God's efforts to save us?

The most obvious answer is that God wants us to have the freedom not only to make certain kinds of choices but to become certain kinds of people.[24] But the power to utterly extinguish our freedom to change is not needed for that. Scrooge is a fictional portrait of someone afforded the freedom to become a miserly, greedy, self-focused, and callous jerk *even though he retained the freedom to change.* And real-life stories of transformation show that this kind of case is not mere fiction. A less immobile form of hard-heartedness is sufficient for allowing us to become the kinds of people we choose, and it doesn't come at the cost of eliminating all future freedom to change our minds about who we want to be.

Perhaps just as importantly, if core Christian teachings are correct, the image of our creator is imprinted on our very being, and only union with God can ultimately satisfy us. But if that is right, then a hard-hearted, God-rejecting character clashes with the deepest longings of our hearts and our most essential nature. There will always be something that grates

---

22. Kronen and Reitan, *God's Final Victory*, 160–67.
23. A point Yang and Davis make in "Choosing Eternal Separation."
24. See Murray, "Three Versions of Universalism," 63–64.

against such a state of character—namely the truth about who and what we are, stamped into our very being.

This fact will render such a state *inherently unstable*.[25] We could make ourselves absolutely hard-hearted, then, only if God gave us the power to wholly destroy within ourselves an essential element of what makes us who we are—the stamp of our creator—thereby effectively annihilating ourselves. But given the stakes, our own foolishness in the pre-saved state, and our inability to fully comprehend the eternal even in relation to our own destinies, wouldn't a God who handed us the power to annihilate ourselves be like a parent who hands their kindergartner a loaded gun?[26] While in the grip of impaired freedom and all the delusions and ignorance and controlling affective states that mar us prior to salvation, such power is beyond our limited wisdom, with consequences whose significance we can't fathom.

Respecting freedom does not mean giving explosives to terrorists so they acquire the power to perpetrate horrors. It does not mean supplying suicidal teens with the means to end their lives. Perfect goodness may call for respecting freedom, but it does not call for supplying to those with impaired freedom the power to do things that so exceed the limits of their understanding they cannot be expected to use that power wisely. A God of love who desires our salvation, but also desires that we choose God freely, might well imbue us with the power to say no to God. But would God imbue us with the power to ensure that the *no* we say at a particular time in our lives—a time when we have no real capacity to imagine eternal consequences and no clear understanding of what the *no* means—can *never* be altered?[27]

If not, then any hard-hearted God-rejecting character we choose will be such that there remains some possibility of change. With *infinite* opportunity to change, and with an infinitely resourceful and loving God on the case, the only reasonable expectation is that, even granted the freedom to reject God, all of us will eventually come around. Some

---

25. For a fuller development of these points, see Reitan, "Eternally Choosing Hell." David Bentley Hart poetically says something similar when he describes hell as a shadow "to which we may flee from the transfiguring light of God if we so wish, but where we can never finally come to rest—for, being only a shadow, it provides nothing to cling to." See Hart, *That All Shall Be Saved*, 129.

26. Or, as Marilyn Adams suggests, leaves a toddler alone in a room full of combustible gas and a gas stove with colorful knobs. See Adams, "Problem of Hell," 313–14.

27. For a fuller development of these arguments, see Reitan, "Eternally Choosing Hell"; Kronen and Reitan, "Annihilation or Salvation?," esp. 151–53.

are perhaps more hard-hearted than Scrooge. But Scrooge only had one night, and God makes the ghosts of Christmases past, present, and future look like amateurs.

And so, even if we grant the radical libertarian view of freedom and God's respect for it, there appears to be a way God can guarantee the salvation of all: create humans so they cannot eradicate the image of God within themselves, and hence make them such that—like Scrooge—their freedom to become hard-hearted God-rejecting persons does not imply the capacity to become so utterly fixed in this state that the freedom to change is erased. Granted this design, the infinitely resourceful God has infinite opportunity to inspire change, and so can guarantee—mathematically if not metaphysically—the salvation of all.

If these arguments are compelling, then there is after all a plausible way to avoid the problem of heavenly grief and so take seriously the divine promise that every tear shall be wiped away and all grief end. Not by holding that the blessed will stop caring about the fate of lost loved ones, the eternal loss of inherently valuable persons, and the eternal thwarting of God's desires. And certainly not by holding that God spares the blessed pain by afflicting them with targeted dementia. Rather, it will be by taking seriously the possibility that all God's precious children will, like the prodigal son, finally come home.

Bibliography

Adams, Marilyn McCord. *Christ and Horrors: The Coherence of Christology.* Cambridge: Cambridge University Press, 2006.

———. *Horrendous Evils and the Goodness of God.* Ithaca, NY: Cornell University Press, 1999.

———. "Horrendous Evils and the Goodness of God." *Proceedings of the Aristotelian Society* 63 (1989) 299–310.

———. "The Problem of Hell: A Problem of Evil for Christians." In *A Reasoned Faith*, edited by Eleonore Stump, 301–27. Ithaca, NY: Cornell University Press, 1993.

Alcorn, Randy. "If Our Loved Ones Are in Hell, Won't That Spoil Heaven?" *Eternal Perspective Ministries*, March 26, 2010. https://www.epm.org/resources/2010/Mar/26/if-our-loved-ones-are-hell-wont-spoil-heaven/.

Anselm. *Why God Became Man.* In *Anselm of Canterbury: The Major Works*, edited by Brian Davies and G. R. Evans, 260–356. Translated by Janet Fairweather. Oxford: Oxford University Press, 1998.

Aquinas, Thomas. *Summa Theologica.* 3 vols. Translated by the English Dominican Fathers. New York: Benziger Brothers, 1947.

Aristotle. *Nicomachean Ethics.* Translated by W. D. Ross. In *The Basic Works of Aristotle*, edited by Richard McKeon, 927–1112. New York: Random House, 1941.

Arnold, Magda B. *Emotion and Personality.* New York: Columbia University Press, 1960.

Augustine. *The City of God.* Translated by Marcus Dods et al. Edinburgh: T&T Clark, 1888.

Aulen, Gustav. *The Faith of the Christian Church.* Translated by Eric H. Wahlstron and G. Everett Arden. Philadelphia: Muhlenberg, 1948.

Baier. *Compendium Theologiae Positivae.* Edited by C. F. W. Walther. Grand Rapids: Emmanuel, 2006.

Baillie, Harold W. "Learning the Emotions." *New Scholasticism* 62 (1988) 221–27.

Barth, Karl. *Church Dogmatics.* Vol. 2.1, *The Doctrine of God.* Edited by G. W. Bromiley and T. F. Torrance. Translated by T. H. L. Parker et al. Edinburgh: T&T Clark, 1957.

———. *Church Dogmatics.* Vol. 4.2, *The Doctrine of Reconciliation.* Edited by G. W. Bromiley and T. F. Torrance. Translated by G. W. Bromiley. Edinburgh: T&T Clark, 1958.

Batson, C. D. "These Things Called Empathy: Eight Related but Distinct Phenomena." In *The Social Neuroscience of Empathy*, edited by J. Decety and W. Ickes, 3–15. Cambridge: MIT Press, 2009.

Bonnano, George. *The Other Side of Sadness: What the New Science of Bereavement Tells Us About Life After Loss*. New York: Basic, 2019.

Bruce, F. F. *The Letter of Paul to the Romans: An Introduction and Commentary*. Leicester, UK: Inter-Varsity Press, 1985.

Calvin, John. *Institutes of the Christian Religion, Volume 1*. Translated by Ford Lewis Battles. Louisville: Westminster John Knox, 2006.

Cholbi, Michael. "Grief's Rationality, Backward and Forward." *Philosophy and Phenomenological Research* 94 (2017) 255–72.

———. "Regret, Resilience, and the Nature of Grief." *Journal of Moral Philosophy* 16 (2019) 486–508.

Craig, William Lane. "Talbott's Universalism." *Religious Studies* 27 (1991) 297–308.

———. "Talbott's Universalism Once More." *Religious Studies* 29 (1993) 497–518.

Davis, Stephen T. "Universalism, Hell, and the Fate of the Ignorant." *Modern Theology* 6 (1990) 173–86.

DeRose, Keith. "Universalism and the Bible: The Really Good News." https://campuspress.yale.edu/keithderose/1129-2/.

De Sousa, Ronald. *The Rationality of Emotion*. Cambridge: MIT Press, 1987.

Doty, Mark. *Heaven's Coast*. New York: HarperCollins, 1996.

Fudge, Edward W. *The Fire That Consumes: A Biblical and Historical Study of the Doctrine of Final Punishment*. 3rd ed. Eugene, OR: Cascade, 2011.

Grenz, Stanley J. *Theology for the Community of God*. Grand Rapids: Eerdmans, 1997.

Griffiths, Paul J. "Self-Annihilation or Damnation? A Disputable Question in Christian Eschatology." *Pro Ecclesia* 16 (2007) 416–44.

Hackett, J. Edward. "Martin Luther King, Jr., and the Legacy of Boston Personalism." *Pluralist* 17 (2022) 45–70.

Hart, David Bentley. *That All Shall Be Saved: Heaven, Hell, and Universal Salvation*. New Haven: Yale University Press, 2019.

Hassoun, Nicole. "Eternally Separated Lovers: The Argument from Love." *Australasian Journal of Philosophy* 93 (2015) 633–43.

Hill, Daniel J. *Divinity and Maximal Greatness*. London: Routledge, 2004.

Kane, Robert. *A Contemporary Introduction to Free Will*. New York: Oxford University Press, 2005.

Kant, Immanuel. *The Fundamental Principles of the Metaphysics of Morals*. Translated by Thomas K. Abbott. New York: Macmillan, 1949.

Kershnar, Stephen. "Hell and Punishment." In *The Problem of Hell: A Philosophical Anthology*, edited by Joel Buenting, 115–32. Aldershot, UK: Ashgate, 2010.

Kimel, Alvin F. *Destined for Joy: The Gospel of Universal Salvation*. No loc: The Works of George MacDonald, 2022.

King, Martin Luther, Jr. "Advice for Living." *Ebony*, November 13, 1957.

———. "The Ethical Demands of Integration." In *A Testament of Hope: The Essential Writings of Martin Luther King Jr.*, edited by James M. Washington, 117–25. San Francisco: HarperCollins, 1986.

———. "Facing the Challenge of a New Age." In *A Testament of Hope: The Essential Writings of Martin Luther King Jr.*, edited by James M. Washington, 135–44. San Francisco: HarperCollins, 1986.

———. "Nonviolence and Racial Justice." In *A Testament of Hope: The Essential Writings of Martin Luther King Jr.*, edited by James M. Washington, 5–9. San Francisco: HarperCollins, 1986.

———. "The Rising Tide of Racial Consciousness." In *A Testament of Hope: The Essential Writings of Martin Luther King Jr.*, edited by James M. Washington, 145–51. San Francisco: HarperCollins, 1986.

———. *Strength to Love*. Philadelphia: Fortress, 1981.

Kronen, John, and Eric Reitan. "Annihilation or Salvation? A Philosophical Case for Preferring Universalism to Annihilationism." *Religious Studies* 58 (2022) 138–61.

———. *God's Final Victory: A Comparative Philosophical Case for Universalism*. New York: Continuum, 2011.

Kvanvig, Jonathan L. *The Problem of Hell*. New York: Oxford University Press, 1993.

Lewis, C. S. *The Great Divorce*. San Francisco: Harper Collins, 2001.

———. *A Grief Observed*. New York: Seabury, 1961.

———. *The Problem of Pain*. New York: Macmillan, 1944.

Levy, Neil, and Michael McKenna. "Recent Work on Free Will and Moral Responsibility." *Philosophy Compass* 4 (2009) 96–133.

Luther, Martin. "The Freedom of the Christian." In *Martin Luther: Selections from His Writings*, edited by John Dillenberger, 42–85. New York: Anchor, 1962.

MacDonald, Gregory. *The Evangelical Universalist*. Eugene, OR: Cascade, 2006.

Mackie, John L. "Evil and Omnipotence." *Mind* 64 (1955) 200–212.

Marshall, Christopher D. *Beyond Retribution: A New Testament Vision for Justice, Crime, and Punishment*. Grand Rapids: Eerdmans, 2001.

McCall, Thomas H. "We Believe in God's Sovereign Goodness: A Rejoinder to John Piper." *Trinity Journal* 29 (2008) 235–46.

Moller, Dan. "Love and Death." *Journal of Philosophy* 104 (2007) 301–16.

Mullins, R. T. *God and Emotions*. Cambridge: Cambridge University Press, 2020.

Murray, Michael J. "Three Versions of Universalism." *Faith and Philosophy* 16 (1999) 55–68.

Na'aman, Oded. "The Rationality of Emotional Change: Toward a Process View." *Noûs* 55 (2021) 245–69.

Nygren, Anders. *Agape and Eros*. Translated by Philip S. Watson. Philadelphia: Westminster, 1953.

O'Connor, Kathleen M. "The Tears of God and Divine Character in Jeremiah 2–9." In *God in the Fray: A Tribute to Walter Brueggemann*, edited by Tod Linafelt and Timothy K. Beal, 172–85. Minneapolis: Fortress, 1998.

Oord, Thomas Jay. "Strong Passibility." In *Divine Impassibility: Four Views of God's Emotions and Suffering*, edited by Robert J. Matz and A. Chadwick Thornhill, 129–51. Downers Grove, IL: InterVarsity, 2019.

Packer, J. I. *Knowing God*. Downers Grove, IL: InterVarsity, 1973.

Parry, Robin A. "A Universalist View." In *Four Views on Hell*, edited by Preston Sprinkle, 101–27. Grand Rapids: Zondervan, 2016.

Pelser, Adam C. "Heavenly Sadness: On the Value of Negative Emotions in Paradise." In *Paradise Understood: New Philosophical Essays about Heaven*, edited by T. Ryan Byerly and Eric J. Silverman, 113–35. New York: Oxford University Press, 2017.

Piper, John. *Does God Desire All to Be Saved?* Wheaton, IL: Crossway, 2013.

Plantinga, Alvin. *God, Freedom, and Evil*. Grand Rapids: Eerdmans, 1977.

Ramelli, Ilaria, and David Konstan. "Terms for Eternity." *Nova Tellus* 24 (2006) 21–39.

———. *Terms for Eternity: Aiônios and Aïdios in Classical and Christian Texts.* Piscataway, NJ: Gorgias, 2007.

Ramsey, Paul. *Basic Christian Ethics.* New York: Scribner's Sons, 1950.

Reitan, Eric. "Eternal Damnation and Blessed Ignorance: Is the Damnation of Some Incompatible with the Salvation of Any?" *Religious Studies* 38 (2002) 429–50.

———. "Eternally Choosing Hell: Can Hard-Heartedness Explain Why Some Remain in Hell Forever?" *Sophia* 61 (2022) 365–82.

———. "Is Annihilation More Severe than Eternal Conscious Torment?" *Southwest Philosophy Review* 38 (2022) 191–98.

Roberts, Robert C. *Emotions in the Moral Life.* Cambridge: Cambridge University Press, 2013.

Rooney, James Dominic. "Hard Universalism, Grace, and Creaturely Freedom." *Church Life Journal*, January 17, 2023. https://churchlifejournal.nd.edu/articles/hard-universalism-grace-and-creaturely-freedom/.

———. "Hell and the Coherence of Christian Hope." *Church Life Journal*, November 29, 2022. https://churchlifejournal.nd.edu/articles/hell-and-the-coherence-of-christian-hope/.

———. "The Incoherencies of Hard Universalism." *Church Life Journal*, October 18, 2022. https://churchlifejournal.nd.edu/articles/the-incoherencies-of-hard-universalism/.

Rosan, Peter J. "The Varieties of Ethical Experience: A Phenomenology of Empathy, Sympathy, and Compassion." *Phänomenologische Forschungen* (2014) 155–89.

Rowe, William L. "The Problem of Evil and Some Varieties of Atheism." *American Philosophical Quarterly* 16 (1979) 335–41.

Ruddick, Sara. *Maternal Thinking.* New York: Ballantine, 1989.

Russell, Bruce. "The Persistent Problem of Evil." *Faith and Philosophy* 6 (1989) 121–39.

Schleiermacher, Friedrich. *The Christian Faith.* Edited by H. R. Mackintosh and J. S. Stewart. Translated by H. R. Mackintosh et al. Edinburgh: T&T Clark, 1928.

Scrutton, Anastasia Philippa. *Thinking Through Feeling: God, Emotion, and Possibility.* London: Bloomsbury, 2011.

Solomon, Robert, C. *The Passions: Emotions and the Meaning of Life.* Indianapolis: Hackett, 1993.

Spaulding, Shannon. "Motivating Empathy." *Mind & Language* 39 (2023) 220–36. https://doi.org/10.1111/mila.12469.

Spiegel, James S. *Hell and Divine Goodness: A Philosophical-Theological Inquiry.* Eugene, OR: Cascade, 2019.

Stump, Eleonore. "Dante's Hell, Aquinas's Moral Theory, and the Love of God." *Canadian Journal of Philosophy* 16 (1986) 181–96.

———. "The God of Love." *Church Life Journal*, April 13, 2023. https://churchlifejournal.nd.edu/articles/can-hell-and-the-god-of-love-coexist/.

———. "The Problem of Evil and the Desires of the Heart." In *Oxford Studies in the Philosophy of Religion, Volume 1*, edited by Jonathan Kvanvig, 196–215. New York: Oxford University Press, 2008.

———. *Wandering in Darkness: Narrative and the Problem of Suffering.* Oxford: Clarendon, 2010.

Talbott, Thomas. "Craig on the Possibility of Eternal Damnation." *Religious Studies* 28 (1992) 459–510.

———. *The Inescapable Love of God.* 2nd ed. Eugene, OR: Cascade, 2014.

———. "Providence, Freedom, and Human Destiny." *Religious Studies* 26 (1990) 227–45.

———. "Towards a Better Understanding of Universalism." In *Universal Salvation? The Current Debate*, edited by R. A. Parry and C. H. Partridge, 3–14. Carlisle, UK: Paternoster, 2003.

———. *Understanding the Free-Will Controversy: Thinking Through a Philosophical Quagmire*. Cascade Companions. Eugene, OR: Cascade, 2022.

Volf, Miroslav. *Exclusion and Embrace: A Theological Exploration of Identity, Otherness, and Reconciliation*. Nashville: Abingdon, 1996.

Wadlinger, Heather A., and Derek M. Isaacowitz. "Fixing Our Focus: Training Attention to Regulate Emotion." *Personality and Social Psychology Review* 15 (2011) 75–102.

Walls, Jerry L. *Does God Love Everyone? The Heart of What Is Wrong with Calvinism*. Eugene, OR: Cascade, 2016.

———. *Hell: The Logic of Damnation*. Notre Dame: University of Notre Dame Press, 1992.

Weil, Simone. "Forms of the Implicit Love of God." In *Waiting for God*, translated by Emma Craufurd, 137–215. New York: Harper & Row, 1973.

———. *Gravity and Grace*. Translated by Arthur Wills. Lincoln: University of Nebraska Press, 1997.

———. "Love." In *Simone Weil: An Anthology*, edited by Siân Miles, 270–76. New York: Weidenfeld & Nicolson, 1986.

Wessling, Jordan. *Love Divine: A Systematic Account of God's Love for Humanity*. New York: Oxford University Press, 2020.

Wolterstorff, Nicholas. *Inquiring about God*. Vol. 1, *Selected Essays*. Cambridge: Cambridge University Press, 2010.

———. *Lament for a Son*. Grand Rapids: Eerdmans, 1987.

Yang, Eric T. "Heaven and the Problem of Eternal Separation." In *Heaven and Philosophy*, edited by Simon Cushing, 153–70. Lanham, MD: Lexington, 2018.

Yang, Eric T., and Stephen T. Davis. "Choosing Eternal Separation: Reply to Gwiazda." *Sophia* 54 (2015) 217–19.

Zagzebski, Linda Trinkaus. *Exemplarist Moral Theory*. New York: Oxford University Press, 2017.

Index

Adams, Marilyn McCord, 6–7, 27–28, 50, 63, 156, 209n26, 211
agape, 62, 74–81, 82–83, 84n36, 85, 86–92; *see* Christian Love
akrasia, 102
Alcorn, Randy, 128–29, 130, 211
annihilation(ism), 1, 3–4, 5, 7n13, 15, 18, 32, 51–52, 68, 107, 121, 128, 144, 150, 163, 184, 189, 191–93
Anselm, 190–91, 192, 211
antecedent and consequent will, 12–13, 16, 71–72
Aquinas, Thomas, 51, 75n11, 79, 81, 105, 181, 184n1, 211
argument from heavenly grief
    Arminian presuppositions of, 10–18
    overview of, 4–6
    premises of, 5, 24, 119–20
    relation to argument from heavenly sympathy, 52–53, 68
    relation to problem of heavenly grief, 5, 19, 24
    versions of, 53, 115–17
argument from heavenly sympathy
    personal version of, 59–63
    universal version of, 53–59
    versions distinguished, 63–68
Aristotle, 87, 94–95, 101–2, 177, 178, 211
Arminian theology, 11–16, 18, 46, 62–63, 124, 125–26
Arminius, Jacobus, 13

Augustine, 2n2, 3n3, 78–79, 81, 211
Aulen, Gustav, 75, 211

beatific vision, 139, 142–45, 162
beatitudes, 45
beloved community, 83
Brés, Madeleine, 21

Calvin, John, 123, 212
Calvinism, 13–16, 18, 62–63, 123–24, 126, 130, 135–37, 157
Cholbi, Michael, 106–7, 169n36, 212
Christian/agapic love
    and attention, 40, 83, 90, 92, 93, 117, 143, 144
    and emotion(s), including grief, 86–93, 106, 110, 114–15
    of enemies, 75, 76, 86
    ethical centrality of, 73–74
    and fellowship, 82–84, 86, 106, 111–12
    and inherent worth, 77–81, 85, 106, 131
    nature of, 73, 74–76, 85–86
    and personal love, 89–93, 116–17, 131–32
    and self-love, 78, 91, 112
    universal scope of, 75, 81, 86, 122, 131–32, 106, 134–35, 138
    value account of, 84–86, 106, 119
conditionalism, 3; *see* annihilation(ism)

Craig, William Lane, 138–48, 162, 185, 212

Davis, Stephen T., 3n5, 208n23, 212, 215
defeat of evil/horror, 6–7, 153, 155–58, 167, 179–82
defense, contrasted with theodicy, 19–23, 138
dementia, ix, xi, xii, 148, 185, 210
desires of the heart, 100, 109–10, 164–68
divine impassibility, 149–51
doctrine of hell, 3, 6–8, 51–53, 59, 66, 68, 144, 184, 192–93
doctrine of limited salvation
    definition of, 2
    impact on consolation of faith, 8, 10, 46, 49
    in conflict with doctrine of perfect blessedness, 4, 8–9, 41, 46, 50, 52, 118, 119–20, 184, 185
    versions of, 3–4
doctrine of perfect blessedness
    definition of, 3
    rejection of, 5, 8–9, 175, 185–88
Doty, Mark, xi, 38–40, 41–42, 43, 45, 47–49, 164, 212

emotion(s); *see also* Christian/ agapic love, grief
    and character, 70, 87–88, 91, 95, 101–3, 105
    defining elements of, 57, 87, 94
    fittingness of, xii, 9, 55–56, 94–99, 100, 102, 103
    in the morally perfected, 70, 92, 106–7, 150–51, 152, 159, 175–79, 181–82
    relation to values, xii, 55–56, 89, 97–98, 99–100, 103–5, 169, 175
    relevance for sound thinking, 27–29, 50, 63
    as truth-discerning, 103–5
emotional blackmail, 158, 163, 173

emotional immune system, xi–xii, 168–69, 172
empathy, 57–58
enkrasia, 102
eudaimonia, 175, 177

felix culpa, 156
freedom
    and Arminian theology, 11, 125–26
    and Calvinist theology, 14, 123
    compatibilist, 11n15, 13, 123–24, 201
    God's respect for, 13, 14, 63, 158, 160, 192, 200, 203, 205, 208–10
    and grace, 11, 14, 46–47, 62–63, 123, 124, 125, 157, 200, 203, 205, 206, 207
    and hard-heartedness, 206, 208–10
    impaired/impairments to, 202, 204, 209
    libertarian, 11, 14, 124, 125, 201, 205, 207, 210
    and rational agency, 201, 204
    and universalism, 17n23, 189, 192, 200–210
Fudge, Edward, 4n6, 212

God's love
    nature of, 11, 15, 17, 77, 85, 150, 160
    relation to human love, 74–75, 80, 84
    universal scope of, 11, 16, 17n23, 18, 125–27, 132–38, 152–54, 185, 200
grace; *see also* freedom
    efficacious/irresistible, 62–63, 123–25, 126, 134, 136
    optimal, 47, 123
    resistible/sufficient, 14, 67, 123–25
    sanctifying, 34, 93
grief
    attenuation of, xi–xii, 32, 113, 114, 169–73

and consolation, 1, 8, 10, 37–38,
    45, 49, 162
and denial, 42
and emotional health, 168
enduring, 5, 8, 65, 112, 114–15,
    119–20, 149, 152, 160, 170
impact on happiness/joy, 1,
    5, 28, 38, 45–46, 61, 72,
    117–18, 120, 154–55, 163,
    173–83, 184, 187–88
and pretense, 42–43, 45, 46, 114,
    170, 172
process of, 33, 45, 112–13, 115,
    168–70
as purgatorial, 34–35
relation to love, xi, 1, 5, 32–33,
    34–35, 36–37, 39–40, 65,
    106–7, 116–17, 119–20,
    128–29, 161–63, 184
and resilience, 40, 114, 169
and self-destruction, 46–49

happiness
    fittingness of, 55, 141, 143
    nature of, 55, 81–82, 141, 177
    supreme vs supremely
        worthwhile, 54–55, 60, 139,
        140–42, 143, 147

Hassoun, Nicole, 51, 59, 63–66, 212
heaven, defined, 2
horror/horrendous evil, 6–7, 8, 156

infernalism, 3
inherent worth (value) of persons,
    10, 41, 77–82, 85, 90–91,
    92–93, 106–7, 108, 115,
    116–17, 119, 126, 129, 131–
    32, 133, 138, 184, 201, 210

Kant, Immanuel, 86–87, 89, 212
Kershnar, Stephen, 190, 212
Kimel, Alvin, xiii, 59, 212
King, Martin Luther Jr., 76–78, 80,
    81, 82–83, 86, 128, 131–32,
    212–13

Kronen, John, xiii, 2n1, 5n8, 17n23,
    71n1, 82n30, 149, 189n3,
    191n7, 208, 209n27, 213

Lazarus, 152, 165
Lewis, C. S., 3, 28, 29–35, 38–39, 41,
    42, 43, 49, 59, 70, 108, 110–
    11, 113, 151, 152, 158–59,
    160, 162, 163, 173, 176, 213
loss(es)
    essential and accidental, 111
    fungible and nonfungible, 108,
        109, 112, 113, 114, 115, 117
    self-regarding and other-
        regarding, 107–8, 112, 114
love; see Christian love, God's love,
    personal love
love webs, 121–22, 124–26, 138
Lutheran theology, 11, 12n16,
    17n23, 75, 191, 192

MacDonald, George, 158, 160, 163
MacDonald, Gregory, 137n24,
    196n11, 198, 199n17, 213
Mackie, J. L., 19, 213
Mary of Bethany, 165
Moller, Dan, xi, 168–69, 171–72,
    173, 213
moral character, development of,
    101–3
Müller-Lyer illusion, 95
Mullins, R. T., 97, 99, 150, 151, 213

Na'aman, Oded, 170–72, 213
Nygren, Anders, 75–76, 77, 79–80,
    81, 83, 213

objective value(s), 33, 78, 92, 103–5,
    111, 113, 127, 163
    relation to subjective value,
        99–100, 108–10, 112, 115,
        129, 164–66

Packer, J. I., 17, 213
Parry, Robin, xiii, 198–99, 213
Pelser, Adam, 175–81, 187, 213
penal substitutionary theology,
    17n23

perfect blessedness, definition of, 2–3
personal love
    in the blessed, 56, 89, 91, 93, 119, 122, 127–29, 131–32
    nature of, 90, 93
    relation to agape, 91, 116–17, 131–32
personalism, 77, 78, 81
Piper, John, 16–18, 135, 136, 213
Plantinga, Alvin, 19–20, 213
problem of hell, 6–10, 27
problem of evil, 1–2, 6–10, 19–20, 27, 165

Ramsey, Paul, 73–75, 76, 77, 78, 81, 82, 91, 214
Rooney, Fr. James Dominic, 152–58, 176, 214
Ruddick, Sara, 88, 92, 214

salvation, defined, 2
Schleiermacher, Friedrich, 51, 53–56, 59, 64, 130, 131, 139, 141, 142, 145, 168, 173, 184, 214
Scrooge, Ebenezer, 76, 206–7, 208, 210
Scrutton, Anastasia, 151, 214
sin(s)
    bondage to, 85, 134, 159, 202
    defined, 2
    God's response to, 3, 4, 135–36, 178, 193, 199, 200
    infinite gravity of, 190–91, 192
    original, 133
    and repentance, 4, 11, 66, 123
    as vitiation/corruption, 71, 81, 133, 161

Solomon, Robert, 97, 214
Spaulding, Shannon, 57–58, 214
Spiegel, James, 51, 66n34, 67n35, 121–32, 135, 136, 138, 147–48, 185, 192n8, 214
Stump, Eleonore, 9, 12, 100, 109–10, 112n28, 113, 117, 160–62, 164–68, 176, 200n19, 211, 214

Talbott, Thomas, 17–18, 51, 54–56, 59–63, 66, 138–41, 143, 144, 146n41, 147, 195n10, 198, 199, 201n20, 202–3, 214–15
Teresa of Avila, 9
theodicy, 19–23, 164, 165
thick affective properties, 96, 98

universalism/universal salvation
    costs of, x, 5, 24, 120, 186, 188–89
    defined, 4
    and divine justice/punishment, 17n23, 182, 190–92, 199
    and freedom, 192, 200–210
    and God's holiness, 192–93
    and Scripture, 137, 193–200

Walls, Jerry, 15n20, 46–47, 123, 136n22, 173–75, 186, 188n2, 200n19, 215
Weil, Simone, 40, 92, 143, 215
Wolterstorff, Nicholas, 28, 29, 35–38, 40, 41, 43–44, 45–46, 48–49, 108, 150n3, 215

Yang, Eric, 149–51, 173–74, 208n23, 215

Zagzebski, Linda, 94–96, 97, 98, 215

www.ingramcontent.com/pod-product-compliance
Lightning Source LLC
Chambersburg PA
CBHW022012220426
43663CB00007B/1055